Women
With
Guns

357 W 20th St., NY NY 10011

Women With Guns

© Copyright 1985 by Broadway Play Publishing, Inc.

All rights reserved. This work is fully protected under the copyright laws of the United States of America.

No part of this publication may be photocopied, reproduced, stored in a retrieval system, or transmitted, in any form or by any means, electronic, mechanical, recording, or otherwise, without the prior permission of the publisher. Additional copies of this publication are available from the publisher.

Written permission is required for live performance of any sort. This includes readings, cuttings, scenes, and excerpts. For amateur and stock performances, and all other rights, consult the opening pages of the individual plays herein.

First printing: April 1986

ISBN: 0-88145-035-9

Design by Marie Donovan

Set in Aster by L&F Technical Composition, Lakeland, FL

Printed and bound by BookCrafters, Inc., Chelsea, MI

Contents

Introduction

The original thought behind this anthology was to put into print the most interesting new playwrights around. These were all plays that I had read or seen over the last three years, and they were writers to whom I wanted to make a commitment.

Then Michael Wolk (*Femme Fatale*) read the other plays that were going into this collection, and noticed that each had a scene with a woman holding a gun (he hadn't read *Sloth* by Bruce Post, but it has both a woman and a gun, though separate). Naturally this set me thinking about the message that these six plays will collectively send to the reader. All six were written by men. They may or may not be expressing ideas held by the majority of men, but they do give us a variety of male visions of female violence directed against men; abstractions using that sacred symbol of virility and power: the gun. Whether collectively these plays make a social/political statement is something the reader will have to decide individually. I know that the unifying factor for me is that, quite simply, I happen to like these plays.

My favorite living American playwrights are Sam Shepard, Lanford Wilson, and David Mamet. I love their imagination and the way they use the language as poetry without being self-consciously poetic. I have already published three playwrights who I believe have the potential of Shepard, Wilson and Mamet. One of them is Mac Wellman (*Harms Way*), whose play *Energumen* is in this collection. (The other two are Dan Therriault, *Battery* and *Floor Above The Roof*, and Eric Overmyer, *Native Speech*.) The other five writers in this anthology also have the talent to join the ranks of America's best contemporary playwrights.

In reading and seeing hundreds of plays each year, I am continually searching for something original. I demand that a playwright present me with a vision that I have *never* seen before. I want to be transported into another world, one no one else has ever even conceived of before. There is no question that both *Energumen* by Mac Wellman and *White Mountains* by Bruce Dale are this type of genuine exercise of the imagination.

On the other hand, if a play is going to be essentially realistic, then I want blood and guts, and powerful soul-ripping passages. Here both *Femme Fatale* and *Skin* clearly exhibit the honest, emotional influence of *Long Day's Journey into Night* and *Virginia Woolf*.

Read them and enjoy them. If you don't think they are new and interesting then I'm in the wrong business.

CHRISTOPHER GOULD
Publisher

Bruce Dale

White Mountains

Bruce Dale was born in Philadelphia, PA, where his first play, *Barnyard Ball*, was produced when he was in high school. He graduated from Tufts University and received an MFA from Catholic University in Washington, D.C. He now lives in Boston, where many of his thirty plays have been produced or workshopped. *Up On the Roof*, which grew out of Ellen Stewart's Boston Massacre Project, won the 1984–85 NEWorks Award and premiered at the New Ehrlich Theatre, as well as being seen at MIT and other Boston-area theatres. *Sins Against the Body*, an epic fantasy freely adapted from interwoven stories by Flaubert, Hawthorne, and Dostoyevsky, was performed at Harvard's Loeb Drama Center and the Boston Shakespeare Theatre. *Wanda and Her Dog* was featured in the "Best of Boston" Playwrights Festival in 1981 and ran in repertory two years later as part of the Boston Playwrights Showcase at the Alley Theatre. In 1985 it played in New York, along with *Memory Olympics*, at the Vortex Theatre. *The Machine Stops* and *Snaps* were produced by Playwrights Platform; *Snaps* also played at the Boston University Threatre Institute and in other parts of the country.

White Mountains was developed at the Nucleo Eclettico Theatre and is scheduled for a New York premiere in 1986. Other works by Mr. Dale include *Mother of Thousands, Take It to the Limit, Woman in a Fur, Into the Future, I Remember Taking a Picture*, and *Famous Among Cockroaches*. Dale furthered his theatrical training as a literary/casting assistant at the Manhattan Theatre Club, and has since been frequently involved in producing. He cofounded Touchstone Productions in Boston and is a charter member of Artists Unlimited in New York. He has produced several plays at Harvard and on Off-Off Broadway, as well as a dance film at the Juilliard. He presently is involved in organizing new theatre companies in New York and Boston, with the aim of creating an exchange program of new plays and experimental theatre between the two cities.

For stock and amateur production rights, contact: Broadway Play Publishing, Inc., 357 West 20th Street, New York, NY 10011. For all other rights, contact: Bruce Dale, c/o Artists Unlimited, 225 West 28th Street, New York, NY 10001.

Author's Note: *White Mountains* is performed without an intermission. The action takes place in multiple scenes, including an overlapping of events, dialogues, and images, and flows continously with as few scene breaks as possible.

Among the special effects called for by the script is a variation in the sound and manner of speaking certain lines, which indicates the distorted and failing hearing of the characters (see Page 11). The chemical poisons are making them go deaf, causing their hands to throb with unbearable pain, stimulating hallucinations based on exaggeration of each person's individual way of looking at the world.

This play was inspired, in part, by a true account of a mother and father who came up with an unusual way to punish their tardy daughter. It backfired.

Cast

MARYANN, 17 years old

MR. BAKER, her father, 40s

MRS. BAKER her mother, 40s

CARLTON, her current boyfriend, late teens

JIMMY, her former boyfriend, late teens

SGT. DAVID ATHERTON, 30

Scene

In the White Mountains of northern New Hampshire: The Baker house, MARYANN's bedroom, various locations outside the town, on the side of the mountain, a cave, a lake, the summit of the mountain, etc.

Time

The present. One night from 11 p.m. till about 4 a.m.

(Lights up on three simultaneous tableaux: (1) MARYANN *in embrace with* SGT. ATHERTON; *(2)* MRS. BAKER *seated in her living room, stroking a cat in her lap; and (3)* CARLTON *and* JIMMY *outdoors, somewhere on one of the mountains, lying on the ground, head to head, facing up, looking at the night sky.)*

JIMMY: I feel better now.

CARLTON: Me too.

ATHERTON: (*To* MARYANN) Promise me you'll think about these things.

JIMMY: The fiend from Flatland can't destroy fifteen years.

CARLTON: Don't call her that.

MARYANN: (*Pause*) If it's . . . if it's all going to happen anyway, what difference does it make what I—

ATHERTON: I want you to be ready.

MARYANN: I have to fight against so much as it is.

JIMMY: You'll find out. One day she'll take you to that cave she likes so much—all dark, damp, and echoey—you'll think you're going there to make love like all the other times. But she'll tell you it's over. And she'll walk out of the cave leaving you all alone to drive yourself nuts wondering why.

CARLTON: That was you. She told me you scared her.

JIMMY: She scared me like nothing I ever knew. I had to talk tough to cover up.

CARLTON: I never could figure what you meant.

MARYANN: I know there must be more. But I'm terribly afraid I could be wrong.

(ATHERTON *kisses her for a long time.*)

JIMMY: We got real close.

CARLTON: I've known her for years.

JIMMY: Not as lovers. (*Pause*) You'll find out.

MARYANN: Let me go now, David.

© *1981 by Bruce Dale*

ATHERTON: Swear to me you won't forget. Watch for the signs. Avoid the traps.

MARYANN: They'll kill me if I don't get back. Please!

(ATHERTON *hugs her again*.)

CARLTON: I'm glad we're friends again.

JIMMY: Carlton, you know what I feel like tonight? I'm always going to know you. If Maryann couldn't end what we have, well, nothing will. I'm going to know you when I die. We'll be together at the end.

(ATHERTON *silently exits*. MARYANN *turns for a last look, but he is gone. She quickly exits in the opposite direction*.)

CARLTON: What are you talking about the end for?

JIMMY: Just a feeling I got.

(MRS. BAKER *puts down the cat, crosses to the window, and looks at her watch.* MR. BAKER *enters with a saw in one hand and a gun in the other. He pauses to watch* MRS. BAKER.)

CARLTON: Those kind of feelings give me the creeps.

JIMMY: I wanted to let you know.

CARLTON: The end. Great. What's that weird smell in the air tonight?

JIMMY: That? Been around for weeks.

CARLTON: It's making me sick.

JIMMY: Just breathe in deep and relax. You get used to it.

MRS. BAKER: What on Earth are you doing with that saw?

MR. BAKER: I have to cut something in half in the basement.

MRS. BAKER: You're lucky. Your hobbies keep you distracted.

(MR. BAKER *puts down the gun and exits with a saw*.)

CARLTON: I think I'm going home.

JIMMY: Home? We're going to watch the sun rise on the mountain.

CARLTON: I feel lousy now. Ears are all stuffed up.

JIMMY: What's the good of going home?

CARLTON: I'll stay in my room, shut the windows. Hate that smell.

JIMMY: Breathe.

CARLTON: Sorry.

JIMMY: Nothing like this air anywhere on Earth.

MRS. BAKER: (*Shouting to* MR. BAKER, *offstage.*) It's after eleven you know.

MR. BAKER: Thanks. I have that bitch of a meeting early tomorrow. Head of the union.

MRS. BAKER: I meant Maryann.

CARLTON: Got to go.

JIMMY: Keep away from that cave.

CARLTON: We'll stay friends.

JIMMY: You'll see.

CARLTON: Till the end comes.

JIMMY: She suggests it, say no.

CARLTON: Night, buddy.

JIMMY: Say no! You say no!

CARLTON: Good-bye, Jimmy.

JIMMY: Carlton—don't forget.

CARLTON: I'll come up and look for you in the morning. (*He exits.*)

JIMMY: Come back! Everything's glowing in the dark. Fantastic! God, I love these mountains.

(JIMMY *breathes in deeply, chokes, coughs. Recovering, he breathes deeply again. He raises his arms to the sky. He opens and closes his hands, and then looks at them.*)

(MRS. BAKER *sits again. She strokes the cat in her lap.*)

(JIMMY *brushes his hands together as if trying to wipe something off.*)

(MR. BAKER *comes back, wiping his hands with a towel, also having trouble getting something off. Standing behind* MRS. BAKER, *he massages her neck.*)

MRS. BAKER: I'm worried sick.

MR. BAKER: You'll make yourself sick worrying.

MRS. BAKER: She ought to know when to be home.

MR. BAKER: She'll flunk school. She hates work. What'll become of her?

MRS. BAKER: Instinct. She knows she's one of the prettiest creatures that ever came into this world. She'll use that.

MR. BAKER: Not very modern, is she?

MRS. BAKER: The nineteenth century, that's when she wishes she'd been born. In Russia no less. Even after all the horror stories her great grandmother told her.

MR. BAKER: We'll make her stay in her room so long the twentieth century will start to seem like the good old days.

MRS. BAKER: She hasn't fed her cat. I sure won't.

MR. BAKER: If that cat stayed out the way she did I'll bet she'd worry. Couldn't fit its whole damn name on a sign.

MRS. BAKER: How can a cat remember a name like that? Elenya Dmitrovna Aleyenta Bacarova Chalyentraika!

(*Cat meows.*)

(JIMMY *runs off.*)

MR. BAKER: Neighbors hear so much Russian gibberish coming out of this house it's a wonder no one sticks a rifle through the window and starts shooting.

MRS. BAKER: She's so smart with the twenty-syllable names. She's flunking that World Affairs course just like everything else.

MR. BAKER: World Affairs sounds about right.

(MARYANN *bursts in.*)

MARYANN: I know, I know! I feel terrible. I lost track of the time.

MR. BAKER: You may feel terrible, young lady, but you made your mother sick as a dog from worry.

MARYANN: Momma, I'm sorry, I didn't have a dime to call.

MR. BAKER: The point is to be in your room where you don't need money to call.

MRS. BAKER: Every—you tell her.

MR. BAKER: Every night for the next month. Weekends too.

MARYANN: A month! Can't you just beat me and get it over with?

MR. BAKER: We're not cavemen like your friends' folks. Beat me, she says.

MRS. BAKER: (*Crying*) . . . your room . . .

MARYANN: (*Pause*) I'll feed Elenya and go right up.

(MRS. BAKER *grabs cat food and spoons it into dish*.)

MR. BAKER: Poor little thing would starve to death if your mother didn't look after it.

(MARYANN *goes to her room*.)

MR. BAKER: She's home, safe and sound now, Linda.

(MRS. BAKER *starts drinking water*. MR. BAKER *buries his head in newspaper*.)

MARYANN: (*Beats pillow, scares cat*) Hate them! Hate him! Hate her! Come back, Eleyna Aleyenta. (*She flips through her World Affairs book*.) How do I know it's as bad as they say over in Russia? Maybe all of school's just some kind of plot to brainwash us. No one's going to force me. Or lie to me, get to me, stop me from finding out. I'll never settle for things the way people here do.

CARLTON: (*Tapping on window*) Psst! Maryann! My folks think I'm camping out with Jimmy.

MARYANN: That's no cover. They must know you and Jimmy hate each other now.

CARLTON: We made a truce.

MARYANN: Jimmy'll say one thing to your face and—he's the one who started telling everyone I was the witch from the lowlands.

CARLTON: Let me in before someone sees.

MARYANN: (*Unlatches window*) Carlton, you couldn't have picked a worse night.

CARLTON: I come every night I can.

MARYANN: The Russians have taken over the town. Now people only come when they're told to.

CARLTON: That's not the Russians, idiot.

MARYANN: Soldiers all over the place. Hiding in the hills. My room is bugged, you can bet on that.

CARLTON: They're a special task force up from Fort Devens. Cleaning up the stuff that spilled.

MARYANN: They're all Russians. Nothing spilled. It's lies to keep us ignorant about the invasion.

CARLTON: The only invasion is from Flatland. Course your folks are both. Russian and Flatlander.

MARYANN: Only the names have been changed.

CARLTON: How come you told Jimmy so much personal stuff and not me?

MARYANN: Don't complain. Jimmy's out. You're in.

CARLTON: Bacarovarich became Baker.

MARYANN: Dad had a lot of prejudice to fight to get ahead in Flatland.

CARLTON: It worked. He got so far ahead there wasn't enough room down there for the Holy Russian Empire to expand.

MARYANN: Stop there. Unless you really want to camp out with Jimmy.

CARLTON: Okay. Let me see your hand.

(*He presses her hand against his crotch.*)

MARYANN: So?

CARLTON: So he's ready and able to stand up to the Russians.

MARYANN: The Russians are the most unpredictable part of World Affairs.

CARLTON: Yeah? If they keep being so unpredictable they might find themselves isolated by the world community.

MARYANN: Russia is strong. She can stand alone.

CARLTON: You haven't stood alone since you moved up here. The list before Jimmy and me is longer than a role call in the United Nations.

MARYANN: Shh! If they hear—

CARLTON: Hell with them! Way they keep browbeating you it's a wonder you have any self-respect left.

MARYANN: Self-respect is evil. The community is everything.

CARLTON: Have they grounded you again?

MARYANN: One month in Siberia.

CARLTON: Don't they have any consideration for me at all?

MARYANN: Carlton, they're so worried about you, that's why they did it. Stuck at home, you're the only boy I can see.

CARLTON: Oh. What's so terrible about that?

MARYANN: There's lots of sexy Russians coming out of the mountains.

CARLTON: Will you stop that shit?

MARYANN: Far from home . . . lonely . . .

CARLTON: I'm going to make noise—

MARYANN: No bubulas to warm their kalashkas against.

CARLTON: Impossible.

MARYANN: I hear the Russians have a better sense of humor than Americans.

CARLTON: Aw, they're a bunch of drunks.

MARYANN: Maybe that's why no one can stop them from making advances. Oh, if only you were a Russian defector. A great Bolshoi dancer. Some heroic free-thinking scientist. A manic-depressive genius novelist.

CARLTON: Or a sexy soldier.

MR. BAKER: Maryann! Your light should be off now.

MARYANN: Okay, Daddy.

MR. BAKER: And cut out all that talking. We know you're cursing us out to that crazy cat. Read yourself to sleep now, honey.

MARYANN: Yeah, Daddy.

(CARLTON *switches off the light.*)

MARYANN: Hey! How can I read my World Affairs in the dark?

CARLTON: (*Getting into bed with her.*) Like this, Babushka.

(MRS. BAKER *has been downing glass after glass of water.*)

MR. BAKER: They haven't said things are safe yet.

MRS. BAKER: I boiled it first.

MR. BAKER: I'm told boiling won't kill it.

MRS. BAKER: Boiling kills everything.

MR. BAKER: Not these chemicals.

MRS. BAKER: Toss out all your vegetables then. No one knows how far back it started. We can't stop living.

MR. BAKER: Animals died from drinking, not eating.

MRS. BAKER: You know I haven't drunk anything but water for five years now.

MR. BAKER: That stomach ailment you think you still have.

MRS. BAKER: If I'm not careful, my intestines could be gone by the time I'm fifty.

(*The rest of what* MRS. BAKER *says comes out garbled, distorted, perhaps sounding the way a deaf person who has never heard speech would sound. Throughout the rest of the play, anywhere this is indicated, it represents a hearing problem in one or more of the characters. The way the one person speaks is the way the other hears it. No one has a speaking problem.*)

I'm amazed you could forget what I went through before we left the city—

MR. BAKER: (*Also distorted*) It's only your nerves again, aggravated by this business with Maryann.

MRS. BAKER: (*Normal speech*) What? Maryann did what?

MR. BAKER: (*First few words are inaudible.*) . . . as if she ever did.

MRS. BAKER: Oh, I'll let her stay up there and stew.

MR. BAKER: Bravo. Ten minutes has gone by and you haven't run to her side to forgive.

MRS. BAKER: We'll make up—after those soldiers are gone.

MR. BAKER: I give you till midnight.

MRS. BAKER: I may be a softie, but I'm not stupid. I remember too well what you were like in the service.

(*Water goes down wrong way and* MRS. BAKER *starts choking.* MR. BAKER *crosses to her, pats her on back. Suddenly, he starts choking too. Her choking stops and she looks at him curiously.*)

(*In the mountains,* JIMMY *enters, still running.* SGT. ATHERTON *enters from another direction, and they collide.*)

JIMMY: Whoa!

ATHERTON: Halt!

JIMMY: Where did you come from?

ATHERTON: Freeze!

JIMMY: Okay!

ATHERTON: (*Drawing weapon*) Back!

JIMMY: Who are you?

ATHERTON: Easy, kid.

JIMMY: I didn't see you. I was just running and—

ATHERTON: You don't do that to a person.

JIMMY: You came out of nowhere.

ATHERTON: Don't get belligerent.

JIMMY: I live here. You soldiers are here on our behalf.

ATHERTON: Theoretically.

JIMMY: What are you doing up here now anyway?

ATHERTON: Patrol.

JIMMY: Well, you got me. Now what?

ATHERTON: Now you walk—back the way you came.

JIMMY: That way I stumble onto something top secret, huh?

ATHERTON: Maybe.

JIMMY: Hey—I know you. You talked to me and my friend in town.

ATHERTON: I felt a duty. To help you both with your problem.

JIMMY: You told us it didn't matter 'cause we were already dead.

ATHERTON: That comes as a surprise to many ears.

JIMMY: How do you know everybody who thinks they're alive is really dead?

ATHERTON: I've learned many useful things since coming up here.

JIMMY: There's nothing like these mountains anywhere. I don't care where in the world you've been.

ATHERTON: The air is . . . unusual. I've never tasted water that made you thirstier the more you drink. Otherwise, a place like any other.

JIMMY: You're not from here. You can never know.

ATHERTON: We've had friendlier welcomes. But we have our job to do.

JIMMY: Like keeping us away from what is ours.

ATHERTON: For the time being. I suggest you follow orders.

JIMMY: I will. (*Pause*) For the time being. (*He slowly backs off and exits.*)

(*Coming out from under covers*, MARYANN *looks across stage toward* ATHERTON, *as if she feels his presence.*)

ATHERTON: It won't change the final outcome if I inform certain . . . specially chosen people. But if I'm powerless to alter your destiny, I can at least let you know what I have found out. Knowing what will happen is a kind of salvation. Isn't it?

CARLTON: Please don't go out with other boys.

MARYANN: It's not other boys I'm interested in.

CARLTON: Please.

MARYANN: Maybe I'll end up liking you more.

CARLTON: If you ran off with a soldier, I'd—I'd—

MARYANN: Kill myself.

CARLTON: I'd kill myself, then I'd kill him.

MARYANN: Those men have killed a lot of people.

CARLTON: There's plenty of cowards in the Army.

MARYANN: Maybe, but they lie so well.

(ATHERTON *jabs the air with his gun, simultaneously to* CARLTON'S *line.*)

CARLTON: They could be gone tomorrow. With the last drum goes the last soldier and—hey! Quit jabbing me!

MARYANN: I'm not touching you.

CARLTON: In my ear.

MARYANN: I didn't.

CARLTON: Ow!

MARYANN: Ouch! It won't help to crunch my fingers!

(CARLTON *gets out of bed, massaging his ears.* MARYANN *holds her hands up over her head. His ears and her fingers continue to throb with pain.*)

MARYANN: What is it? I hope you don't have some disease.

CARLTON: Do you?

MRS. BAKER: Maryann, let me in.

(CARLTON *goes under the bad to hide.* MARYANN *lets her mother in.*)

MRS. BAKER: He's turning in now. He blows up but he's more hurt than mad.

MARYANN: I'm not cursing you out.

MRS. BAKER: You've been quiet as a mouse. (*Pause*) He's playing the tyrant. Tomorrow he'll cut the time.

(MARYANN *is silent.*)

We don't know anything about these soldiers.

MARYANN: I'm only watching what's going on.

MRS. BAKER: I believe you. And still (*The next words are garbled, inaudible.*)

MARYANN: What?

MRS. BAKER: (*First words inaudible*) . . . of exposing yourself to that kind of danger. You don't have to give me that sarcastic look of yours.

MARYANN: Look?

MRS. BAKER: I'm trying, Maryann. And you're not even listening.

(MARYANN's *response is distorted*) Don't mumble! It stinks up here. (*She crosses to close the window.*)

MARYANN: Momma, my fingers . . . look at them. They're killing me . . .

MRS. BAKER: What's wrong? Well, let me see.

MARYANN: Like some animal's biting, chewing—

MRS. BAKER: No marks anywhere.

MARYANN: Just started throbbing when I tried to go to sleep.

MRS. BAKER: Don't tell me you've got venereal disease already.

MARYANN: This can't be VD!

MRS. BAKER: I've read it mimics other ailments. What are you doing to us?

MARYANN: Oh . . . oh . . . I think it's going away.

MRS. BAKER: (*Pause*) I hope that wasn't a play for sympathy.

MARYANN: (*Hugging her*) I don't deserve sympathy.

MRS. BAKER: I try to keep in mind what it's like at your age, honey. I know all the feelings, they're so powerful. I want you to have as much freedom as possible. But I get so scared.

MARYANN: I'm scared too. But I want to push on out, not close myself in.

MRS. BAKER: I know you'll be gone in a year. Maybe less.

MARYANN: Not out like that, Momma.

MRS. BAKER: From the day you were born you were the most uncontrollable thing. Energy like I never saw. How did that fireball come out of you, your dad would ask me.

MARYANN: That why you didn't want anymore after me?

MRS. BAKER: Didn't want? God, how we tried!

MARYANN: What you get is what you want.

MRS. BAKER: Who ever told you that?

MARYANN: No one. (*Pause*) Just seems the way things have always been. What I read.

MRS. BAKER: Your World Affairs book proves just the opposite. Everyone has to live through what they didn't ask for.

MARYANN: The people who wrote it thought that. The people who lived it knew otherwise.

MRS. BAKER: Who do you know who LIVED World Affairs?

MARYANN: I can imagine, that's all.

MRS. BAKER: You've left nothing to the imagination.

MARYANN: I'm not going to be a nobody forever, Momma. I'll be in a book like that in fifty years.

MRS. BAKER: Screwing soldiers is no ticket to the history books!

(SGT. ATHERTON *on patrol*.)

ATHERTON: People don't die. I've seen hundreds, thousands of dead bodies. And I've met the people on the other side.

MARYANN: Momma, I'm not afraid of anything. I want us to stay close, but I'm sure I'll do a lot worse in my time.

MRS. BAKER: Let's see you try to screw anybody in here, smarty.

MARYANN: So you won't get Dad to let me out?

MRS. BAKER: If I had my way, you'd spend the rest of your life right in here READING the history books. Honestly—admiring all that war and killing.

ATHERTON: This isn't life. People feel strange, crazy, frustrated, confused because this is only a prelude. We're all impatient for the dawn. The killing speeds up the coming of the resurrection.

MARYANN: Momma, please don't go away mad!

MRS. BAKER: (*Facing away*) Damn it, I cry too easily.

MARYANN: It's only because you're so impatient.

MRS. BAKER: I'll tell your father that one. The hellcat calls me impatient.

MARYANN: Dad calls me a hellcat?

(MRS. BAKER *turns around. She is crying blood.*)

Momma!

MRS. BAKER: Stop trying to win me over.

MARYANN: Look! You're bleeding!

MRS. BAKER: I opened my cut somehow.

MARYANN: Cut?

MRS. BAKER: A knife fell on my cheek. Let me go now. (*She crosses back to* MR. BAKER.)

MRS. BAKER: She's a tramp. The worst kind.

MR. BAKER: I know. But you should try and calm down. Come to bed.

MRS. BAKER: My nerves are shot.

MR. BAKER: That kid gets her moodiness from you. I've never been depressed a day in my life.

MRS. BAKER: You're not getting into bed all dirty like that.

MR. BAKER: (*Coughing, some distortion*) Sure I am. It's my knocking around in the basement that keeps me fit. I've worked damn hard, dealt with the biggest men in the business, just to get her this house, take the pressure off her. My firm has altered the way people live on this planet, but a hammer and nails are all I need to keep happy.

MRS. BAKER: She'll never be happy.

MR. BAKER: Stop torturing yourself.

MRS. BAKER: I'm keeping a big pitcher of water right by my head.

(The BAKERS in bed.)

ATHERTON: When blood flows out of the White Mountains, great rivers, geysers, torrents, oceans of blood, you'll know your own resurrection is near. Look around you, Maryann. It's already beginning.

(CARLTON *jumps out from under bed. He rushes to open the window.*)

CARLTON: I almost suffocated!

MARYANN: She didn't see you. She was too afraid to even look.

CARLTON: I'm boiling hot. Must be sick. But I've got so much energy I could climb all nine mountains tonight.

MARYANN: Don't go now, Carlton. Please stay overnight.

CARLTON: Hot . . . horrible . . . hot. I've got to feel the wind at the top of the mountain. I'll dive off thousands of feet into the lake. Cold freezing water all over me!

(*Putting on his trousers, he drops his wallet.*)

MARYANN: Did you see Momma's face?

(CARLTON *kisses her, then takes off through the window.*)

Wait___

ATHERTON: For some the waiting becomes unbearable. The lesser souls fear death and hide in a million disguises. But those of us who know have to shed all the trappings, let ourselves die again and again, just to forget—we're still only waiting.

MARYANN: (*Stepping into remembered scene with* ATHERTON.) I'm surrounded by liars, Sgt. Atherton. David. They won't shed their disguises. Can't, maybe? Like Momma. All the time so afraid.

ATHERTON: You're alone in this world. Don't let anyone tell you otherwise. It's a test. Whoever bears the loneliness best can cross over a thousand times, come back with knowledge, each time stronger.

MARYANN: I love them! I'm not alone.

ATHERTON: The dead don't lie, Maryann. They're the only ones who can't. The dead are your closest friends. The honest and real family your own can never be.

MARYANN: It's getting terribly late, David. I have to go home. Meet me here tomorrow night.

ATHERTON: Resist! Your family wants you in a hole in the ground. They'll bury you with their love, their fear. Stay with me tonight, Maryann. I'll show you the place where people are beyond love.

MARYANN: (*Running away from him.*) I don't want to ever see that place!

(*The* BAKERS *in bed. They cough continually.*)

MRS. BAKER: I can't sleep.

MR. BAKER: Neither can I.

MRS. BAKER: We probably caught this cough from Maryann. Running around in the damp night air.

MR. BAKER: We've got to be strict or there's no hope.

MRS. BAKER: She's got venereal disease. Pain all over. Seeing things.

MR. BAKER: It takes years for those symptoms to show up. You know what that means. Where's all this blood coming from?

MRS. BAKER: She got me so upset my knife cut opened up.

MR. BAKER: (*Coughing, choking*) I told you not to go up to her.

MRS. BAKER: Here, have some water.

MR. BAKER: NO!

MRS. BAKER: I'll sleep in the other room then. You'll keep me up all night with your coughing. (*Drinking constantly*) You're more stubborn than me. Water's the best thing for you at a time like this. It's fresh, pure. Comes out of the White Mountains. You can't tell me they've poisoned the White Mountains.

(MR. BAKER *keeps coughing miserably.* MRS. BAKER *goes to a separate bed.* MARYANN *sits in her darkened room, listening to the coughing sounds coming from below. She looks through the World Affairs book, reading by flashlight.*)

(*As she reads from the different chapters,* MR. BAKER, MRS. BAKER, CARLTON, *and* SGT. ATHERTON *perform the indicated actions.*)

MARYANN: Oppression. Struggle. Underground. Backlash. Hunger. Catholicism. Military. Resurgence. Power. Throne. Ascension.

(CARLTON *is climbing to the top of Mt. Washington. He reaches the summit and raises both arms over his head.*)

MARYANN: Resistance. Assassination. Marxist. Desegregation. Inflation. Bombing. Murderer. Territorial. Rapist.

(MRS. BAKER *pours glass after glass from her seemingly bottomless pitcher, with no end to her thirst. The towel on her lap is dabbed with blood.*)

MARYANN: Abortion. Starvation. Rioting. Terrorist. Imprisonment. Suicide. Dignity. Slavery. Nuclear. Refugees.

(MR. BAKER *wraps himself in blankets. He is sitting up in bed, shivering.*)

MARYANN: Burial. Invasion. Arson. Kidnapping. Eviction. Execution. Famine. Stockpiling. Multinational. Space. Devastation.

(SGT. ATHERTON *uncovers a broken chemical drum from which a shimmery substance oozes out onto the ground. He wears thick protective gloves as he removes the drum.*)

MARYANN: Panic. Fascist. Explosive. Impeachment. Border. Republican. Guns. Oil. Pope. Espionage. Persecution. Treaty. Treachery.

(CARLTON, *now naked, dives off the mountaintop.*)

(MRS. BAKER *drops her pitcher, spilling water all over everything.* MR. BAKER, *looking deathly ill, struggles out of bed, gets his shotgun, and gets back into bed, laying it by his side.*)

(SGT. ATHERTON *disposes of another container of toxic substance. He has a look of insane glee. He takes off the protective gloves and dips his hands into the leaking fluid. He licks his fingers.*)

MARYANN: Equal. Independence. Freedom. Rights. Salvation. Humanity. Future. Bountiful. Agreement. Peace. Hope.

(*Having reached the end of the book,* MARYANN *writes something of her own on its final blank page. She writes quickly, passionately.*)

(CARLTON, *dripping wet, lies on the ground, chilled, relieved.*)

(MRS. BAKER *refills her pitcher with blood and goes in to* MR. BAKER.)

MR. BAKER: No water!

MRS. BAKER: It's not water. It's safe.

(SGT. ATHERTON *is kneeling, praying in front of the leaking chemical drum.*)

MARYANN: (*As she writes*) Evolution. Maryann. Insurrection. Maryann. Militaristic. Maryann. Political. Maryann. Annihilation. Maryann. Discovery. Maryann. Fanatic. Maryann. Energy/Upheaval/Shortage/Accident/Crisis/Armageddon/Negotiations/Liberal/Disproportionatedecentralizedstabilityrevolutionarystriking allegationconservativewarfareregimesucidalwelfarepopulation diplomaticautonomypowerminority skirmishessupportersplague radicalsetbackgovernmentalsecession shakyunrestdeescalation guerrillaethnictroopshutdownimperialistic mistreatmentdeportationhostageviolationmechanizationabomination maryannMARYANN MARYANN MARYANN!!!

MR. BAKER: I can't take this pain!

MRS. BAKER: You're not dying—drink this.

MR. BAKER: Fast death better than slow!

MRS. BAKER: You're going to drink!

MR. BAKER: You're poisoning me—

MRS. BAKER: You're delirious.

MR. BAKER: You're a witch! You aborted all my children.

MRS. BAKER: Your sickness made them die inside me. Drink!

MR. BAKER: Only that daughter who's no daughter of mine—you let her survive. For her to disgrace me. To humiliate me. No sons! No daughters! Only Maryann.

MRS. BAKER: She's our most loving child. She's not beyond help. Your sickness is talking.

MR. BAKER: Let me die.

MRS. BAKER: I won't leave your side. You're going to make it through this night.

MR. BAKER: I'm burning inside. My head is glowing red hot. See it? See it?

(MRS. BAKER *pours water all over his face, trying to get some down his mouth.*)

MRS. BAKER: Water from the White Mountains will cool you completely.

(MARYANN *takes off her clothes and stuffs them into a bag. She puts on a beautiful white dress that looks like something worn in nineteenth-century Russia, perhaps by a princess in the court of the Czar. All that is left in her room is her World Affairs book, open on the bed. She picks up her cat in one arm, the bag full of belongings in the other. The cat jumps free. She throws the bag out the window, then climbs out.*)

(SGT. ATHERTON *comes upon* CARLTON, *lying naked on the ground.*)

ATHERTON: You're in a restricted area.

CARLTON: I had to cool off. The lake was freezing. Perfect.

ATHERTON: The lake is out of bounds. All those signs are up for your safety.

CARLTON: I didn't see any signs. I jumped into the lake. From way up there.

ATHERTON: The mountain?

CARLTON: The very top.

ATHERTON: You can lie to me, kid. I don't care. It's your life that's in danger.

CARLTON: I was burning up. Trapped like an animal. I don't feel that now. The danger was before.

ATHERTON: (*Drawing his gun*) Get up. Put your clothes on.

CARLTON: I left them up there.

ATHERTON: We'll get you some spare gear. Let's go!

(*Brought abruptly out of his blissful state,* CARLTON *walks off with* ATHERTON.)

(BAKERS *in bed together again.* MR. BAKER *wakes* MRS. BAKER *from a deep sleep.*)

MRS. BAKER: Mmm? What are you doing?

MR. BAKER: I just had a nightmare.

MRS. BAKER: You're overheated. Congested. You won't drink water.

MR. BAKER: In the nightmare you forced me to drink blood.

MRS. BAKER: Drink blood? Boy, you are worried about the water!

MR. BAKER: I was so feverish I wanted to shoot myself. You wouldn't let me.

MRS. BAKER: I'm such a good wife to you.

MR. BAKER: I woke up with the shotgun in bed with me.

MRS. BAKER: Just 'cause I wouldn't sleep next to you for one night—honestly.

MR. BAKER: I must've walked in my sleep.

MRS. BAKER: You're upset over Maryann. All the soldiers out there. Memories of the war.

MR. BAKER: This was even worse than the Army.

MRS. BAKER: The war is long over.

MR. BAKER: In the dream you climbed into bed with me. Even with my burning fever.

MRS. BAKER: You stay right here with me now.

MR. BAKER: (*Stepping in water* MRS. BAKER *spilled earlier.*) What did you do here? We'll slip and break our necks in the middle of the night.

MRS. BAKER: I don't remember doing that. (*Pause*) Maryann unsettled me so. She actually thinks we stopped having children because she was too much for us.

MR. BAKER: Well she was.

MRS. BAKER: Let's not exaggerate.

MR. BAKER: Can't shake that dream. Like it's still happening.

MRS. BAKER: Did you put the shotgun away?

MR. BAKER: Trigger's locked. The cat can't set if off.

MRS. BAKER: Good. And Maryann won't blast us in our sleep.

MR. BAKER: I'll go put it away.

(*He crosses to get the shotgun. Upstairs,* JIMMY *is sneaking in through* MARYANN'S *open window.* MR. BAKER *hears a noise and heads upstairs.*)

(*Looking around,* JIMMY *finds only the World Affairs book. Astonished by what* MARYANN *wrote, he tucks the book under his arm. He sees* CARLTON'S *wallet on the floor near the bed. He looks inside.*)

(*Startled by* MR. BAKER, JIMMY *drops the wallet.*)

MR. BAKER: Where did you come from?

(JIMMY *speaks but his words are garbled and distorted in the manner previously described.*)

Come downstairs, you.

(JIMMY *starts down ahead of* MR. BAKER, *who notices that* MARYANN *is not in her room.*)

Linda! Wake up! Is Maryann down there?

(*The distraction gives* JIMMY *the chance to bolt out of the house.*)

Damn it! Maryann! Where are you?

MRS. BAKER: She's not down here.

MR. BAKER: Call the police. That man made off with all her things.

MRS. BAKER: Where is she!

MR. BAKER: Maybe she ran off when she heard him coming through the window. (*He finds the wallet.*) He dropped this. Goddamn it! I didn't get a good look at him. That was Carlton. (*He meets Mrs. Baker in the living room.*) Get the police anyway. I bet they find the two of them together someplace.

MRS. BAKER: Her window was open when I went up. Carlton must have been hiding in there all the time.

MR. BAKER: This is the end of her. (*He suddenly drops the shotgun and twists his hands together in pain.*)

MRS. BAKER: What is it?

MR. BAKER: Like arthritis. I don't know. Go make that call.

(CARLTON *and* ATHERTON *re-enter, in the mountains.* CARLTON now is dressed in Army fatigues.)

CARLTON: Sorry about all this, Sergeant. I know about the off limits. I got crazy or something.

ATHERTON: See your family doctor tomorrow. Have him check your blood. Might not be anything wrong. Or you could die.

CARLTON: Hey, what about all my clothes and things I left on the mountain?

ATHERTON: I can't let you go back up there now.

CARLTON: I could die? That what you said?

ATHERTON: It might only be temporary.

CARLTON: In the papers they didn't make that spill sound so awful. Routine poison.

ATHERTON: I'm saying for your own good. Privileged information. No need to start a panic. You run on home now.

CARLTON: Listen, what is this chemical stuff anyhow?

ATHERTON: You read the papers.

CARLTON: I want to know exactly what I took a bath in tonight.

ATHERTON: I wish to hell we knew. Looks like it could be bigger than all these nine mountains.

CARLTON: Come on, cut the Big Brother routine. I know where you really hail from.

ATHERTON: Narrowminded New England snobs. You think Oklahoma's a different country.

CARLTON: Oklahoma? Ha! I pledge allegiance to the flag of the Union of Soviet Socialist Republics. So much for your poison cover story, "Sergeant."

ATHERTON: (*To himself*) Hallucinations. (*Pause*) Do your hands tingle? Any pain in the ears? How about unexpected bleeding from strange places?

CARLTON: Yeah, your face, you Commie turd.

ATHERTON: When you trespass on military property we have total control over what happens to you, boy.

CARLTON: What can she possibly see in the likes of you? Bunch of leadheaded morons.

ATHERTON: You'll spend the night in lockup.

CARLTON: Red-bellied, vodka-puking—

ATHERTON: Move, kid!

CARLTON: You don't push me around, socialist scum.

(CARLTON *is jabbed in the gut by* ATHERTON's *rifle. He is tripped and then pinned on the ground.*)

Wake up, everybody! Hey! Out of your houses! You're being tricked!

(ATHERTON's *hands are glowing like the substance he's been cleaning up. He places a hand over* CARLTON's *face.*)

ATHERTON: One life is nothing when thousands are at stake.

(CARLTON *is unconscious.* ATHERTON *drags him off.*)

(JIMMY *enters, still clutching World Affairs book.*)

JIMMY: Lived here all my life. No one's going to ruin it for us. Soldiers. Factory people. Rich Flatland families from the south. Scare them off. Drive them out. White Mountains stay pure. Clean. Free.

(*His hands start hurting so much he has to drop the book. His next few sentences are distorted. Perhaps the audience members' hearing is going also.*)

JIMMY: They lie, tell us it'll be safe again soon. It's all a fake to get more soldiers, more strangers in here. People from the south already poisoned. Illness and death their natural way of life. Boston, Concord, Cambridge, Cape Cod—all the contaminated regions of Flatland—moving in, spewing their poisons everywhere.

(*His speech alternates between low, roaring animal sounds and the clear intonations of a heroic rebel.*)

Must be pushed back. Forced out. Plague started before I was born. Signs of it mysterious, remote. Then Maryann seduced me in the schoolyard. Her family carried in the full dose. She fucked me on the football field. Her poison's in my blood now. She made me love her with the kind of witchcraft mountain people can't understand, can't fight. My best friend was next, while she left me to die in her underground cave. It won't end with us either. All the boys in the mountains will fall to the southern eroticism of that contagious bitch. Only a thing so unbearably pretty as Maryann could make slow death so appealing. Only a fast death can put a stop to what she came here to do. The Flatland fiend must be destroyed if the White Mountains are ever to fluorish again!

(*He picks up the World Affairs book and throws it in the lake. He drops down on his belly, dips his face into the water, and drinks.*)

(MR. *and* MRS. BAKER *are waiting again.* MRS. BAKER *still drinks constantly from her "bottomless" pitcher of water.* MR. BAKER *is rubbing ointment all over his aching hands. The cat is in* MRS. BAKER'S *lap. She strokes it and lets it drink water also.*)

MRS. BAKER: You have to worry about all those poor soldier boys, too.

MR. BAKER: Linda, don't mutter to yourself.

MRS. BAKER: She's spreading VD to every one of them she touches.

MR. BAKER: (*Distorted sound, partly inaudible*) . . . to Carlton . . . always . . . boy was decent . . .

MRS. BAKER: Then they spread it in every foreign port. Children around the world cursed with VD from the word go.

MR. BAKER: Stop your nagging! Sure I'm only a VP now, but they'll make me president soon. I've stood by the firm during this crisis.

MRS. BAKER: VD! VD! I'm proud of what you are. I moved here with you because of the place. I never expected you to become the king of industry.

MR. BAKER: What were we supposed to do with ten thousand drums? Shoot them into outer space?

MRS. BAKER: You leave the city. It follows you up into the mountains. They come after you with tanks.

MR. BAKER: The White Mountains will be here forever. What we make can't destroy nine mountains. Let the waste wear itself out. So simple. A war with Nature. Nature always wins. White Mountains are eternal.

(*The cat scratches* MRS. BAKER.)

MRS. BAKER: Nyet! Monster! Ow!

JIMMY: (*Bobbing his head out of water.*) I am the savior of the mountains. Leading my people higher and higher. At the summit we will turn, look down upon the poisoned creatures of the south. We will send an avalanche to crush them. Bacarovarich and his hordes will be buried forever and White Mountains shall be saved!

(*As he jumps to his feet, his voice now distorted:*)

Hear me now! People of Franconia, Lincoln, Conway! Friends along the Kancamagus! Stop the legions moving in among us! The life of eight mountains has already been annihilated. Don't let them destroy the only one we've got left! Rise up to save White—

(*"Mountains" is inaudible, even though he screams it. As* JIMMY *continues shouting, his voice is gone and there is only silence.*)

(*Another area on the mountain:* MARYANN *enters in her white Russian gown. She waits by a steaming pool.*)

MARYANN: David? David! Are you there? (*Silence*) David.

(SGT. ATHERTON *appears.*)

MARYANN: They'll kill me. I wasn't supposed to go out again.

ATHERTON: In the morning I'll talk to your parents. Tell them you had to be disinfected.

MARYANN: I still don't believe your story, you know.

ATHERTON: Even the others in my platoon doubt me. But you must believe it.

MARYANN: I love denying the truth. Other people think you're crazy for it and then you can be as crazy as you like. They'll let you do anything because that's all they expect from you.

ATHERTON: It's not to be taken lightly, Maryann. I thought was immune, but now I find the antidote is imperfect. I feel the symptoms. I don't know how much longer I'll survive to spread the word.

MARYANN: Don't tell anyone what we two know. Let's lose ourselves in the mountains!

ATHERTON: You can lose yourself only so much in this life. It's nothing once you've seen the next.

MARYANN: I don't care about that life. I want to immerse myself in this one. Be a part of World Affairs. Revolution. Anarchy. Socialism. Summit conference. Invasion.

ATHERTON: Poison. Running all through your system. You want to be a part of everything, Maryann, but soon there won't be anything of you left.

MARYANN: Wonderful poison! I breathe it, drink it in, let it consume me. I feel more alive tonight than I ever have.

ATHERTON: When I talked to the dead I knew how ignorant all the people of this world really are. I could finally sense what had escaped every genius who ever lived. The resurrection, Maryann! When we'll be lovers in a way that's impossible here. It doesn't matter that we poison the White Mountains in this life. The next life is where we reach the summit.

MARYANN: I'm young! The next life can wait. You, too—they've forced you to think old ahead of time. Take me back to Russia with you. I've got to see for myself how my World Affairs book tells lies.

ATHERTON: I've never been to Russia. I hear it's very gray.

MARYANN: Don't talk down your motherland. She still loves you even though you've done horrible things across the world.

ATHERTON: I don't remember where I come from. But it *was* dismal and gray.

MARYANN: Then let me take you into the White Mountains. Look around you! Every color except gray! If I show you the White Mountains, will you take me around the world?

ATHERTON: You don't want to see what's left of it. Gray all over.

MARYANN: Gray can be beautiful. Gray is the color of my cat, Elenya Dmitrovna Aleyenta Bacarova Chalyentraika. She's lived through three czarist empires, four Communist regimes, and one capitalist spree in Flatland. This is her ninth life, here in the White Mountains. Where we haven't suffered as much, but at the same time can never be so happy as those who have truly known pain.

(*She suddenly raises both hands to her ears, in apparent distress.*)

ATHERTON: You've definitely been exposed. In most people the hands start to go first. But the ears quickly follow.

MARYANN: Why does it hurt so much? Tonight! I finally have the chance to escape and now this!

ATHERTON: Listen to me! (*His speech distorted.*) In a short while you won't need your body anymore. There's no reason to endure pain when right around the corner—

(*His words are not only distorted beyond recognition—now, each sound from his mouth reverberates with a resonance that is unbearable to her ears.*)

MARYANN: Stop telling me about the next life! I'm in pain right now, right here! I want it to stop! Now! Not in some wonderful other place.

(SGT. ATHERTON *guides* MARYANN *to a secluded spot where he put one of the leaking drums. He has her immerse her trembling hands into the chemical substance. Her hands glow as his did before.*)

ATHERTON: The antidote I told you about is . . . an excess of the chemical itself.

MARYANN: Pain is a major part of World Affairs. I can learn to live with it. Better to feel it than not be a part of anything.

ATHERTON: Shh. Be calm now. Soon it will all be gone.

MARYANN: Treachery. Starvation. Poverty. Batallions. Firebomb. Barbarism. Coup d'etat. Squalor. Holocaust.

ATHERTON: Sleep. Rest. Tranquility. Dreams. Adrift. Doze. Forever. Peace. Death.

(MARYANN *has passed out.*)

(JIMMY *moves in from the shadows.* SGT. ATHERTON *is absorbed in* MARYANN, *and his hearing is failing him as it is all the others.*)

(JIMMY *brings a rock down on* ATHERTON's *head.* ATHERTON *falls.*)

JIMMY: (*Caressing* MARYANN) So you weren't helping these foreigners, were you? You're their victim, too. (*He splashes water from the pool onto her.*)

JIMMY: Maybe the poison's been happening for years. Long before any of us knew. Maybe that's what made you not love me all of a sudden after telling me we'll be together forever. The poison made you so crazy you couldn't tell one boy from the next. Carlton was my best friend—I never liked a guy that much my whole life. Maryann! White Mountains can't be like the rest of the dying world. I remember being two years old. Even younger. The beauty was astounding me already. It was in the people too. You can't tell me there was ever family closer than mine. Never friends like Carlton and me.

(MARYANN *is waking up.*)

What can I do! Love you or kill you? It's the poison confusing me. I waited too long . . .

MARYANN: David? (*Pause*) Carlton?

JIMMY: Guess again.

(MARYANN *looks shocked.*)

What's the matter? Say my name!

(MARYANN *says "Jimmy" but it is utterly distorted to his ears.*)

Jimmy! Jimmy! Jimmy! Why won't you say it?

(MARYANN *is talking in a frenzy but it's all coming out like a record being played backwards.* JIMMY'S *ears are hurting and he wails with pain.* MARYANN *sees* ATHERTON *and throws herself on him.*)

MARYANN: What have you done!

(JIMMY *climbs on top of* MARYANN.)

Get off of me! I loved him.

JIMMY: You don't know who you loved.

MARYANN: I know who I didn't.

JIMMY: What?

MARYANN: And never ever could.

JIMMY: You tell me that now?

MARYANN: I'm telling you I hate everybody in the White Mountains. Everyone I've been forced to associate with since my family dragged me up here. Each and every boy, girl, teacher, hunter, preacher, trucker, animal, rock, tree that ever got in my way. None of you live! Nobody here understands.

JIMMY: You are a witch from the south. The lowliest fiend Flatland ever sent to destroy what we have.

MARYANN: If only that was true. If I only had the power to blast you off this mountain!

(SGT. ATHERTON *opens his eyes like he's been awake all along. He scrambles out from under them, grabs his rifle.* JIMMY *goes for his rock, pushes* MARYANN *aside, and attacks* ATHERTON. ATHERTON *shoots him.*)

MARYANN: JIMMY!! Oh—what is happening? What's going on! Jimmy . . . Jimmy . . . Is that what it's like? That's how it happens? People everywhere dying—being butchered, slaughtered—JUST LIKE THAT? World Affairs end like Jimmy?

ATHERTON: Just like Jimmy.

MARYANN: But—everybody heard. You can't get away with that. You'll be arrested. Jailed. Executed.

ATHERTON: Nobody heard anything.

MARYANN: An explosion! A sound like I never heard. World Affairs right outside their windows. A mob will come.

ATHERTON: They're all stone deaf by now. Holding their ears. Screaming.

MARYANN: His body here. Dawn in a couple hours.

ATHERTON: His body will get shipped out with the others.

MARYANN: Shipped out?

ATHERTON: (*Picking up* JIMMY's *body.*) Follow me. I'll show you. World Affairs right under your nose.

(*Dumb with fear,* MARYANN *follows* ATHERTON *off. The* BAKERS *are making sounds again: whispers and grunts, gradually coming back to identifiable speech.*)

MRS. BAKER: I can't blame her. Carlton forced her.

MR. BAKER: So quiet tonight. No wind. No animals.

MRS. BAKER: Maybe they're all gone. The clean-up's over sooner than expected.

MR. BAKER: There was no clean-up. Just an excuse. Competition saw the chance to close us down.

MRS. BAKER: Then why you beg me not to drink water? Why you up with chills all night? Where's the poison coming from if not your factories?

MR. BAKER: Don't complain to me about poison and such when it's my punishing Maryann that's got you upset.

MRS. BAKER: She's so dreadfully lonely up here.

MR. BAKER: How's that scratch?

MRS. BAKER: Hurts like the devil. Little Russian monster.

MR. BAKER: She sits up in her room and tells that damn furry thing everything she hates about us.

MRS. BAKER: She loves us.

MR. BAKER: She loves the cat more. Just see if she had to choose.

MRS. BAKER: Where's that ointment? My hands are acting up again.

MR. BAKER: Instead of worrying yourself to death—imagining you've got what I do—do like I said. Try to get that cat into a box of some kind. We'll give Maryann a lesson she'll remember.

(SGT. ATHERTON, *carrying* JIMMY, *enters the cave ahead of* MARYANN. *Inside there is a pile of bodies, many in advanced states of decay.*)

MARYANN: How do you know this cave?

ATHERTON: It was my job to learn every inch of these mountains.

MARYANN: This is where Jimmy and I used to come. Before we found out my parents were so deaf they couldn't hear us fooling around right in my room.

ATHERTON: I don't think you'll want to bring anybody here from now on.

(*They see the bodies.*)

MARYANN: Who are they?

ATHERTON: Some people would say they've lost their identity.

MARYANN: They're dead!

ATHERTON: Another name for it. (*He puts* JIMMY's *body with the others.*)

MARYANN: Did you kill all these people?

ATHERTON: Hey, I'm not some kind of monster.

MARYANN: The burning of Rome. Excavation of the concentration camps. Hiroshima. The starving of Cambodia. Avalanche of poison in White Mountains.

ATHERTON: All these people reached the truth by different paths. A couple exposed to a hundred times the amount your family was. Not everyone survives the antidote. With some it's even a mystery to us how they ended up here so fast. And people like this fellow here—from being where they had no business.

MARYANN: Carlton!

ATHERTON: Knew him too? Popular girl.

MARYANN: He's dressed like a soldier.

ATHERTON: I found him buck-bathing in the lake. No hope after that.

MARYANN: You killed him! Just like Jimmy! Only Carlton did nothing!

ATHERTON: Where he is, I wouldn't mind.

MARYANN: Where he is—you should be! Murderer!

ATHERTON: What I've been all along, Maryann. I thought it was what you liked in me.

MARYANN: Carlton was my first friend here. When everyone else called me the fool from Flatland. We didn't become lovers till five years later. That ruined it, of course. But Carlton was the best. The only one who never condemned.

ATHERTON: You really believe he's gone, don't you?

MARYANN: Well he is!

ATHERTON: Everything I've told you the last few nights—none of it's penetrated. Carlton is resurrected.

MARYANN: World Affairs has nothing to say about that. You won't convince me otherwise. In my book even the one famous resurrection didn't rate a single chapter, not a footnote, a purple box even.

ATHERTON: It's the chapter that hasn't been written yet. I told you—everything thus far has been a prelude. In our time, Maryann, history will become inverted, stretched out, relived thousands and thousands of times. It will end and begin again. The final war between Ignorance and Enlightment will be fought in our time. This life will fade and the Next will become a reality.

MARYANN: Liar! You lie to cover up why you killed Carlton.

ATHERTON: I'm a savior, not a killer.

MARYANN: And I'm the witch from the lowlands. The fiend who flew into White Mountains to pollute the only pure place left on Earth.

ATHERTON: I love you, Maryann. THEY call you witch. Why won't you believe me instead of those who will never understand you?

MARYANN: You know when I'll love you again? When I SEE Carlton resurrected.

ATHERTON: But of course you will.

MARYANN: Yes?

ATHERTON: When you are resurrected. I only show you all this—because you and I will never walk out of this cave again.

MARYANN: What? You promise to show me the world—

ATHERTON: And then some.

MARYANN: What did you have in mind—a double suicide?

ATHERTON: In your case, it won't have to be suicide, my love.

MARYANN: I just fell out of love with you.

ATHERTON: I can tell you loved this Carlton far more than you could ever feel for me.

MARYANN: Did I say that? You could easily win back my love, David.

ATHERTON: How?

MARYANN: I want YOU to resurrect Carlton. Bring him back.

ATHERTON: How do you know I can do that?

MARYANN: Because you did it to me. You have the knowledge. Carlton can't have been dead more than a couple hours. We made love tonight. You've talked to the dead on battlefields. You can bring back Carlton.

ATHERTON: So if I bring him back? Then what? You'll reject him?

MARYANN: I could hardly remain indifferent to you then.

ATHERTON: And you'd come with me.

MARYANN: When I hear from Carlton's own lips that the next life is better than this one. Sure, then I'm with you totally, David.

ATHERTON: You'll hear from him.

(SGT. ATHERTON'S *hands start glowing again as he raises them over* CARLTON'S *body.* ATHERTON *hesitates, then lifts* CARLTON'S *body and moves it away from the pile of bodies to a different part of the cave.*)

MARYANN: What are you doing?

ATHERTON: I only promised you Carlton. I don't want a mob scene in here. (*He lays his glowing hands on* CARLTON'S *face.*) Talk to me, Carlton. Tell us what it's like.

MARYANN: This is a little like me asking my cat for her opinion.

ATHERTON: Give me a chance, Maryann. I'm no faith healer. This is pure technology.

(ATHERTON *lays atop* CARLTON, *head to head, toe to toe, putting his mouth against* CARLTON'S *mouth.*)

MARYANN: If anyone from school was watching, that would get a rise out of Carlton.

(ATHERTON *breathes in deeply, then exhales the air into* CARLTON. CARLTON'S *body seems to glow. He stretches and opens his eyes.* MARYANN *joyously hugs him.* CARLTON *is startled, disoriented.*)

MARYANN: You're back! Oh you're back!

CARLTON: Mary—Maryann—what's going on?

MARYANN: You weren't dead. You couldn't have been!

ATHERTON: He was quite dead.

CARLTON: What's that guy doing with you?

MARYANN: He saved you. Brought you back. You got poisoned or something.

CARLTON: Yeah, and he's the one who did it!

ATHERTON: Never mind that. Maryann wants to know what it's like to be dead.

CARLTON: Then tell her!

(*He charges* ATHERTON. MARYANN *comes between them.*)

MARYANN: Carlton, honey, he did you a favor. I saw. You'd have been left on this pile of dead people.

CARLTON: Where he dragged me in the first place.

ATHERTON: How did you know that?

CARLTON: I watched you!

ATHERTON: I rest my case.

CARLTON: That's right! After you smothered me—

MARYANN: Smothered you?

CARLTON: Just a few seconds later . . . I was swimming again. Diving deep into the lake. I was able to see clear to the bottom and then beyond that, right through the earth and out the other side. I knew that with one stroke and a kick I could torpedo myself through all the oceans. But no sooner did I think that—when the exact opposite happened. I went exploding out of the water, shot up like a geyser, landed back on top of the mountain. Everything that happened to me tonight happened over again in reverse. I was naked on top of Mt. Washington looking south—no, north! I was able to turn my back on the threat from the south as if there was an unlimited distance north to escape no matter what happened. Then I was looking both directions at once. How did I do that? What an incredible sensation! Everyone in the world had been down there in the lake with me and now they were following me up, wooshing up out of the whirlpool, spinning around my head as I spun over the highest peak of the highest place in the universe. I was flying over the White Mountains, cold wind wonderfully beating my face, tears shooting out all over, I was freer than I ever felt in my whole life. Then comes this heavy weight bearing down on me. I couldn't stay aloft, I went careening downwards toward jagged rock I knew would split me in two. And then there's Maryann, her face pressed against mine, screaming at me in some foreign language. (*To* MARYANN) What did you do? Why did you bring me back?

MARYANN: You were dreaming. You weren't dead yet. We got to you just in time.

ATHERTON: She made me do it, Carlton. I'm a buddy. I'd have just as soon leave you dead.

MARYANN: You did this to him in the first place! I could never go with you now.

CARLTON: I don't know which of you to hate more. You who killed me . . . or you who made him bring me back.

MARYANN: If you hate me—after all I went through tonight for you—my decision becomes that much easier.

(*She moves to* ATHERTON.)

CARLTON: But, Maryann, it was the most fantastic feeling. Like being in love, only with no limits.

MARYANN: Being dead is—

CARLTON: Like skiing down the mountain and no bottom in sight. A thrill that never ends.

MARYANN: Better than our love used to be? Before I got dissatisfied. Before you started complaining about—

CARLTON: Being perfect. Not like feeling it's ME trying to be perfect. I mean BEING perfect. The thing itself.

MARYANN: The way I felt running to meet David tonight.

CARLTON: He made you feel that good?

ATHERTON: It wasn't me. It was the anticipation of what we would soon go through together.

MARYANN: That's right . . . it was not you. I thought it was love. Love like I'd never felt. But it was totally inside me. A feeling of myself. Beyond all World Affairs.

ATHERTON: Part of everything at last.

(*Silence.* CARLTON *and* MARYANN *look at each other for a long moment.*)

CARLTON: We don't need each other, Maryann.

MARYANN: No. Not at all.

CARLTON: If you had told me that a few hours ago I would have gone crazy. I did go crazy—climbing the mountain naked, swimming in what I knew was poisoned water. But now . . . I don't need you or anyone else. I've flown over White Mountains.

ATHERTON: I'm glad you're accepting it, boy. Some people get confused. They'd rather go back to living their life of fear. Settle for the kind of lesser love you and Maryann shared.

CARLTON: I see now I haven't had a happy day all my life.

MARYANN: Not even one?

CARLTON: Wait till you see, Maryann.

ATHERTON: Yes, it's good you accept it. Because you'll soon be back there.

MARYANN: What? But you had the power to—

ATHERTON: Temporarily resurrect Carlton.

MARYANN: Temporary?

ATHERTON: To prove to you.

MARYANN: You've been on the plains of Armageddon! You talked to the dead.

ATHERTON: A few words. A flash of the eyes. Moments of insight.

MARYANN: And what I'm seeing of Carlton now is just another one of those? A moment?

ATHERTON: You're very lucky. What a moment.

MARYANN: Carlton, I love you!

CARLTON: I can love you too. But you can't possibly feel what I do yet.

MARYANN: He lied to me, Carlton! He said he'd bring you back.

CARLTON: I didn't want to come back.

MARYANN: But you love me—

CARLTON: Forever. Even beyond that. Wait till you see it.

MARYANN: That man . . . the soldier . . . don't go away and leave me alone with him.

CARLTON: You're going to run away with him to Russia. I heard you.

MARYANN: Not with him. I'm going to go alone. By myself I'll fly over the mountains of Russia. Please! Don't die without taking him with you.

CARLTON: I haven't got much time left. I can't waste it on killing. Just let me watch you as I go. I have no reason to do anything else.

MARYANN: No reason? Look! Look what he did to your best friend.

CARLTON: What?

MARYANN: Or who was your best friend before you split over me. That's all over now. Jimmy did not deserve this.

CARLTON: He shot Jimmy!

ATHERTON: So you could be best friends in the next life. With all my blessings.

CARLTON: (*Kneeling over* JIMMY's *body*.) No. It's not like that. THERE ... I'm alone. No friends. *I'm* everything. All I need. But here—in the White Mountains—friendship means something. What people are to each other—that's everything. What I had with Maryann ... what I had with Jimmy before her—there's nothing to compare.

ATHERTON: The sentimentality of the moment is nothing. How could I kill as many as I have and not seen through all the lies you people use to go on living?

MARYANN: (*Trancelike*) And you have killed ... so many. The battlefields ... the caves ...

(CARLTON is crying over the body of JIMMY.)

ATHERTON: Your friend tried to kill me with a rock. But his hands were shaking so much from the poison he couldn't hit with any force. And besides, I'm so close to the dead now rocks go right through me. A whole mountain could fall on me. I'd feel nothing. White Mountains means nothing to me.

(*Screaming with rage,* CARLTON *attacks* ATHERTON *and strangles him.*)

(MARYANN, *still in a trancelike state of shock, sits next to* JIMMY's *body, stroking him, touching the wound, resting her head against his.* CARLTON *crawls back over and hugs her.*)

CARLTON: All lies. All lies he told you. He didn't know what he was talking about. It's not like he said. What I've seen—you can only see for yourself.

MARYANN: I'll follow you. Immediately.

CARLTON: No. You won't even be able to see me. IT'S NOT LIKE HE SAID. No lovers united forever. No friends. Nothing. Perfection. But nothing.

MARYANN: You want me to go back to my World Affairs book. Read it all again from Chapter One. As though there's something I've missed. Now I know what I've been missing.

CARLTON: You don't know! I can't tell you anything. Just that he was a liar. White Mountains IS something. Live out your life here.

MARYANN: Nothing's left for me here. I wasn't born here. I'm the fiend from Flatland.

CARLTON: Flatland is lost. You were lucky to escape. White Mountains is pure. Climb to the top. Take off your white dress. I can't see you anymore. You're high in the mountains . . .

(*He dies.*)

(MARYANN *lets the tears come, crying over all three men.*)

(*At home,* MRS. BAKER *holds a box in which they have imprisoned the cat.* MR. BAKER *sits with his hands stretched uselessly before him, the shotgun in his lap. The World Affairs book is on the table between them. It is drenched.*)

(*Both the* BAKERS *are now experiencing horrible discomfort in their ears, and their hearing has been reduced or distorted to the fullest degree. All their dialogue must be intelligible, but the sound of their speech can be intermittently muted, echoed, intensified, whispered, made strange.*)

MRS. BAKER: I'm worried sick.

MR. BAKER: You'll make yourself sick if you keep on.

MRS. BAKER: So cruel to us.

MR. BAKER: Past four now.

MRS. BAKER: She's run away for good. All her things gone.

MR. BAKER: She'll learn not to hurt you.

MRS. BAKER: I never could punish her. It's lucky you're so firm.

MR. BAKER: We're both sitting here with flu, sick as a pair of dogs. She's out having herself a hell of a time.

MRS. BAKER: Teach her good so she'll know how to take care of herself when we're gone.

(*Silence.* MARYANN *enters, blood and dirt on her white dress.*)

MARYANN: (*Pause*) I'll just go upstairs.

MR. BAKER: Wait a minute, Maryann.

MARYANN: I'll stay in my room a month. Two months. Forever if you want.

Mrs. Baker: Maryann . . . can you hear me?

Maryann: Yes, Momma.

Mrs. Baker: Can you? Maryann!

Mr. Baker: She said yes, Linda.

Maryann: How did my World Affairs book get like this?

Mr. Baker: Police found it. Dredging the lake for your body.

(Maryann *picks up the ruined book. The pages are stuck together so she can't open it.*)

Mrs. Baker: Your cat isn't in your room.

(Maryann *turns to her.*)

Now she listens.

Mr. Baker: Maryann, there's something we'd like you to do before you go to your room.

Maryann: I'm so tired, Daddy. If you make me stay up any later I won't make it to school tomorrow.

Mr. Baker: You care about school?

Maryann: I hate it. But I'm learning how to be patient.

Mrs. Baker: Why is she just talking to you?

Maryann: I said I HATE SCHOOL, MOMMA! But I can be just as patient as the rest of you.

Mrs. Baker: Don't spare the rod after she talks to me like that.

Maryann: School, Momma, school! (*Pause*) Not you.

Mrs. Baker: Tell her about this box.

Mr. Baker: You won't be cursing us out to that little Soviet cat of yours tonight.

Maryann: I don't talk to my cat. I don't hate either of you. I only want to sleep. Feel no pain. Like the dead.

Mrs. Baker: What? WHAT IS GOING ON HERE?

Mr. Baker: SHE SAID SHE'D JUST AS SOON SEE US DEAD!

Maryann: Whatever you say. I don't know anything.

Mr. Baker: Open the box, Linda. You'll have to hold it up. My hands are useless. Maryann, take this gun from me.

MARYANN: Why do you have that out?

MR. BAKER: I said take it.

MARYANN: For whoever I came home with?

MR. BAKER: Take it, girl!

(MARYANN *takes the shotgun.*)

Now open that box, Linda. LINDA!

(MRS. BAKER, *hearing nothing, does nothing.* MR. BAKER *crosses to her and lifts off the cover with trembling hands.* MRS. BAKER *gets the idea and holds up the cat.*)

MR. BAKER: Maryann. This is the only fair way we could think up to punish you. So you'd learn. Once and for all. Our feelings count for something.

MARYANN: I know that. Why can't you believe I love you?

MR. BAKER: Well, there's only one way to prove that to us. Shoot your kitty.

MARYANN: (*Not hysterical; a slow, thoughtful reaction.*) You . . . want me . . .

MR. BAKER: Simple as that. One two three. Bang.

MRS. BAKER: Hurry up. Please.

MR. BAKER: You're killing your mother worse than that damn cat will ever feel. Now shoot, girl. Shoot!

(MARYANN *takes a long look out the window, up into the mountains. She looks back at her parents, then finally at her little cat that is meowing pathetically.*)

(*She turns the gun on herself and shoots.*)

(MR. BAKER *utters a long scream that fades into silence while his mouth is still wide open.* MRS. BAKER *sits frozen with horror. The cat meows.*)

(CARLTON, JIMMY, *and* SGT. ATHERTON *speak overlapping lines as lights fade.*)

ATHERTON: White Mountains are absolutely nothing!

CARLTON: Live out your life here!

JIMMY: The fiend from Flatland has become the martyr of the mountains . . .

ATHERTON: When they fall I'll feel nothing . . .

CARLTON: Live out your life . . . Maryann—war—annihilation—tranquillity—peace—

ATHERTON: Death has freed you from this nothingness!

JIMMY: The invaders are retreating.

CARLTON: Death—tragedy—loss—go South—go South—forget—forget—

JIMMY: Her martyrdom—their loss—drove them out. Away. Forever. And White Mountains are saved. White Mountains are saved!

(*The cat meows.*)

FADE TO BLACKOUT

Calvert Parlato

Billings for the Defense

Calvert Parlato believes that a varied past helps to round out a writer. His experiences include graduation from New York University; working in jazz and classical music; serving in the U.S. Navy; and teaching elementary school in Los Angeles.

Billings for the Defense had its world premiere at The Richmond Shepard Theatre in Hollywood, CA, on July 16, 1983, with the following cast:

Douglas Billings	Angus Duncan
John Cloud	Jim Lefebvre
Masters	Paul McGibboney
Sherry	Lisa Marie

Bruce Gray directed the play; Richmond Shepard and Richard Gastelum were the producers; the set, light, and sound design were executed by W. Lansing Barbour; Armina Shepard was the stage manager; and the costumes were designed by Halima McMaster.

Parlato's other plays include *Ambrosia and Arthur* and *Antic Love*.

For stock and amateur production rights, contact: Broadway Play Publishing, Inc., 357 West 20th Street, New York, NY 10011. For all other rights, contact: Calvert Parlato, 8800 Kester #103, Panorama City, CA 91402.

Cast
John Cloud
Douglas Billings
Sherry
David Masters

The action is in any American city. Two acts. The time is now. Any place names can be changed to suit the locale where the performance is held.

Act One

Scene One

(At rise: Stage right, on split-level set, is seen a modest section of office in a police station. Sirens are heard in background. There is a desk and file cabinet. Detective Sergeant John Cloud stands at a desk talking on the telephone. Cloud, 34, is of modest build and Indian ancestry. He is soft spoken, with an engaging shy smile but intense and intelligent eyes. He is the kind of man whose intelligence is often overlooked because he is not exhibitionistic in behavior. His suit jacket is draped over his desk chair, thus revealing his shoulder holster with handcuffs on the back of his belt.)

(The lower part of the stage is occupied by the funky yet luxurious law office of Douglas Billings, 53, who possesses a trim moustache and patrician good looks and attire—the diametrical opposite of Cloud. His office is a strange combination of contemporary furnishings mixed with Native American artifacts such as a small sharp tribal spear, tomahawk, quiver of arrows, a bow, a handsome Navajo rug on the wall, etc. A large cigar store Indian stands near the entry door. Billings has a small selection of law books either on the wall or on the miniblind-covered window sill (stage right).)

(Parallel action: While Cloud is on the phone, Billings methodically peels an apple with a spear blade; the apple peel, which is in one piece, falls into a wastebasket downstage in front of Billings' desk. Cloud has a police file on the desk before him.)

Cloud: Yessir. I been going through the stuff . . . What've I come up with? No more than the rest of the guys who worked the case. Four deaths in seven years . . . The only common thread is: all four were successfully defended by the great Douglas Billings. Maybe someone's trying to scare off business. Be defended by Billings and die . . . has anyone interviewed Billings in any kind of depth, sir? . . . What's insulting? He might shed some light . . . Doesn't the P.D. also have friends on the city council? . . . Yessir . . . I will, sir. Thank you. *(Hangs up. Sighs in disgust.)* In a pig's eye, I will. *(Puts on his jacket with determination.)*

(Lights off Cloud. There is a warning buzz on Billings' intercom. David Masters, 28, blond, handsome, and wearing an expensive white suit lets himself into Billings office. Masters, while entering, looks askance at the Indian statue. Billings pays no attention and continues peeling.)

MASTERS: Gal outside said I could come in. I have an appointment.

BILLINGS: (*Godlike*) Hmnn.

(BILLINGS *makes a minimal gesture to the client chair in front of his desk.* MASTERS *sits.* BILLINGS, *while seated, continues to concentrate on the apple as if he is excoriating it.* MASTERS *is ill at ease.*)

MASTERS: I . . . I'm David Masters.

(BILLINGS *peels*)

MASTERS: The valley murders last week. You heard about them, didn't you?

(BILLINGS *shakes his head, finishes with the apple, holding the body of the fruit, and puts down the spear.* MASTERS *reaches over to shake his hand and* BILLINGS *indicates he cannot shake while holding the apple.* MASTERS *moves back.*)

MASTERS: Don't you read the papers?

BILLINGS: Rarely.

MASTERS: How about the T.V. news?

BILLINGS: I'm not fond of T.V.

(MASTERS *gestures around the room.*)

MASTERS: What are you some kind of Indian nut?

BILLINGS: I have fondness for the Native American.

MASTERS: Custer died for our sins, eh?

BILLINGS: As a matter of fact, he did.

MASTERS: You got any Indian blood in you?

BILLINGS: (*Look of contempt*) Do I look like an Indian?

MASTERS: You look more like General Custer. (*Chuckles—but* BILLINGS *is not receptive.*) What the hell am I doing talking about Indians?

(MASTERS *reaches inside his jacket and slaps a roll of bills on the desk.* BILLINGS *speaks sophisticatedly while munching on the apple delicately.*)

BILLINGS: Ah, wampum.

MASTERS: There's more where that came from.

BILLINGS: You dabble in Indian herbs.

MASTERS: Yeah, but that's not why I need a lawyer.

Billings: Ah, yes, the valley murders.

Masters: The blue flus are about to make an arrest.

Billings: Who were the victims?

Masters: An asshole named Vanek, his wife, and kid.

Billings: How old was the child?

Masters: Five or six.

Billings: Boy or girl?

Masters: Girl.

Billings: Why did Mr. Vanek incur someone's ire?

Masters: He was mixing horseshit with his herbs.

Billings: So, then, he died for reasons of quality control.

Masters: You could say that.

Billings: Why the wife?

Masters: Bitch was in on the operation.

Billings: Surely not the little girl?

Masters: Nah.

Billings: Was the little girl molested?

Masters: I don't know.

Billings: Come, come, Mr. Masters, the medical examiner's report will reveal all.

Masters: (*Matter of fact*) Yeah.

Billings: The little girl makes it a despicable crime. (*Throws money roll off desk.*) Please leave.

(Masters *talks while retrieving bills.*)

Masters: You can't do this to me.

(Billings *rises, takes up bow and arrow from the wall, and aims it at* Masters.)

Billings: I'm quite a marksman with this. Out!

Masters: What kind of bullshit?

Billings: Keep moving toward the exit.

MASTERS: (*Hand on doorknob.*) You defend some of the worst scumbags on earth . . .

BILLINGS: Quite so.

MASTERS: And get them off.

BILLINGS: I ply my trade well.

MASTERS: You're the best there is.

BILLINGS: Flattery gets you nowhere. (*Draws back on bowstring.*) Turn the knob and flee rapidly.

(MASTERS *beats out the arrow as it hits the door.* BILLINGS *lets out a warhoop and places the bow on the wall in its usual place. Then, under the bow, he takes a drink from a portable bar with several bottles atop it. Pause. Then a knock on the door.*)

BILLINGS: Yes?

MASTERS: (*Outside door*) Give me a break, Billings.

BILLINGS: (*Drinking*) Disappear. I have another arrow at the ready.

MASTERS: I'll give you three times what I showed you.

BILLINGS: The next arrow'll go through the door. I'm aiming at your heart.

MASTERS: Every penny I got.

(BILLINGS, *drinking, walks slightly toward door.*)

BILLINGS: You better leave, Masters. You're about to be scalped.

MASTERS: I'll sell my Ferrari, my Mercedes sedan. I'll borrow from everyone I know.

(*Sipping his drink casually,* BILLINGS *walks to window to look out and lets* MASTERS *sweat a bit.*)

BILLINGS: You may open the door, Masters.

(MASTERS *peeks in nervously and glances at the arrow in the door.* Billings *does not look at him.*)

BILLINGS: You got what you came for. Make your next appointment with my secretary.

MASTERS: Thanks, I . . .

(BILLINGS *cuts him short with a brushing gesture. Leaving the door ajar,* MASTERS *exits.* BILLINGS *walks to the door to call out.*)

BILLINGS: Don't bother to sell the Mercedes. Sign over the pink slip. I know a tribe that can use it as a minibus. (*He closes the door, removes the arrow, and smiles to himself. He replaces the arrow in its quiver on the wall. Then he walks to the window and peeks out the miniblinds while drinking. He is intoxicated.*) Oh, teaming metropolis. Who knows what evil lurks on your streets? Who knows what rapscallion will soon require legal intervention? (*Buzzer sounds on intercom. He moves shakily to speaker.*) Listen, counselor. Straighten up. (*Appearing more sober, he presses button.*) Yes?

SHERRY'S VOICE: Detective Sergeant John Cloud, Mr. Billings.

BILLINGS: The name again?

VOICE: Sergeant Cloud.

(BILLINGS *caps the expensive vodka he has been drinking, places it back on the bartop.*)

BILLINGS: Does the gent have an appointment?

VOICE: No, Mr. Billings.

BILLINGS: Can't see him.

CLOUD'S VOICE: Please, sir. I'm a fan of yours. I'd appreciate a few minutes.

BILLINGS: The name again?

CLOUD'S VOICE: John Cloud.

BILLINGS: (*Sighs*) Very well.

(BILLINGS *walks to the bathroom door and takes out a brown paper-wrapped picture of Cherokee Chief Sequoia and places it on the desk before him. He is unwrapping the painting as* CLOUD *enters, proffering a shy smile.*)

CLOUD: Thank you, sir.

(BILLINGS *looks over the Sequoia painting.* CLOUD *walks to desk and looks at it. There is also a framed citation in the brown paper wrapper.*)

BILLINGS: Do you know whose picture this is?

CLOUD: No, sir.

BILLINGS: Chief Sequoia, one of the most brilliant men who ever lived . . .

CLOUD: Named a tree after him.

BILLINGS: (*Does not like* CLOUD's *remark*.) He invented an alphabet capable of conveying deep symbolic thought. He was as sophisticated as the white man's most advanced thinkers. For God's sake, don't you know anything about your priceless heritage?

CLOUD: Not into that, sir.

BILLINGS: A white Indian, eh?

(CLOUD *picks up the framed citation*.)

CLOUD: To Douglas Billings, in thanks for his many contributions to the Cherokee nation. Hmnn, a Robin Hood. Take from your clients and give to the poor.

BILLINGS: I'm an Indian giver.

CLOUD: (*Smiles*) Very good, sir.

(CLOUD *has a complicated attitude toward* BILLINGS. *He puts* BILLINGS *on with the humble detective routine, yet he respects* BILLINGS *as a lawyer.* CLOUD *sits as* BILLINGS *tries to find a suitable spot to hang the Sequoia picture.* BILLINGS *is not satisfied and replaces the picture in its brown paper wrapper in the bathroom.* BILLINGS, *restless, does not sit.* CLOUD *rises and follows him around the room as they talk.*)

BILLINGS: Your name again?

CLOUD: Detective Sergeant John Cloud. Homicide.

BILLINGS: Are you here on official business? (*Satiric*) If so, I want my lawyer present.

CLOUD: May I act as your attorney, sir? I'm in my final year at law school.

BILLINGS: Ah, bettering yourself.

CLOUD: Slow but sure, sir.

(*He follows* BILLINGS, *who perambulates again*.)

CLOUD: I go nights. And, may I say, sir, that you are often cited as an example of skilled advocacy.

BILLINGS: (*Stops to look at* CLOUD.) You plan to follow in my footsteps?

CLOUD: Nosir.

BILLINGS: Why not? I'm a legend in my time. (*Looks out windows*)

CLOUD: That you are. You're larger than life, sir. Me, if anything, I'm smaller.

BILLINGS: The secret, sergeant, is believing in yourself. If you believe in yourself, this is communicated to the world around you.

CLOUD: Save your breath, sir. I know my place. The tortoise and the hare. I'm the tortoise, you're the hare.

BILLINGS: Don't undersell yourself. You have your own gift. There's room for all kinds in the family of man.

CLOUD: (*Putting him on*) You really think so, sir?

BILLINGS: (*Goes to bar for another drink.*) I do. So long as they're good people. I make that a condition.

CLOUD: Good people, sir?

BILLINGS: Indeed.

CLOUD: Then why do you keep so many rotten apples out of the penal system?

BILLINGS: What alternative do I have?

CLOUD: You could become a D.A., y'know, a prosecutor.

BILLINGS: Is that your aim?

CLOUD: Yessir.

BILLINGS: Unfortunately, civil service pay is very poor. (*Holds up finger*) I have you there, don't I?

CLOUD: I guess you do, sir.

BILLINGS: You think I bend the law too much?

CLOUD: Uh-huh.

BILLINGS: The law is not a fixed entity. It's there to be created.

CLOUD: This may sound naive, but I worship the law.

BILLINGS: A strict interpretationist.

CLOUD: I am. I hold to the straight and narrow. I guess that's all a tortoise can do.

BILLINGS: Perhaps when you learn more, you'll change.

CLOUD: Not likely.

BILLINGS: You didn't come here to discuss the philosophy of jurisprudence, I take it.

CLOUD: I've just taken over the file on Filmore, Sissler, Baker, and Donato. You recall the names, sir?

BILLINGS: Indeed. Former clients.

CLOUD: All mean dudes.

BILLINGS: I've heard rumors to that effect.

CLOUD: I requested the file.

BILLINGS: Why?

CLOUD: It's a challenge. Been sitting on my butt too much lately.

BILLINGS: You wish to resolve questions about their deaths, is that it?

CLOUD: Yessir.

BILLINGS: But why, sergeant? They were the rotten apples you accuse me of keeping from the penal system.

CLOUD: At least two of the deaths were definite homicides, therefore not legal.

BILLINGS: If they had been done in by the state gas chamber you would be satisfied?

CLOUD: Uh-huh.

BILLINGS: So what do you want from me?

CLOUD: (*Rubs his chin*) Well, sir, I . . .

BILLINGS: Before you proceed, who authorized you to question me?

CLOUD: I don't hold with all of the P.D.'s formality, Mr. Billings. Especially in the early stage of an investigation. Certainly, you don't expect me to serve you with a warrant.

BILLINGS: Warrant, indeed. Who authorized you?

CLOUD: May I tell you a little story, sir? When I was a kid, I stole some oranges from a neighbor lady's tree. The lady collared me and called the police. She was something else; she wanted me thrown in jail, the whole bit. Anyway, this Irish cop took the call—my dad knew him; his name was Carmody—and he told the lady to calm down, it would all be taken care of. Carmody got me outside, kicked me in the pants, and said to never do it again. I never did. To this day, I don't eat oranges; they make me sick. Officer Carmody made me a believer in easygoing police procedure.

BILLINGS: Ah, but he murdered your taste for oranges. So then, you're not authorized to talk to me about Filmore, Sissler, Baker, and Donato?

CLOUD: I was hoping for an informal pow-wow.

BILLINGS: A pow-wow.

CLOUD: Please.

BILLINGS: (*Sits at desk*) I'm inclined to like you, Sergeant, probably because you have Indian ancestry, so it would be with reluctance that I would report this harrassment of me. You realize I have friends in high places in this fair municipality . . .

CLOUD: So I've heard.

BILLINGS: And I could register a protest with said friends.

CLOUD: Without a doubt.

BILLINGS: (*Voice gets slurry, elbow slips off desk.*) How do I know you're what you say you are?

CLOUD: Excuse me, sir, but are you intoxicated?

BILLINGS: Whom are you calling intoxicated? (*Stands, faces* CLOUD.) Smell my breath.

CLOUD: That won't be necessary.

BILLINGS: (*Slightly reeling; makes hand gestures.*) Come on. I insist.

CLOUD: (*Leans over desk, sniffs.*) Vodka.

BILLINGS: Nobody can smell vodka.

CLOUD: I can, sir. I have a sensitive nose.

BILLINGS: You're no cop. You've been misrepresenting yourself. (CLOUD *takes out wallet with badge and starts to open it.*) Never mind that. We'll settle it Indian style.

CLOUD: Why don't you think I'm an officer?

BILLINGS: You don't meet the height and weight requirements. (*Sets up his arm for Indian wrestling.*) Come on.

CLOUD: (*Reluctant*) My height, my weight's O.K. Please sir.

BILLINGS: You're the one who likes easygoing police procedure. Am I quoting correctly?

CLOUD: Yessir, but . . .

BILLINGS: Get your goddamn arm on this desk, jockey!

CLOUD: Jockey? I must warn you, sir. I'm not large but I'm strong.

BILLINGS: Fine. Put your arm where your mouth is.

(CLOUD *shrugs and sits, positioning himself for arm wrestling. They wrestle and it is obvious that* CLOUD *could take command but he lets* BILLINGS *win.* BILLINGS *at the end is exhausted but settles his clothing with pride.*)

BILLINGS: Hah! How'd you ever get in the department?

CLOUD: They had an Indian quota. I was the only applicant.

BILLINGS: Let me see your i.d.

(CLOUD *hands over wallet.* BILLINGS *scrutinizes it and reads somewhat woozily.*)

John Cloud, eh?

CLOUD: As advertised. May I have it back?

(BILLINGS *hands him the wallet and* CLOUD *pockets it.* BILLINGS *reaches for a vodka bottle and plants it on the desk.*)

BILLINGS: Have a drink. (*Removes cap and pushes bottle to* CLOUD.)

CLOUD: No firewater, sir. It's against the treaty my tribe signed.

BILLINGS: Archaic law. Are you going to insult your host?

(CLOUD *shrugs and pretends to sip.* BILLINGS *takes the bottle from him and has a large swig.*)

Are you surprised I drink from the same bottle as an Indian? (*Irony mixed with affection*) Nothing to fear; the alcohol kills any germs.

CLOUD: I wondered why you were so bold, sir.

BILLINGS: (*Inebriated slip*) So what did you want to know about Masters?

CLOUD: Masters?

BILLINGS: Y'know, the valley murders.

CLOUD: David Masters isn't my case. Filmore, Sissler, Baker, and Donato, sir.

BILLINGS: Those names again?

CLOUD: Filmore, Sissler, Baker, Donato.

BILLINGS: By George, you have a good memory for an Indian.

(CLOUD *tries to maintain his patience and it is obvious to* BILLINGS.)

Are you impatient with me?

CLOUD: Not at all, sir. Take your time.

BILLINGS: Whether I'm slow or not, the taxpayers foot the bill anyway.

CLOUD: You're a taxpayer, sir, and I'd like to deliver your money's worth. Forgive me, but I think you're giving me the runaround . . .

BILLINGS: Is that so?

CLOUD: And trying to avoid talking about Filmore and the others.

BILLINGS: Never discuss a pending case.

CLOUD: Pending? The men are all dead.

BILLINGS: Dead you say?

CLOUD: Very much so, sir.

BILLINGS: Oh! Who done it?

CLOUD: I'm determined to find out.

BILLINGS: Determined?

CLOUD: Yessir.

BILLINGS: How'd they expire, sergeant?

CLOUD: Filmore was strangled, Baker was shot, Sissler hit by a car, Donato—the body was too badly decomposed to fix cause of death.

BILLINGS: Why are you lumping them together? Only two are homicides.

CLOUD: They all happen to be your clients. (*Beat*) You have any reason to believe that the victims may have . . . er . . .

BILLINGS: Which victims?

CLOUD: (*Puffs impatiently*) Filmore and the others.

BILLINGS: Oh, them.

CLOUD: Do you have any reason to believe their deaths are connected?

BILLINGS: I most certainly do.

(CLOUD *looks at him in anticipation—maybe he will finally get something tangible.*)

BILLINGS: They were called by the big chief in the sky.

CLOUD: Please, Mr. Billings, I'm serious.

BILLINGS: (*Stands shakily*) The interview is at an end.

CLOUD: A few more questions, please.

(BILLINGS *finds the spear with which he pared the apple and shows it to* CLOUD.)

BILLINGS: This spear isn't large but it's strong.

CLOUD: You may be obstructing justice. (*Starts for door*)

BILLINGS: My dear fellow, that's what I'm paid handsomely to do.

CLOUD: Maybe this has to go to the Grand Jury.

BILLINGS: Sergeant, sergeant, you're violating your sacred oath of easygoing police procedure. Now, please take easygoing leave.

(BILLINGS *half menaces with the spear.* CLOUD *turns to exit and bumps into the cigar store Indian statue. He knocks his knuckles on it.*)

CLOUD: I thought these things were solid.

BILLINGS: Keep moving into the corridor.

(CLOUD *takes a business card from his wallet.*)

CLOUD: Here, sir. (*Gingerly tenders card.*) If you change your mind, give me a call.

(*Holding the spear,* BILLINGS *takes the card.* CLOUD *eases out.* BILLINGS *stalks him.*)

CLOUD: Goodbye, sir. I hear you're quite a racquetball enthusiast.

(BILLINGS *slams entry door in* CLOUD'S *face. He puts the spear on the desk, tears the business card, and dumps it in his wastebasket. He then makes a three-finger evil sign at the torn card. He looks to the door from which* CLOUD *exited.*)

BILLINGS: Fare thee well, vanishing Indian. (*Removes a pocket handkerchief, covers the vodka bottle from which* CLOUD *drank with kerchief, and drinks some vodka. Then he holds the bottle—covered by the handkerchief—over his heart in mock reverence.*) Alas, poor Filmore, Sissler, Baker, and Donato. I knew them well, sergeant—before I killed them. (BILLINGS *opens small door stage left bathroom. He walks in and dabs water on his face. He is heard from inside the bathroom.*) Sober up, counselor. (*Offstage: Sounds of water splashing.*) I've got to massacre that poor dumb Indian. (*Exits from bathroom, carrying a face towel and wiping his face. He places the kerchief-covered vodka bottle on bartop.*) Oh, great Hiawatha, forgive me for what I am about to do. (*Presses intercom button.*)

SHERRY'S VOICE: Yes, Mr. Billings.

BILLINGS: Sherry, get me the chief. (*Places towel on desk.*)

VOICE: Running Deer, Joseph Woodchuck, or Bob Toltec?

BILLINGS: No. Paleface chief. Use the hotline. (*Pause*)

VOICE: Ringing.

(BILLINGS *picks up phone. Intercom switches off.*)

BILLINGS: Hello, Ed. Doug here . . . One of your finest just left my office. By the way, Ed, up to now I've been staunchly opposed to civilian review boards . . . Brutality? The guy's a one-man Little Big Horn . . . All right, I'll begin at the beginning. First, he barged into my office shoving my secretary against the wall. Then he barged into my cubicle muttering incoherently about some sort of murder investigation. Threatened me with everything including the Grand Jury . . . he was obviously under the influence . . . I'll say this for him: for an Indian he sure can hold his liquor. By the way, if your lab wants I have his fingerprints on the bottle . . . (*He leans up against the wall holding his neck.*) Got me in a choke hold. Ed, I'm afraid I'll have to cancel racquetball tomorrow; the savage damn near broke my right wing . . . What? I didn't say his name? (*Reaches into wastebasket for card.*) Cloud. Detective Sergeant John Cloud. If that's what you're turning out in Homicide these days, God help our city . . . Internal affairs, eh? That's fine, Ed, real fine. It'll go no further than here, Ed . . . Ed, Ed, don't get that upset. Any organization occasionally finds itself saddled with a rotten apple. Pardon the mixed metaphor . . . No, no, don't mention it. Listen, give me a few days. Then maybe the old wing'll be up to handling a racquet . . . God bless you, Ed.

(*Hangs up. Presses intercom.* SHERRY *enters. She is lovely, 24, petite, of mixed Indian and White ancestry. She is dressed in a stylish outfit which like her is half Indian, half Vogue.*)

SHERRY: Yes, Mr. Billings?

BILLINGS: Take the rest of the day off, Sherry.

SHERRY: (*Delighted*) Really? But I have these letters you wanted to . . .

BILLINGS: No, no, my dear. After what you've been through today.

SHERRY: What've I been through?

BILLINGS: Sherry, please, don't indulge in heroics. I know how hard it is dealing with the brutes who pass through this office.

SHERRY: It is a regular rogue's gallery.

BILLINGS: Don't I know it, dear, don't I know it. Ta, ta.

SHERRY: See you tomorrow, Mr. Billings.

(SHERRY *walks off down the hall. He calls after her.*)

BILLINGS: Thanks again, Sherry, for all you endure. (*He closes the door. He walks over to vodka bottle and lifts it to his lips, making sure to employ the handkerchief.*) Damn shame the way this country treats its Indians.

BLACKOUT

Scene Two

(CLOUD *is sitting at his Homicide desk, casually looking through file. His jacket is draped over a chair. He gets interested in a detail in the file and riffles back and forth through some pages. Then he pushes one of the buttons on his phone and talks.*)

CLOUD: Crime lab, please. (*Pause*) Bernie? . . . John . . . How are things going, Shakespeare? No kidding? You're going to play Hamlet at the recreation center. T.B. or not T.B., eh Bernie? Me? Forget it. I'm too knobby-kneed for black tights . . . Listen, I'm puzzled by something in the Filmore, Sissler, Baker, Donato file . . . Yeah, the four horsemen of the apocalypse—that's good, Bern. Anyway, in each guy's file I see the letters and numbers D-A-T-2-5-0. Some kind of computer thing? . . . Sure, go ahead. I'll hold . . . (*Pause. Sings softly.*) Ah, sweet mystery of life, at last I found you. Da-da-da-etc. (*Sits up*) Yeah? Cedar wood fibers. Let me get this straight, Bernie. Each of these dudes had cedar fibers in his hair and on his clothing . . . Where the heck is a cedar forest around here? . . . You want the truth? It's going crummy. I'll probably bomb out like the rest of the guys who worked this case . . . Thanks, Bern. (*Hangs up. Thinks aloud*) Cedar fibers, eh? (*Phone rings once and a button lights on phone.* CLOUD *presses it and speaks.*) Cloud, here. (*Jumps up and stands at attention.*) Yessir . . . (*Pause. He is being read out.*) Please, sir, may I say . . . Sorry, sir. Sure, go on . . . (*Annoyed, he shows his temper.*) Now, just a minute, sir. You want my badge, you can have it for breakfast. But you listen to me. (*Sits*) He was intoxicated, stoned to his ears. I didn't touch his secretary. He arm wrestled me and I let him win . . . What? He forced me to handle the vodka bottle . . . (*Softens*) Pardon me, sir, but he's out and out lying . . . I don't know why. Wait, I do know why. He likes to put everybody on. He impresses me as a great game player. He ties the court system in knots and now he'd like a go at the Police Department . . . Not true, sir. I admire the man. What Shakespeare is to actors, Billings is to me. Y'know, sir, Shakespeare had his shady side, too. Bernie in the crime lab told me The Dark Lady of the Sonnets was really a guy . . . (*Pause.*

Nods sometimes, shakes his head at other times.) Please, sir, don't pull me off Filmore and Sissler. If you do, forgive me, but I'll file a grievance . . . Of course, he isn't a suspect. Why would he pull the brilliant strategy he does when all he had to do was shave a few points and the bums would've gone to the showers? . . . A firm promise, sir. I'll stay away from the great Mr. Billings . . . Thank you, sir. I apologize for sounding off but, y'know, what's fair is fair . . . have a nice day, sir. (*Hangs up and breathes a sigh of relief. He takes a pencil and taps his file as he thinks.*) If Mohammed can't go the mountain, I'll go around him.

CURTAIN

Scene Three

(*Depending on the physical setup of the theatre, this scene can be enacted in front of the curtain, or* PEREZ's *office can be altered to reveal a prison conference table or booth. At scene start,* BILLINGS *is meeting with* MASTER, *who is in prison garb.*)

MASTERS: When this trial started, I thought you had it in the bag, especially when I saw the judge walk down from the bench and bow and scrape in front of you.

BILLINGS: An old acquaintance. I got his wife off on felony arson some years back.

MASTERS: Now, I'm not so sure.

BILLINGS: What's bothering you?

MASTERS: That guy who's foreman of the jury. He hates the sight of me.

BILLINGS: What evidence do you have for asserting that?

MASTERS: That crooked look he gives me all the time.

BILLINGS: Nonsense, Masters. The man has had a stroke and it distorts his face.

MASTERS: His mind is distorted against me, not only his face.

BILLINGS: Pure imagination on your part.

MASTERS: I never in my life got along with old geezers.

BILLINGS: Let's say for the sake of argument that this "geezer" does have it in for you.

MASTERS: He does, I tell you.

BILLINGS: Fine.

MASTERS: What do you mean "fine"?

BILLINGS: A prejudiced jury foreman could be grounds for a mistrial or the basis of an appeal should you be found guilty. It all works out from a legal point of view.

MASTERS: Hey, I didn't hock everything including my jockstrap to be found guilty (*Contemptuous*) Mr. Billings.

BILLINGS: Dear lad, you place a great burden on me.

MASTERS: You don't get me off, I got friends.

BILLINGS: What will your friends do?

MASTERS: Ream your ass.

BILLINGS: Sounds intriguing. Tell them to be careful. I do suffer from hemorrhoids.

MASTERS: Hemorrhoids, my ass.

BILLINGS: Oh, dear, you have them too?

MASTERS: Cut the games, Billings. Level with me.

BILLINGS: As your advocate, I'm legally bound to.

MASTERS: Am I going to beat this rap?

BILLINGS: I'll do my level best.

MASTERS: You seem awfully casual about my ass.

BILLINGS: Can we get off the subject of posteriors? It's rather depressing.

MASTERS: Depressing. (*Gestures around*) This place is depressing. That courtroom is depressing. When I saw that judge kiss the ground you walk on I thought they'd throw out the case.

BILLINGS: They can't. There's a lot of evidence that must be heard. The police and the D.A. aren't mongoloid, you know. If they take someone to trial, they feel reasonably sure of winning.

MASTERS: The evidence is depressing, too. What you going to do about that?

BILLINGS: David, David, stop fretting so. Did you know that the name "David" in ancient Hebrew means "beloved"? Are you beloved?

MASTERS: You don't like me, Billings . . .

BILLINGS: Nonsense. Have you ever heard me say a bad word about you? Just you listen carefully to my summation when the time comes; why, even that geezer with the crooked face will light up with a smile for you—granted it may be a crooked smile, but then again I'm a lawyer, not a plastic surgeon.

MASTERS: You may as well know I don't like you.

BILLINGS: You resent the fee.

MASTERS: Damn right.

BILLINGS: You could've hired a cheaper lawyer or even acted as your own attorney.

MASTERS: Don't try to be funny. How you going to get me off?

BILLINGS: It's all rather technical. You wouldn't grasp it. (*Sardonic*) David-beloved.

MASTERS: What about the evidence?

BILLINGS: Let me say this: we are not wild Apache country; we live in a civilized society and it has rules for the gathering of evidence . . . (*Unseen by* MASTERS, BILLINGS *gives him a three-finger evil sign.*)

MASTERS: Like a bloody shirt.

BILLINGS: Uh-hum. Sometimes, the police in our civilized society in their zeal to do the job forget the rules of evidence gathering.

MASTERS: Hey, it was my blood. They proved that.

BILLINGS: My, it's a good thing you didn't act as your own attorney. David-beloved, it's not your blood; it's merely blood type B. Blood type B is found in ten percent of the population. Let's see, the population of these United States is somewhere in the neighborhood of 230 million. So you see, there are 23 million people walking the streets who could have commited the crime for which you are charged. Even the stringent scientific methods employed by the F.B.I. can only narrow blood typing down to one percent of the population. You see how slight the chances are of your being guilty?

MASTERS: Then why'm I worrying?

BILLINGS: Because you don't comprehend statistics. Further, you don't understand how law operates on the gathering of evidence.

MASTERS: Screw the legal bullshit. Am I going to get off?

BILLINGS: I repeat: I'll do my level best. Keep in mind, too, that I have a reputation to uphold. If I don't win for you, I may not get such fine clients as you in the future.

(MASTERS *gives* BILLINGS *a worried look. He is still not convinced that he will get off, and he dislikes* BILLINGS' *cavalier attitude.*)

MASTERS: One more thing: I don't pay you to come to court drunk.

BILLINGS: If I appeared in court sober, David-beloved, I might just decide to let you act as your own attorney.

(MASTERS *scowls.*)

CURTAIN

Scene Four

(*Sketchy. The rudimentary indication of a cocktail bar.* SHERRY *is seated on a stool with her legs crossed and jazz music is playing. She is looking off toward the audience and something that can be assumed is interesting.* CLOUD *walks over to her with two drinks in his hand. His is whisky and soda and hers is vodka and orange juice. He looks over with her at the interesting occurrence. Then he offers her the drink.*)

CLOUD: Here you are. Vodka and . . .

SHERRY: Vodka and orange juice. Vitamin C mixed with the sin.

CLOUD: The juice'd be the sin for me.

SHERRY: Really?

CLOUD: Vodka and . . . (*Shrugs*) I can't say it.

SHERRY: You can't say orange juice?

CLOUD: Oh, I can but I'd prefer not to. When I was a kid, I got in trouble stealing oranges. To this day I can't abide them. They make me retch.

SHERRY: Laying a guilt trip on yourself.

CLOUD: I guess.

SHERRY: Probably why you became a cop. Vitamin C for cop.

CLOUD: Never thought of that. That's deep.

SHERRY: Deep is my trip. I'm majoring in psychology.

CLOUD: Going to school, eh?

SHERRY: Nights.

CLOUD: Me, too. Studying law.

SHERRY: Law? (*Beat*) Funny, you don't look like a lawyer.

CLOUD: Now you tell me, when I'm practically finished.

SHERRY: Don't look like a cop either.

(*They sip their drinks.*)

CLOUD: What do I look like? I'm afraid to ask.

SHERRY: (*Studies him*) If I didn't know, I'd take you for a . . . a teacher.

CLOUD: Teacher?

SHERRY: Uh-huh. Little kids.

CLOUD: Kindergarten?

SHERRY: Or first grade.

CLOUD: I like kids.

SHERRY: Ever had any?

CLOUD: Nah. Never been married.

SHERRY: Doesn't stop you from having kids.

CLOUD: Does me.

SHERRY: You're very moral.

CLOUD: How about you?

SHERRY: You mean, am I moral?

CLOUD: (*Smiles*) No. Ever have kids? (*She shakes her head.*) Ever been married?

SHERRY: No.

CLOUD: Never know these days. I got a sister. Twenty-three. Been married thrice.

SHERRY: Thrice!

CLOUD: Starting on number four.

SHERRY: I'm old-fashioned. Once is enough.

CLOUD: That's the way I feel.

SHERRY: Ever come close to marriage?

CLOUD: Couple times.

SHERRY: What happened?

CLOUD: A policeman's wife is not a happy one.

SHERRY: Gilbert and Sullivan.

CLOUD: You recognized my pun.

SHERRY: I'm a G and S freak.

CLOUD: (*Sings*) When a coster's finished jumping on his mother, he loves to lie a basking in the sun. But take one consideration with another, a policeman's life is not a happy one.

SHERRY: It's a "policeman's lot."

CLOUD: I know but life sounds better than lot.

SHERRY: You have a nice voice.

CLOUD: Not really.

SHERRY: (*Studies him*) I don't usually like police officers.

CLOUD: How come?

SHERRY: A lot of them have this . . . I don't know.

CLOUD: Wha . . . what?

SHERRY: Maybe you're different because you're going to be a lawyer.

CLOUD: If I pass the bar.

SHERRY: You'll pass.

CLOUD: What are you, psychic?

SHERRY: You have this real shy, nice-guy manner. Underneath you get what you want.

CLOUD: (*Playful, takes her off bar stool and starts to dance with her.*) And little girl, little girl I want youuuuuu.

SHERRY: (*Blushes*) You're making me blush.

CLOUD: I love it. Underneath that gorgeous exterior lies a demure young lady.

SHERRY: Sergeant, please.

CLOUD: Call me John.

SHERRY: If you call me Sherry.

CLOUD: How do you spell it?

SHERRY: Like the wine.

CLOUD: I once busted a hooker with that name. Spelled it C-h-e-three rs-i-e.

SHERRY: Three rs?

CLOUD: That's a hooker for you.

SHERRY: The three rs made her stand out.

CLOUD: Wasn't the only thing that stood out. (*Sincere*) Excuse me, I'm getting vulgar.

SHERRY: That's it. That's what I like about you.

CLOUD: That I'm vulgar?

SHERRY: Silly. That you're not. Most police officers are vulgar.

CLOUD: Fictitious belief. I had a partner once who acts Shakespeare. Another cop I know does macrame. Another is studying to be an opera singer.

SHERRY: No wonder they don't catch crooks anymore.

CLOUD: Can't win with you, Sherry.

SHERRY: Only teasing.

CLOUD: You like to tease?

SHERRY: Sometimes.

CLOUD: You're not just all talk, are you?

SHERRY: (*Seductive*) Try and find out.

CLOUD: Whew! You're spooking me. (*Gestures to drinks*) How about another?

SHERRY: Better not.

CLOUD: Why?

SHERRY: I can't hold my liquor.

CLOUD: (*Calls out*) Waitress. Couple more, please.

SHERRY: Naughty. You have a lot of facets to you.

CLOUD: Doesn't everybody?

SHERRY: Some people are pretty much what they seem.

CLOUD: Then they're dull. (*They get a little closer as the music gets more romantic.*) Sherry, your boss is a real interesting guy. Tell me a little about him.

(SHERRY *stops cold and puts her hand on his chest, pushing him off.*)

SHERRY: I should've known. Orange juice, vodka, romantic music. Phoney!

CLOUD: Who you calling "phoney"?

SHERRY: It's my boss you want a romance with.

CLOUD: What does that mean?

SHERRY: I don't mean you're gay. You want to get next to the great god attorney. Let me tell you something: he isn't interested in a junior partner. Two years ago, there was this guy: boy, did he give me the buildup. What did he want? He wanted me to check the files so he could learn where Mr. Billings got his ideas for winning. (*Turns on her heels, starts to exit.*)

CLOUD: (*Grabs her.*) Just a second. (*Turns her to face him.*) Look me in the eyes. You're a psychology major, right? (*She nods.*) Study me as I speak. I do not want a job out of your boss. I do not want to kiss his royal rear end for any reason. I'm not interested in his research on legal strategy.

SHERRY: In the first place, he doesn't write anything down. He has a mind like a data bank. It's all in his head.

CLOUD: All I was going to ask was how long you worked for him.

SHERRY: Four years.

CLOUD: You seem super loyal.

SHERRY: He's a fabulous man.

CLOUD: You got a crush?

SHERRY: Come on. He's old enough to be my father.

CLOUD: That's the kind of stuff I wanted to know. I can't compete with God. (*Beat*) What about what I said?

SHERRY: What'd you say?

CLOUD: I'm hot for your corpus delectable, not Billings.

SHERRY: What about the corpus of his knowledge, lawyer?

CLOUD: Forget it. I do it my way. You want me to sing that, too? I do a rotten imitation of Sinatra.

SHERRY: (*Softening*) I'll bet you do.

(*He senses her pliability and grabs her and starts to nuzzle her neck. They dance romantically.*)

CLOUD: Who's your favorite psychologist?

SHERRY: Sigmund Freud.

CLOUD: Old Ziggy. Cool, baby. Let's go find a couch.

(CLOUD *gives her a stylish floor spin and bends her back to kiss her neck in tango style.*)

CURTAIN

Scene Five

(BILLINGS' *office. He is holding a picture of a woman to his chest and chanting in Indian style as he faces the wall. There is a knock at the door. He takes a swig of vodka and puts the bottle back on the bar and replaces the picture on his desk.*)

BILLINGS: Just a minute. (*He wipes his tearful eyes.*) Come in.

SHERRY: May I talk to you?

BILLINGS: Certainly. Important?

(SHERRY *nods and enters with papers for* BILLINGS *to sign during the scene. He picks up his phone, presses a button, dials.*)

Alex? . . . Billings, here. Am I still clear on your scanner? . . . Thank you. (*Hangs up.*)

SHERRY: Afraid you're being bugged again?

BILLINGS: My dear, America lives from day to day where electronic surveillance is concerned. Gone are the days when innocent smoke signals relayed messages across the continent. What sayest thou, Indian maiden?

SHERRY: Maiden? This is the twentieth century.

BILLINGS: Alas, the tribal ways no longer hold sway with women. I'm afraid it's all swing and sway. Don't overdo, my dear. You must think of marriage some day and a swaybacked woman finds it harder to capture a cowpoke.

SHERRY: I'll keep that in mind . . . Sergeant Cloud and I met . . .

BILLINGS: The Indian sleuth.

SHERRY: And had rather a fun time.

BILLINGS: On whose initiative?

SHERRY: His. He asked me out for a drink.

BILLINGS: Did he manage to stay sober this time?

SHERRY: What do you mean "this time"?

BILLINGS: Rumor hath it that he drinks in excess.

SHERRY: No, he doesn't. He's fine as long as he stays away from orange juice.

BILLINGS: I recall he has an aversion to oranges.

SHERRY: He was very interested in you. I got mad at first; I thought he might be using me to get in your good graces. You know, he's going to law school.

BILLINGS: I do know.

SHERRY: He convinced me he wasn't a fortune hunter. He had me look in his eyes. He sure is appealing . . .

BILLINGS: To me he's a swarthy bugger.

SHERRY: I don't think, I really don't . . . I mean, he's not trying to milk you for a scholarship or a junior partner thing. Maybe he just wants to touch shoulders with a great attorney.

BILLINGS: No. The man's not a celebrity seeker.

SHERRY: You sure?

BILLINGS: Positive.

SHERRY: But he does want something?

BILLINGS: (*Evasive*) He wants you, little girl.

SHERRY: Exactly what he said. Rather, he sang it. He also sang Gilbert and Sullivan.

BILLINGS: Hmnn. A singer, eh? He's a man of more parts than he at first reveals.

SHERRY: He is sort of a private person. It takes a while to know him but it's worth the wait.

BILLINGS: Sherry, did you mean what you just said about his being a "private" person?

SHERRY: I did.

BILLINGS: My errant sense of humor is rubbing off on you.

SHERRY: Should I stay away from him?

BILLINGS: How nice of you to ask.

SHERRY: My job comes first.

BILLINGS: Smart girl, what with the economy the way it is.

SHERRY: Well?

BILLINGS: I'm thinking. (*Pause to reflect.*) No, no. Don't stay away from him. I'd like to be apprised of his significant movements—the vertical ones, that is.

SHERRY: Not the horizontal?

BILLINGS: The horizontal's your affair. The new feminism has taught this old bird that a woman's body is her castle. Modern ladies don't feel a man is taking advantage of them when they go to bed. It's a mutual exploration of sensuality. Do I have it right?

SHERRY: You've been reading *Ms* magazine . . . Is he interested in you as a policeman?

BILLINGS: I doubt it. I already told him civil service pay is too low.

SHERRY: I'm serious.

BILLINGS: Don't worry your pretty head. Just keep tabs on him.

SHERRY: I wouldn't want you to be in trouble.

BILLINGS: Nor I you. I assume you're taking your quota of little marshmallows from Upjohn Laboratories.

SHERRY: Parke-Davis.

BILLINGS: Parke-Davis, eh?

SHERRY: And sometimes Ortho.

BILLINGS: Hmnn, Ortho. Do you know the meaning of "ortho"?

SHERRY: No, I don't.

BILLINGS: It means straight and upright.

(SHERRY *smiles and shakes her head.*)

BILLINGS: See how difficult it is to keep the horizontal and the vertical separate?

CURTAIN

Scene Six

(CLOUD *is in the cocktail bar and there is jazz music playing. He dials the phone on the wall, with a toothpick in his mouth.*)

CLOUD: Crime lab, please. (*Pause*) Bernie? . . . John. Did you run David Masters profile through the computer? . . . How does he compare to the four horsemen of the apocalypse? . . . Point 8-9. That's great. This is the boy to watch. (CLOUD *starts jabbing his arm with the toothpick to simulate drug needle marks.*) Macbeth? You gotta be kidding. I'm not interested in when Birnam wood comes to Dunsinane unless Birnam wood has a grove of cedar trees . . . Sherlock Holmes? Hah. Bugs Bunny is more like it. See you, Bern. (*Hangs up.*) Filmore, Sissler, Baker, Donato, and David Masters. (*Sings*) When constabularly duty's to be done—to be done! (*Hums*) Da-da-da-da-de-da-de-da, etc.

CURTAIN

Scene Seven

(*Duplicate of Scene Three except* CLOUD *will meet with* MASTERS. MASTERS *is at table when* CLOUD *walks up.* CLOUD *will at first play* MASTERS *with respectful approach.* CLOUD *appears, holding open his wallet.*)

MASTERS: Christ, the blue flu.

CLOUD: May I talk to you a minute?

MASTERS: Does my lawyer know you're here?

CLOUD: This doesn't involve your lawyer. May I call you David?

MASTERS: Call me sir.

CLOUD: As you wish, sir.

MASTERS: (*Triumphant smile*) Say it again.

CLOUD: What?

MASTERS: Sir.

CLOUD: Sir.

MASTERS: Again.

CLOUD: Sir.

MASTERS: I like it when blue flu are respectful.

CLOUD: I'm with you sir. My second year of service I won officer of the month because of my courteous attitude.

MASTERS: Yeah, yeah. When you book assholes you kiss them on the lips.

(CLOUD *takes his measure. The previous conversation has been his way of feeling* MASTERS *out.*)

MASTERS: What you looking at?

CLOUD: (*Tough*) Hey, peckerhead, who you think you're talking to?

(MASTERS *now looks at* CLOUD *with interest.*)

CLOUD: Don't call me blue flu anymore, got it?

MASTERS: Why the hell not?

CLOUD: Blue flu is a disease. Being a cop is not a disease.

MASTERS: That's a matter of opinion.

CLOUD: Being a cop can be a benefit to you, peckerhead.

MASTERS: Hey, since we're being respectful, don't call me peckerhead.

CLOUD: I'll try to remember.

MASTERS: How can you being a cop help me?

CLOUD: If you beat this rap . . .

MASTERS: I'll beat it. I got the best defense money can buy.

CLOUD: My buddies and I . . .

MASTERS: Who're your buddies?

CLOUD: You don't have to know that.

MASTERS: Other cops?

CLOUD: No comment.

MASTERS: (*Contemplates* CLOUD) You're a narc, right?

(CLOUD *holds his fingers to his lips. He feels around the edge of the table for possible bugs, then he feels the edge of the light that is over them.* CLOUD *takes the gum he has been chewing and places it on the rim of the light.* MASTERS *is impressed.*)

MASTERS: I get the picture.

(CLOUD *moves closer to* MASTERS.)

CLOUD: You have any idea how much shit there is in the property room at P.D. headquarters?

MASTERS: Enough to keep this city high for a century.

CLOUD: You a user?

MASTERS: (*Pride, holds out arms.*) You ever see cleaner limbs than these, man?

CLOUD: Very good.

MASTERS: The only thing I'm hooked on is health food.

CLOUD: Into health, eh?

MASTERS: Bet your ass. Never put salt in my food.

CLOUD: Salt?

MASTERS: Causes high blood pressure, man.

CLOUD: That a fact?

MASTERS: You don't expect me to break into the property room, do you?

CLOUD: And set off the alarms! What a dumb question. (*Beat*) You ask another dumb question, I'm blowing.

MASTERS: Give me some smart answers, I don't have to ask dumb questions.

CLOUD: When you get out, come to me.

MASTERS: You're the business agent.

(CLOUD *does not deny it.*)

MASTERS: How do I find you?

CLOUD: (*Proffers business card.*) If you lose this, look me up in the white pages.

(MASTERS *grabs* CLOUDS *arm and pulls up the sleeve. He sees the ersatz needle marks and is satisfied.* CLOUD *feigns embarrasment.* MASTERS *gives him an evil smirk.*)

MASTERS: Don't tell me this is a dumb question, or you can go hump yourself. Why come to me?

CLOUD: That's not a dumb question. You answer it.

MASTERS: (*Pride*) I'm the shit king.

CLOUD: I heard the term "emperor" used.

MASTERS: Get one thing straight: if you're setting me up, it won't stick. This is entrapment, man.

CLOUD: Goddamn! Talking like a peckerhead again.

MASTERS: Got a cash flow problem, right? All the little boy blues don't have the scratch to make the deal go down.

CLOUD: You don't get rich being a cop.

MASTERS: Yeah. Well, I got a cash flow problem, too. Sonofabitch Billings drained me dry.

CLOUD: You're breaking my heart. You got connections.

MASTERS: I'm a lone wolf. I stay away from loan sharks, man. They are poison.

CLOUD: Soon as you get out, come to see me. No promises, but I'll see what I can do.

MASTERS: Get this straight: when I'm on the outside, don't tail me—ever! I spot tails like radar . . . (*Makes spiral gesture with his finger.*) spots airplanes.

CLOUD: I won't know where you are unless you come to me.

MASTERS: Never struck a deal with a cop before.

(CLOUD *extends a hand to shake with* MASTERS.)

CLOUD: Call me sir.

MASTERS: Sir.

CLOUD: Again.

MASTERS: Sir.

CLOUD: (*Offers a pretend toast of champagne.*) To a productive future.

MASTERS: (*Plays the game.*) I'll buy that.

CLOUD: A joint venture.

MASTERS: They got "joints" in the property room, too?

CLOUD: (*Finger to his lips.*) Shhh . . . Peckerhead.

MASTERS: (*Nods*) I'm cool, I'm cool.

CLOUD: Don't forget. After the trial, come to me my melancholy baby.

MASTERS: Melancholy? I'm coming with a big old smile, man. Ear to ear.

CLOUD: Very good, sir. (*Starts to rise and exit.*) Let a smile be your umbrella.

MASTERS: See you soon, blue flu.

CLOUD: (*Annoyed*) What'd you say?

MASTERS: Excuse me. Sir!

CLOUD: That's more like it. (*Beat*) You gotta have mutual respect for a productive future.

MASTERS: I'm hip.

(CLOUD *exits.* MASTERS *smiles to himself.*)

MASTERS: Emperor David. Beloved by his people.

CURTAIN
END OF ACT ONE

Act Two

Scene One

(CLOUD's office. SHERRY *is in a seat at the side of the desk, waiting impatiently for* CLOUD. *Her eyes spot a memo; she picks it up and reads it. Her face registers alarm.* CLOUD *enters with books.*)

CLOUD: Sorry, I'm late, hon. The professor kept us overtime.

SHERRY: When'd you get this? (*Hands him the memo.*)

CLOUD: This morning.

SHERRY: Who's this county jail informant? That means a stool pigeon, doesn't it?

CLOUD: Uh-huh.

SHERRY: Why do they call him "highly reliable"?

CLOUD: He's usually on target. (*Puts the memo on the desk.*)

SHERRY: Do you know this informant?

CLOUD: No. He reports directly to the prison authorities. His identity is secret.

SHERRY: Why don't you tell Mr. Billings yourself?

CLOUD: I'm under orders to stay away from him.

SHERRY: So send a mailgram.

CLOUD: Figured I'd kill two birds. One: I know his loyal secretary will give him the information, and two: I get to feast these tired eyes on said secretary during a dull working day.

SHERRY: Mixing murder and romance.

CLOUD: Don't come unglued, hon. It's not yet "code blue."

(*She looks quizzical*)

CLOUD: That's hospital lingo for lifesaving measures. Masters is still in custody.

SHERRY: The case goes to the jury any day.

CLOUD: After the verdict, we go code blue. (*Beat*) Sherry, this is important: I've felt from the beginning of my work on this case that your boss was the ultimate target. Whoever has been eliminating his clients has been waiting for the right moment to finish him. It would've been great—I tried but it wasn't in the cards—if Billings and I could've worked together.

SHERRY: You don't dislike him for getting them off?

CLOUD: He's not to blame. He just works the system.

SHERRY: You hate the system, then?

CLOUD: I love the system. The human race is going to be around a while—unless we do something stupid. We can plug the holes in the system. We learn as we go along.

SHERRY: Let me get this straight. You don't hate my boss?

CLOUD: You kidding? I admire him. If I had a fourth of his ability, I'd consider myself lucky.

SHERRY: (*Touches the memo.*) Make me a copy.

CLOUD: Can't. This isn't a press release.

SHERRY: Then you couldn't have told Mr. Billings?

CLOUD: Not directly. Look, I'm sticking my neck out telling you.

SHERRY: (*Considers him*) John, you're not pulling something, are you?

CLOUD: What, for instance.

SHERRY: This is a real memo?

CLOUD: (*Crosses his heart*) Hope to die.

SHERRY: Honest?

CLOUD: You want to look in my eyes again?

SHERRY: (*Faces him*) I'd like to do that anyway.

(*They stand and embrace. She pulls off to look in his eyes.*)

SHERRY: Are you able to fake sincere eyes?

CLOUD: No. When I tell lies, they cross. Dead giveaway.

SHERRY: I'm in big trouble.

CLOUD: How so?

SHERRY: I think I'm in love with you.

CLOUD: This a confession?

SHERRY: Uh-huh.

CLOUD: Under Miranda, you had a right to remain silent.

SHERRY: Thanks a lot.

CLOUD: It's a good thing you owned up. (*Takes her closer.*)

SHERRY: Why's it a good thing?

CLOUD: If you didn't, I'd have had you arrested.

(*She touches him gently on the face.*)

BLACKOUT

Scene Two

(BILLINGS' *office. The attorney is taking a law book from a shelf and perusing it.* SHERRY *knocks.*)

BILLINGS: Sherry?

SHERRY: (*Outside door.*) Yes.

BILLINGS: Come in.

(*She enters.*)

SHERRY: Some vertical news.

(BILLINGS *walks over to his desk. Gestures* SHERRY *to seat.*)

BILLINGS: How is our Indian brave?

SHERRY: Fine. I saw an important memo in his office.

BILLINGS: Never mind the memo. What's the current state of affairs with you two?

SHERRY: I told him I'm in love.

(BILLINGS *makes an unhappy face and considers her before he speaks.*)

BILLINGS: How does he feel about you?

SHERRY: He said if I didn't own up soon, he was going to have me arrested. Wasn't that a darling way to put it?

BILLINGS: (*Sarcastic*) Hello young lovers. As your employer and I hope friend, I'd like to interject one thing: he isn't good enough for you.

SHERRY: He's the top.

BILLINGS: Please. He's a plodding sort; probably not too high an I.Q. Even he characterizes himself as a tortoise.

SHERRY: I see a side of him you don't.

BILLINGS: (*Smirks*) Granted.

SHERRY: I'm not talking about that.

BILLINGS: Let me finish. With your beauty, brains, and personality, you can do infinitely better than a gendarme.

SHERRY: He'll be a lawyer soon.

BILLINGS: If—and it's a big if—if he passes the bar. I checked on him. He's near the bottom of his class. I don't foresee a brilliant career in jurisprudence.

SHERRY: Considering he has a full-time job, he's doing all right. Don't worry, he'll pass the bar.

BILLINGS: Why do women invariably go for losers? Must be inborn maternal protectiveness. I've known more marvelous females who married dullards. (*Sighs*) The old cliché love is blind, is true I guess.

SHERRY: He's no dullard.

BILLINGS: That's how he impressed me.

SHERRY: Look, I don't go for high-toned, flashy, big talkers.

BILLINGS: Like me, you mean.

SHERRY: Present company excepted. Y'know, you're very irritable today.

BILLINGS: Guilty as charged. (*Beat*) What's this about a memo?

SHERRY: John let me see it on his desk. It was from county jail to the Police Department. It said, "Highly reliable informant reveals he was asked to kill Attorney Billings at conclusion of Masters Case."

BILLINGS: That's all it said?

SHERRY: Just that one sentence.

BILLINGS: Who's the informant and would-be hit man?

SHERRY: John didn't know. He said that would only be known by the jail authorities. Does that make sense?

BILLINGS: (*Nods*) Good informants get protection.

SHERRY: John is worried about you.

BILLINGS: (*Chuckles*) I'll bet.

SHERRY: He really is. (*Beat*) Who has it in for you?

BILLINGS: My firm hunch'd be David Masters.

SHERRY: But you're saving him.

BILLINGS: The verdict hasn't been rendered yet.

SHERRY: Is he that hard to defend?

BILLINGS: Pardon my Iroquois, but he's a shit. He's threatened retaliation if I lose. If I win and he's free, he's going to hate me for impoverishing him.

SHERRY: So give him a rebate.

BILLINGS: Rebate? (*Thoughtful*) I just might do that.

BLACKOUT

Scene Three

(CLOUD *is in the bar in which he met* SHERRY. *He is seated on a stool drinking whiskey and soda. Frantic music is playing.* MASTERS, *in far-out outfit, wearing sunglasses, approaches him from behind.*)

MASTERS: Hey, my man.

CLOUD: Hello.

MASTERS: Dig my threads?

CLOUD: Far out.

MASTERS: Just like me. Far out of stir, man. (*Beat*) What about the deal your business agent for?

CLOUD: I'm agent for zilch.

MASTERS: Couldn't raise the lubrication money, eh?

CLOUD: Unless you can lubricate with swamp water.

MASTERS: Everything else about the setup still cool?

CLOUD: Hey, without funding, I'm a bride waiting at the altar.

MASTERS: Here comes the bride, man. Got on my wedding outfit. (*Scrutinizes* CLOUD) I want to study all the details. You got written plans?

CLOUD: Some. Mostly it's in my head.

MASTERS: Gotta make sure the plan is feasible, man. You know what "feasible" means?

CLOUD: It is unfeasible. Strictly cash operation.

MASTERS: (*Looks off*) Be here ten o'clock. Sit in the last booth over there.

CLOUD: You putting me on?

MASTERS: (*Smiles evilly*) My counselor has a gift for me.

CLOUD: Money?

MASTERS: A partial refund.

CLOUD: Isn't that unorthodox? Y'know, returning the fee.

MASTERS: I'm unorthodox, man. Saving his ass. When I was in the cooler, I went to the local finko and made a deal to kill Billings.

CLOUD: All right. Figuring it'd get back to him.

MASTERS: That's what finks are for, man.

CLOUD: Clever.

MASTERS: Thank you. See you at ten bells.

CLOUD: Gotcha.

MASTERS: Remember, I don't like the plan, I don't finance it. Be ready with some heavy details.

CLOUD: How long should I wait for you?

MASTERS: Let's see. Meeting my counselor at nine. Eh, I may have to listen to his monologue before he kicks over the loot. I'll cut it short.

(*Rises and starts to slink out.* CLOUD *extends a hand and* MASTERS *gives him skin.*)

CLOUD: See you later.

MASTERS: (*Winks and makes a clicking mouth sound.*) In a while, crocodile.

(MASTERS *makes an amusing exit.* CLOUD *smiles at the antics, then waxes serious and goes to corner pay phone and dials.*)

CLOUD: Sherry? . . . Code blue . . . You keep your promise, hon? Billings mustn't know . . . Leave the office door unlocked when you go home . . . My crystal ball tells me it's coming together tonight . . . Of course, I'll be careful . . . No, no, don't worry about Masters. He is no threat; as of the moment he's a happy man. I've got to nail the third party who wants to take out both Masters and Billings . . . Thanks, babe. Stick by your phone . . . Bye.

(*Hangs up. He feels the pistol in its shoulder holster for reassurance. Then he pulls up his jacket to check the handcuffs which hang on the rear of his belt.*)

BLACKOUT

Scene Four

(BILLINGS' *office. Night.* CLOUD *lets himself in and surveys the room with a small searchlight. He switches off the searchlight, then goes to the window and looks out of the miniblind. From offstage we hear the sound of a van pulling up.* CLOUD *hides in the Indian statue, closing the case. After a minute* BILLINGS *enters, switching on the room lights. He is pushing a large dolly. He pats the Indian statue as he passes it.*)

BILLINGS: Hail, chief. Are you ready for your white man's burden?

(BILLINGS *moves to the bathroom and opens the door. The noise of the moving dolly covers* CLOUD'S *opening the statue slightly to observe* BILLINGS *hiding of the dolly.* CLOUD *recloses the statue.* BILLINGS *closes the bathroom door. Next is heard the sound of a knock on the outside entry door.*)

BILLINGS: Come in.

(MASTERS *enters.*)

BILLINGS: Ah, my client.

MASTERS: (*Sullen*) Former client.

BILLINGS: How's it feel to be walking the streets a free man?

MASTERS: Damn good.

BILLINGS: I should imagine.

MASTERS: Well?

BILLINGS: Well what?

MASTERS: Don't crap around. Let's talk money.

BILLINGS: I never talk money without a drink. Name your poison.

MASTERS: Booze is your trip, man.

BILLINGS: You're not going to imbibe with me on this memorable occasion?

MASTERS: (*Reluctant, gestures to bar.*) I'll try the orange juice.

BILLINGS: Nothing to sweeten it?

MASTERS: Just the O-J.

(BILLINGS *pours the orange juice and passes over a glass of it to* MASTERS, *who gets ready to drink instantly.*)

BILLINGS: Please. Wait for me.

(BILLINGS *pours vodka and tonic into a glass; he holds up the glass.*)

BILLINGS: Cheers.

(MASTERS *nods, then drinks the juice.* BILLINGS *watches for the effect of the mickied juice, which will sneak up on* MASTERS.)

MASTERS: Now, let's talk money.

BILLINGS: Ah, yes. Moolah, lucre, greenbacks.

MASTERS: Cut the chatter. I've heard enough of your bull to last a lifetime.

BILLINGS: Don't you, at least, wish to thank me for having a lifetime?

MASTERS: (*Speech starts slurring*) Save the words and the word games for people who dig it. Frankly, I don't.

(MASTERS *gestures for the money owed him.* BILLINGS *puts pile of bills on the desk.*)

BILLINGS: Cash, as you requested.

(MASTERS *picks up and flips through bills.* MASTERS *shakes his head groggily.*)

MASTERS: W . . . wh . . . what about my M . . . Mercedes? It was in m . . . mint condition.

BILLINGS: Alas, no longer. This tribe, well, they carry sheep and goats, occasionally chickens. On the other hand, if you want it back . . .

MASTERS: Forget it. I'm not into barnyard smells.

BILLINGS: That's right; you prefer less wholesome odors.

MASTERS: (*Looks at the money with effort.*) Y'know, I think you better give me, oh, twenty percent more.

BILLINGS: Don't be greedy. Help the needy.

MASTERS: I'm needy! I may be bankrolling a massive deal.

BILLINGS: Promoting nefarious schemes already?

MASTERS: Grass doesn't grow under me! (*Pockets money*)

BILLINGS: How about *over* you?

MASTERS: Don't try to be funny. You like that cute little whatsit who's your secretary?

BILLINGS: Indeed.

MASTERS: Maybe you donate a little more money so she keeps her pretty face.

BILLINGS: That's right, David-beloved. You do have a penchant for carving up female anatomy.

MASTERS: Let's compromise. M...m...make it ten percent m...more.

BILLINGS: Sorry. (*Raises hands for search, watching.*) You wish to search me?

(MASTERS *foggily ponders* BILLINGS. *His legs get rubbery as he walks toward* BILLINGS.)

BILLINGS: Surely, you don't want my Visa Card?

(MASTERS *falls flat on his back, unconscious.*)

BILLINGS: I guess not.

(BILLINGS *rushes to the wall for a tomahawk and is readying to crash in* MASTERS *skull.* CLOUD *has been struggling to get out of the jammed Indian case. At the moment when* BILLINGS *will hit* MASTERS, CLOUD *bursts out with a revolver on* BILLINGS)

CLOUD: Drop it. Raise your hands. (*Cutting*) Sir!

(BILLINGS *drops the tomahawk and raises his hands.* CLOUD *moves toward him.*)

BILLINGS: What do you think you're doing?

CLOUD: Apprehending a murderer, sir.

BILLINGS: Murderer? Masters was threatening bodily harm. Surely, you heard.

CLOUD: Heard and I smelled, sir.

BILLINGS: The long nose of the law. What did you smell?

CLOUD: Cedar, sir. (*Removes fibers from his hair and drops them.*) Cedar has a strong odor.

BILLINGS: That makes me a murderer?

CLOUD: Filmore, Sissler, Baker, Donato had cedar fibers on their persons.

BILLINGS: Weak circumstantial evidence.

CLOUD: (*Shakes his head*) Evidence as strong as the odor. Bernie at the lab'll match cedar fibers with clothing fibers and hair samples . . . Up against the wall.

(BILLINGS *complies.* CLOUD *takes out handcuffs and is readying to lock them.*)

Forgive me, sir. I realize this is no way to treat a man who's a legend in his time.

BILLINGS: I daresay.

(*Unknown to them,* SHERRY *has entered, with her face registering surprise.* CLOUD *pats* BILLINGS *for weapons.*)

SHERRY: John, what's going on?

CLOUD: (*Intent on* BILLINGS.) Stay out of this. Turn around and leave.

(SHERRY *draws a small protection pistol from her purse and puts her purse aside.*)

SHERRY: Don't hold a gun on my father.

(CLOUD *registers surprise.*)

BILLINGS: I told you never to use that word. Never!

SHERRY: Drop it, John.

CLOUD: (*Simultaneous*) Father? You two've been having a good laugh at me.

(*Reluctant and discouraged,* CLOUD *drops his gun.* BILLINGS *picks it up, also training it on* CLOUD. SHERRY *gestures to* MASTERS.)

SHERRY: What happened?

BILLINGS: Masters violated the highest of laws: the no deposit, no return law. (*Reaches for* CLOUD'S *handcuffs.*) I'll take those.

(CLOUD *hands him the cuffs.*)

Hands behind you.

(BILLINGS *secures the cuff on* CLOUD.)

Sit down, Sergeant.

(CLOUD *sits in client chair near* MASTERS, *then he looks at* SHERRY.)

CLOUD: You help with the others, too?

SHERRY: What're you talking about?

CLOUD: His dead clients.

SHERRY: (*To* BILLINGS) What's he talking about?

BILLINGS: Your boy friend—I hope I may use the adjective "former"—seems to think I murdered Mssrs . . . The names again, Sergeant?

CLOUD: (*Sighs in disgust*) Filmore, Sissler, Baker, Donato.

BILLINGS: Considering your aptitude, I suggest you seek employment as a railroad conductor.

SHERRY: Ridiculous.

BILLINGS: Not really; Amtrak is reviving trains.

SHERRY: How can you think my father . . .

BILLINGS: (*Annoyed, half to himself*) Mr. Billings!

SHERRY: How can you think he murdered those men?

CLOUD: You weren't party to it?

(*He searches her face for the truth. Her face reveals she is trying to comprehend.*)

CLOUD: Take a look—the bathroom.

(*Still holding the pistol,* SHERRY *walks to and opens bathroom door, revealing the dolly. She pulls it out to look at it. She turns to* BILLINGS.)

SHERRY: What's this for?

BILLINGS: Ask your friendly sleuth.

(SHERRY *pushes the dolly back in and closes the door.*)

CLOUD: (*Wheeling the mummy case around.*) Exhibit B: smell the inside.

SHERRY: (*Walks to the statue and sniffs.*) Pine?

CLOUD: Cedar.

SHERRY: What they make hope chests out of.

BILLINGS: Abandon all hope ye who . . .

CLOUD: (*Cuts him off.*) Case closed.

BILLINGS: Incorrect. The case is open, else you couldn't smell it.

CLOUD: Sherry, all four had cedar fibers on them. (*He gestures to* MASTERS.) He was next for a cedar treatment.

BILLINGS: (*Needling*) Procedure, officer. You haven't read my rights.

CLOUD: (*Going along with the game.*) You have a right to remain silent. Any statement you make may be used against you in a court proceeding.

(SHERRY, *now grasping the enormity, looks horrified from* CLOUD *to her father as* CLOUD *drones on.*)

CLOUD: You have a right to remain silent. Any statement you make may be . . .

BILLINGS: Repeating yourself, dummy.

CLOUD: Excuse me.

(CLOUD *upset, looks at* SHERRY *and tries to gather his thoughts. She refuses to look at him.*)

CLOUD: Where was I? (*Beat*) You have a right to be represented by counsel and to have counsel present during any questioning. If you cannot afford counsel, the court will appoint counsel to represent you.

SHERRY: Stop it. Stop it! (*She is at the breaking point; both men watch her. She gasps for breath, holding her chest, and the next word explodes from her lungs.*) Father! (*In a breaking voice.*) You killed those men.

BILLINGS: Easy, easy, my dear. Calm yourself. (*Smirks*) The cat isn't out of the bag. In fact, there is no bag.

CLOUD: (*Rebuttal*) Just a cigar store Indian with a cedar lining.

SHERRY: (*Holds her ears in pain, and then her jaws.*) Father, tell me you didn't kill those men.

BILLINGS: Didn't you hear? I have a right to remain silent.

SHERRY: What'd you say?

BILLINGS: (*Louder*) I have a right to remain silent.

SHERRY: You just answered.

CLOUD: Sorry.

BILLINGS: (*The clown*) For me?

CLOUD: For her!

SHERRY: You're sorry.

CLOUD: I am, baby.

BILLINGS: She's my baby; don't you forget it.

CLOUD: I love you.

SHERRY: Used me, John, you used me!

CLOUD: Please. I had no idea. I thought I was *protecting* Billings.

BILLINGS: To protect and serve.

CLOUD: That's right, sir. Don't make fun of something I'm proud of.

SHERRY: (*Obviously pondering*) Hmnn. What now? (*Looks at pistol*) The psychology books never deal with this. What would Jung or Adler say? (*To* BILLINGS) My wonderful loving father. (*To* CLOUD) My John.

(*At this point,* MASTERS *moves and reaches for* SHERRY'S *legs. She screams and moves back.* BILLINGS *moves to* MASTERS *with the gun.*)

BILLINGS: Up against the wall! Hand on your head.

MASTERS: (*Complies, looks at* CLOUD.) What the hell you doing here?

CLOUD: I saved your life, man.

MASTERS: What about our deal?

CLOUD: Made it up.

MASTERS: You bullshitted me?

CLOUD: I lied to protect you.

MASTERS: Protect me? (*Gestures around*) How the hell'd you do that? Christ!

BILLINGS: Is that a way to address your knight in shining serge?

MASTERS: (*Furious at* CLOUD) You want to protect me—screwup— (*Touches* CLOUD's *handcuffs*) You let me know what he's doing, I come in here with a three-fifty-seven magnum!

CLOUD: (*Angry at himself*) I didn't know.

MASTERS: Screwup!

CLOUD: (*Bitter acknowledgment*) You're right, you're right. I'm the dumbest cop in history.

(*Looks heavenward for strength in his despair. Sighs.* MASTERS *pans all thoughtfully, wondering where his self-interest lies.*)

MASTERS: What happens now?

(*Silence.* Billings *looks at* Sherry, *then* Cloud *looks to her. She squirms.*)

Masters: What the hell happens now?

Cloud: Good question, your honor.

Sherry: Your honor! What's that supposed to . . .

Cloud: In your hands, baby.

Sherry: My hands? What about your hands?

(Cloud *holds out his handcuffed hands.*)

Sherry: John, don't lay a trip on me.

Cloud: A trip? Just obey the law.

Sherry: The law?

Masters: You gotta turn in your boss.

Sherry: (*Mordant laugh*) My boss.

Masters: What's so funny?

Cloud: He's her father.

Masters: (*Beat to* Cloud) You and I are dead meat, man.

Cloud: Why didn't you want Sherry known as your daughter?

Billings: A man in my situation, a daughter is a window of vulnerability.

Cloud: And I opened the window.

Billings: Not wisely, not well—but you opened it (*Beat*) You don't have to die, Sergeant. Incompetency is a misdemeanor. (*To* Sherry, *building his case.*) In your studies, what've you learned about psychopaths?

Sherry: Oh, er . . . antisocial, incorrigible . . .

Billings: How about the fact that their neural circuits, their brains, are different from the rest of us?

Sherry: Some of the research says that.

Billings: Your Iroquois mother, this might be the time to tell you how she died. (*Picks up the photo from his desk. He is on the verge of tears, and shows true emotionality.*) You find my daughter attractive, Sergeant?

Cloud: You know I do.

Billings: (*To* Cloud, *with a deep sigh, working to gain him as an ally.*) Her mother was even more beautiful. (*He holds the photo against his chest*.) Her cheekbones were a little higher . . . (*Cries*) Her eyes were . . . (*Sob*) Larger . . . and . . . (*Sniffs*) A deeper brown, almost black. She was as gentle as a fawn. She had a quiet dignity that illuminated every path she walked upon. (*He walks toward* SHERRY.) She loved you, Sherry. She called you her gift to the universe.

(*Moved,* SHERRY *wipes tears from her eyes. Somber,* BILLINGS *walks to the bar, takes a belt of vodka, and wipes his mouth. Then he walks closer to* MASTERS, *continuing to stand sentry with the pistol. He takes a deep breath and lets out a pained sigh.*)

BILLINGS: She was raped and murdered by a white man when you were twenty months old, Sherry. A butcher. The word "squaw" was carved on her torso.

CLOUD: Brooded all these years.

BILLINGS: (*Recovers composure*) Brooded? No. I worked. Worked to rid society of psychopaths. My criminal practice was my bait and my cover.

CLOUD: You hate all your clients?

BILLINGS: Don't be absurd. Only the likes of him—the irredeemables. (*To* MASTERS) Tell them about the valley murders, the crime of which you are innocent. Tell them about the wife, tell them about the little girl.

MASTERS: Thanks to you, counselor, it's off the books.

BILLINGS: In an Anglo-Saxon court; never an Indian court.

MASTERS: Yeah. Redskins woulda castrated me.

BILLINGS: Which is why I believe in the justice of your people, Sergeant.

CLOUD: I'm part Indian, O.K.? I don't buy murder; I never will.

BILLINGS: I beg you—and I'm not a man who likes to beg—let me finish what I started. (*Gestures at* MASTERS) Keep your mouth shut, Sergeant, and I'll give your liaison with Sherry my blessing.

MASTERS: (*Fear registers on his face.*) Don't buy this, Cloud! You took an oath. He looks down on me. I always knew it. Well, I look down on him. He's no better than I am.

BILLINGS: Heaven strike me dead.

MASTERS: For all your fancy talk, the tailormade suits, you're a killer, man. You enjoy it.

BILLINGS: Quite right.

Masters: (*To* Cloud) What'd I tell you?

Billings: Ah, but whom do I kill?

Cloud: Irrelevant. I agree; you're no better. Erase that. You're worse. The legal genius, strangling and shooting. (*Shakes his head*) "Hokie," sir.

Billings: Get something through your head. Native American law sacrifices lawbreakers for the good of the community. Take note, Sherry, take note.

Masters: You're the lawbreaker, pops.

Billings: Not the true law! Listen carefully, Sherry. (*Beat*) My days of hypocrisy are over.

Cloud: What hypocrisy, sir?

Billings: Pleading in court for scum.

Cloud: Without you, they might've been convicted. Isn't that, y'know hypocrisy?

Billings: I had to intervene. Can't trust the system. As a cop you know what walks our streets, stalking us. (*Gestures out the window*) Walk in the park at night, take your life in your hands. You deny it?

Cloud: No. (*Beat*) Forgive me, sir, but how about a walk in your office?

Billings: A walk in my office?

Cloud: Shouldn't it be safe to walk into your office?

Billings: No honest citizen need fear me.

Cloud: I'm an honest citizen. You scare me to death! (*Beat, rational*) Come on, now, make it easy for Sherry. You love her, don't you?

Billings: Rhetorical question.

Cloud: Undo the cuffs. You and Sherry hand me your weapons.

Billings: (*Gestures to* Masters *with the gun.*) And he gets away scot free!

(Masters *cringes*).

Cloud: Had a brilliant defense and a fair trial. Have to catch him next time.

Billings: Did you read the autopsies on his victims?

Cloud: Nosir.

BILLINGS: Well, I did!

CLOUD: Come on, release me. Hand over your weapons.

BILLINGS: You're in no position to make demands.

CLOUD: Oh, yes I am. I'm an officer of the law.

BILLINGS: The wrong law, Sergeant, the wrong law.

CLOUD: I'll see you get a fair trial.

BILLINGS: (*Puffs*) A fair trial!

SHERRY: John, he could go to the gas chamber.

BILLINGS: If I don't, friends of my victims'd kill me in prison.

CLOUD: Now, you think of the consequences. Why'd you decide to play God?

BILLINGS: (*Measured*) Because I'm extremely good at it!

CLOUD: When I write this up, no one'll believe me.

BILLINGS: I can't let you write it up, you know that.

SHERRY: (*Dutiful daughter*) John, go along with Father. It's the only way.

MASTERS: (*Worried face*) Holy shit!

CLOUD: (*To* SHERRY) You can't be serious!

SHERRY: Father, say something. Reassure him.

BILLINGS: Very well. After Masters, no more.

SHERRY: See, John?

CLOUD: I want to forget what you just said. (*Points to* MASTERS) What about him? This is a living, breathing man, not a statistic. Tell you what, Sherry, I'll buy it if you shoot Masters right now.

MASTERS: What kind of . . . !

CLOUD: (*Pressing*) Pull the trigger, come on!

SHERRY: In cold blood?

CLOUD: The way daddy does.

SHERRY: (*Leans against the wall, tearful.*) I . . . I can't.

MASTERS: (*Moves toward* BILLINGS) Look, you people are going about it . . .

BILLINGS: (*Aims at* MASTERS) Sit down!

MASTERS: (*Sits in* BILLINGS' *chair.*) Look. Listen. You people are going about it the wrong way. (*Puts the money gotten from* BILLINGS *on the desk.*) I'm on your side.

BILLINGS: God help us.

MASTERS: Hear me out. Look, one of us can't walk outta here. You both have it all wrong. I'm not your enemy. (*Gestures to* CLOUD) He is! (*Beat*) Even if he promised not to—you know he'd talk. He's a cop through and through.

BILLINGS: (*Smiles at* CLOUD) Listen to the man you're bent on saving.

SHERRY: John, he's a snake.

CLOUD: Fine. So pull the trigger.

(MASTERS *studies everyone with calculation. He understands* CLOUD'S *strategy but he thinks he can defeat* CLOUD *because of familial loyalty.* SHERRY *studies her pistol.*)

SHERRY: Will you keep quiet if I do?

CLOUD: Sorry. If I live, this gets handled legally.

MASTERS: (*To* BILLINGS *and* SHERRY) What'd I tell you? He's the one has to die! (*Fast talking*) Look, I'm known in the trade—you know damn well, Billings—I'm known for keeping my trap shut.

BILLINGS: True.

MASTERS: They can kill me before I fink.

BILLINGS: You do have a felon's honor.

MASTERS: Give me the gun. I'll be trigger man. That way you know you can trust me. I'll have a stake.

SHERRY: A gun for him, Father?

MASTERS: What's the matter? You don't trust me?

SHERRY: You'll turn it on us.

MASTERS: Why would I do that?

BILLINGS: The money.

MASTERS: Screw the money. We're talking my life.

BILLINGS: Good logic, Sherry. He's smarter than Cloud.

MASTERS: (*Insistent*) Look, keep a gun on me. I'll drop the pistol soon as I blast him. If I don't, shoot me. Now, for chrissake, use your brains.

BILLINGS: Very interesting. I'd like to hear from the potential victim.

CLOUD: What am I supposed to say?

BILLINGS: Have you heard the preceding?

CLOUD: I'm not deaf.

BILLINGS: Your reaction?

CLOUD: Fear.

BILLINGS: What happened to the brave officer of the law?

CLOUD: He sees his life rushing before his eyes.

BILLINGS: Good. (*Beat, claps hands once.*) Let's make a deal. Variation of the Golden Rule: you do to Masters what he wishes to do to you.

(CLOUD *shakes his head.*)

BILLINGS: Listening to Masters, you still have scruples?

CLOUD: I don't change with the breeze.

BILLINGS: (*Sighs*) You're impossible.

CLOUD: Shoot me, sir.

BILLINGS: I? (*Shakes his head, points to* MASTERS.) There's an executioner at the ready.

SHERRY: John, please, I didn't want this situation.

CLOUD: (*Gestures to* BILLINGS) He created the situation, not I.

SHERRY: Can I let you take him to jail and God knows what? Suppose he were your father?

CLOUD: Toughest question in the world, hon. (*Deeper into his strategy*) Tell you what: *you* shoot me, *not* Masters.

SHERRY: (*Distraught*) Oh, for the love of . . .

CLOUD: (*Pressing*) Right between the eyes, Sherry.

SHERRY: Reconsider, John. Please. (*She utters a pained sigh.*)

BILLINGS: (*Gun on* MASTERS) Sergeant, I'll make it easy on you. You don't have to shoot him. I will. Promise to keep your mouth shut.

CLOUD: No way.

MASTERS: He's an asshole! All three of us are in the soup because of him and his stupidity. Give me the gun!

(BILLINGS *looks like he may give the weapon to* MASTERS. *He is still hoping to win* CLOUD *over.*)

BILLINGS: Last chance.

SHERRY: John, please.

CLOUD: (*Stalling*) May I have a drink?

BILLINGS: Wouldn't you prefer a blindfold and a cigarette?

CLOUD: My throat's dry.

(BILLINGS *gestures to* MASTERS *to give* CLOUD *the drugged orange juice which has been sitting on the desk.* MASTERS *does a take and then* BILLINGS *gives him a reassuring look.* BILLINGS *hopes to get* CLOUD *to sleep so he can still finish off* MASTERS. MASTERS *approaches* CLOUD *with the glass of juice.* CLOUD *laughs.*)

BILLINGS: (*To* MASTERS) Help him drink.

(MASTERS *holds out the juice.* CLOUD *looks at* SHERRY)

CLOUD: (*Wry smile*) Finally coming to terms with orange juice.

(SHERRY *looks at her father with pain in her face. She is torn in both directions. Her look conveys a question to* BILLINGS. CLOUD *drinks.*)

BILLINGS: He has only himself to blame, Sherry.

CLOUD: You're not getting off that easy, sir. This all started when you decided to play God way back when. God has branched out. From psychopaths to policemen!

(*The potent word "policemen" shakes* BILLINGS *and he is momentarily off guard.* MASTERS *the opportunist goes for* BILLINGS'S *gun.* SHERRY *simultaneously shoots and screams, acting instinctively, and with one shot kills* MASTERS. CLOUD *breathes a sigh of relief since his strategy worked.* BILLINGS *recovers and holds up the weapon.* SHERRY *takes aim at her father.*)

SHERRY: Drop the gun, father.

(*There is a tense moment.* BILLINGS *is torn. Of course, he cannot shoot his daughter. He puts the gun on the desk top.* SHERRY *covers* BILLINGS.)

How do I undo the cuffs?

CLOUD: Key's on my belt. (*The drugged juice is starting to take effect.*)

BILLINGS: What now, daughter?

(SHERRY *is momentarily silenced by the shock of killing* MASTERS. *She is preoccupied and stares at the body.* CLOUD, *when he is released by* SHERRY, *gathers up the two guns and takes up the verbal slack.*)

CLOUD: That depends on the jury.

BILLINGS: Jury? (*Starting to crack—or is he? He takes off his shirt and tie and throws them on the desktop.*) What do you mean?

SHERRY: (*Abstracted*) Please. You heard.

BILLINGS: Spell it out for me, Sherry love.

(SHERRY *sighs and shakes her head. She is still upset over the killing.* BILLINGS *works to bare his chest.* CLOUD *is trying to maintain command but the drug is taking a greater toll on his faculties.*)

CLOUD: A jury, a fair trial.

BILLINGS: A jury-jury. (*To* SHERRY) A jury of my peers?

CLOUD: A superior court jury, sir.

BILLINGS: (*To* SHERRY) Is that right? You accept the white man's law over Indian law?

SHERRY: I do, father.

BILLINGS: (*Crescendo as he moves to the wall and puts on the headpiece with feathers and a neckband.*) A superior court jury? You deny your heritage?

(SHERRY *tries to touch and reassure* BILLINGS *but he shoves her away.*)

BILLINGS: You're not an Indian. You don't have a clue what it means to be an Indian. (*He slaps his chest to emphasize each word as he moves to exit.*) I protected the tribe. I'm an Indian! (*He takes a last look at the two of them. He gives a warhoop, then exits. The warhoop is punctuated by the palm of his hand. The eerie sound trails off.*)

(CLOUD, *almost out from the drug, falls on the floor.*)

SHERRY: (*Points to* MASTERS' *body, devastated.*) I . . . I just killed a man.

CLOUD: (*Groggy, shaking his head*) Justifiable homicide. (*Touches* SHERRY) The phone. (*He gestures for her to give the phone to him. He is barely able to dial. He blinks his eyes in an effort to stay awake.*)

Dial for me.

(*Unresponsive because she is on her own beam,* SHERRY *hands the phone to* CLOUD.)

SHERRY: He's crazy, John. He's liable to get hit by a car. (*Exits*)

CLOUD: (*Chuckles groggily, in measured speech*) *Crazy like a fox!* (*He tries to focus on the phone.*) O.K., Sherry. You won't dial for me, I deal—excuse me—dial myself. (*Dials with difficulty, speaks*) Defective—pardon me—Detective Sergeant Cloud, Homicide. (*Drops receiver, then picks it up.*) Never mind the badge mumbler—I mean, number! Get car to Fifth and O . . . O . . . Olive. Suspect on the loose. (*Again almost drops the receiver*) What's that? (*Beat*) Prescription? (*Fading mentality*) Oh, description! (*Beat*) Look for a white Indian!

(*Chuckling drunkenly,* CLOUD *falls to the floor while dropping the phone. In a last burst of energy he replaces the receiver on the phone cradle. He then lapses into unconsciousness with a silly, yet triumphant smile on his face.* SHERRY *is his, the crimes are solved, and he beat the master attorney in "court." The last sound we hear comes from the street. It is the incongrous howl of an abandoned "Indian"—the loser in the action.*)

CURTAIN
END OF PLAY

Bruce B. Post

Sloth

Bruce B. Post is a playwright and a caterer. He lives in Connecticut with his mother, his sister, and his dogs. He possesses a college degree and a Honda Civic. He has always wanted to be a science fiction writer. This is not his first play; nor will it be his last. If you don't like his writing then you probably wouldn't like his cooking, either. Bruce is a member of the Dramatists Guild and of the Roundabout Theatre Conservatory.

For stock and amateur production rights, contact: Broadway Play Publishing, Inc., 257 West 20th Street, New York, NY 10011. For all other rights, contact: Bruce B. Post, 2 Marli Lane, West Redding, CT 06896.

Characters

Harvey Sloth, an old man
Sally, his granddaughter
Herb McGoon, Harve's best friend
Huey, Harve's stableboy
Meg, Harve's sister

The time is the present. The place is northern New England.

Act One

Scene One

(An outdoor set. Stage left is the porch of an old colonial house. There are steps up to the porch, but it has no railing. There is a rocking chair and a few caned chairs on the porch. The wall behind the porch has one screen door and one window. Center stage, overhanging the porch, is an apple tree. There is a yard, with flowers, in front of the porch. Everything looks pretty and very well kept. We hear katydids.)

(It is early evening. Meg and Sally sit on the steps of the porch.)

SALLY: Have you been over here at all?

MEG: Not since the funeral. The place looks great, Sally. Your mother and your father'd be so proud to see this.

SALLY: I like to think they can.

MEG: Me too.

SALLY: I wish I didn't have to leave.

MEG: How long you think it'll take?

SALLY: Couple of months, maybe. If I was just going to spend the money, I could do it in a week. Less, in New York. But I've got to invest it, and that could take some time.

MEG: Sure you know what to do?

SALLY: We'll find out soon enough.

MEG: You be careful. Don't get taken in by one of those shysters.

SALLY: I'll be very careful, Aunt Meg.

MEG: You want me to peek in on things here?

SALLY: Grandpa will be here.

MEG: Exactly.

SALLY: You still don't like the idea, do you?

MEG: I don't feel well about it at all, Sally. Harve's likely to ruin this place.

SALLY: I don't think he's going to leave any permanent damage.

MEG: Never underestimate your grandfather.

SALLY: I can trust him.

MEG: Sally, I love my brother dearly, but the man hasn't done a thing with himself for over a decade. I think he's gone senile.

SALLY: Harve? Senile? He's as sharp as a whip.

MEG: He's peculiar. Has been ever since your grandmother died.

SALLY: But that was twenty years ago!

MEG: You grew up with it, Sally. You never knew the difference.

SALLY: What difference?

MEG: Harve turned sour after Sarah died.

SALLY: I think he's sweet.

MEG: It's true, he's got a soft spot for you. You look a lot like your grandmother. But Harvey isn't going to change for anyone. The man's becoming more and more odd as the years go by.

SALLY: I can't leave the place empty. And somebody's got to feed the horses.

MEG: I wouldn't trust him.

SALLY: Harve loves horses.

MEG: Just the same . . .

SALLY: What else can I do, Aunt Meg? I don't want a stranger in here. You can't move out of your place. Grandpa's the only one who can do it.

MEG: I'll stop in as often as I can.

SALLY: I appreciate it, Aunt Meg, but I don't think it's necessary.

(HARVE *drives in, stage right. He drives an old car, from the fifties. It is dull and rusty, but clean. On its bumper is a plate reading "Manado-nock Rescue Squad."* HARVE *parks the car in one of the flowerbeds.*)

MEG: Look, he's started already.

SALLY: Grandpa, look out!

(HARVE *doesn't seem to hear. He cocks his head, listening to the engine idle.*)

MEG: What is he doing?

SALLY: Harve!

(HARVE *listens to the engine for a few more beats. He stops the engine and slowly gets out of the car. He is dressed in green workpants and a flannel shirt. He is not in a hurry.* HARVE *is never in a hurry. He heads for the porch.*)

HARVE: Did you listen to that car? She still hums like the day I bought her. What a hellish motor!

MEG: Harvey, you parked your old clunker on top of the geraniums.

HARVE: Hello Sally, dear. You're looking very well.

SALLY: Hi Grandpa. Thanks for coming.

MEG: Harvey.

HARVE: 'Lo Meg. I'd be lyin' if I said I was surprised to see you here.

MEG: I came to persuade Sally not to leave this place in your hands.

HARVE: Eyuh. And were you successful?

MEG: She won't listen to reason.

HARVE: Hate to disappoint you, Meg.

MEG: Don't you worry about me. Don't disappoint Sally.

HARVE: Mind if I sit down?

(SALLY *makes room for him on the steps.* HARVE *sits.*)

Beautiful evening.

SALLY: Yes, it is.

HARVE: Quiet. Peaceful. Always was up here.

MEG: Did you hear me, Harvey?

HARVE: I heard you, Meg. What you gonna be doin' in New York, Sally?

SALLY: Try to find a good way to invest the money Mother and Daddy left me.

HARVE: They leave you a lot, did they?

SALLY: Quite a bit.

MEG: You'd know that if you'd come to hear the will.

HARVE: I couldn't be there. How'd I make out?

SALLY: Mother left you the horses.

HARVE: (*Brightening*) Did she? Meg, you never told me.

MEG: I was hoping you wouldn't find out.

SALLY: Do you want them?

HARVE: 'Course I do.

SALLY: I thought you would.

HARVE: My own horses. That's somethin' I never had.

SALLY: Think you can take care of them?

HARVE: Course I can. Though I'll have to keep them here for a while.

SALLY: That's fine with me.

HARVE: Place looks healthy, Sal. You been livin' here alone?

SALLY: I did it all myself.

HARVE: Good for you. You got a boyfriend? Or don't you go in for that sort of thing?

MEG: Oh, Harvey.

HARVE: Oh, Meg.

SALLY: Sure.

HARVE: How many?

SALLY: Grandpa.

HARVE: Good-lookin' woman like you's bound to have more than one.

SALLY: I can't afford more than one.

HARVE: Don't give me that. Bet you got one in every state.

SALLY: Only one. He was at the funeral.

HARVE: I don't recall him.

SALLY: You met him at the funeral.

HARVE: You mean I shook his hand and said hello. Am I supposed to remember a man on account a that?

SALLY: No matter. He isn't permanent.

MEG: You should get yourself married, Sally.

SALLY: I'm not ready yet.

HARVE: Don't do it till ya are.

SALLY: I don't have anybody to do it with!

MEG: You'll meet someone nice in New York.

HARVE: I doubt that, Meg.

SALLY: You will take good care of the place?

HARVE: I ain't lame.

SALLY: You won't mind living here?

HARVE: Why should I mind? I built this house.

MEG: You did not.

HARVE: Well, I helped an awful lot.

SALLY: I hope it's not too much trouble for you.

HARVE: Sally, dear, if you want to sell this place, then sell it. Won't bother me none. I can always go on welfare and live in one a them trailer parks.

MEG: Oh, Harvey.

HARVE: Oh, Meg.

SALLY: I couldn't sell it. I grew up here.

MEG: Then why don't you live here?

SALLY: I might.

HARVE: I doubt you could stand the quiet.

SALLY: I like the quiet.

HARVE: Eyuh.

SALLY: Do you need any money?

HARVE: Are you threatening to pay me?

SALLY: Don't get huffy. I thought . . .

HARVE: I will not be paid by my own granddaughter.

SALLY: Okay, take it easy. (*Pause*) I could send some for the bills.

HARVE: You could do that.

SALLY: They're all paid so far.

HARVE: That's good.

SALLY: Will you write me?

HARVE: I doubt it.

SALLY: Will you call me at least?

HARVE: Let's say you call me.

MEG: She can't! If she puts a phone in here you'll just unplug it.

HARVE: Eyuh. But she could put one in anyway, on the off chance it might ring, and I might answer it.

SALLY: I'll call the phone company tomorrow.

HARVE: Okay.

SALLY: I want to hear from you, Harve.

HARVE: Whatever for?

SALLY: Because I do!

HARVE: Then you'll have to come see me. If you can't make it yourself, then I guess you won't hear from me.

MEG: Harvey, you're not going to sit up here and do nothing, are you?

HARVE: I might.

SALLY: Grandpa.

HARVE: Don't worry, Sal. I'll take care of things, like I said I would.

SALLY: I'm worried about you being here by yourself.

HARVE: Afraid I'll die?

SALLY: No! I just . . .

HARVE: Do I look like I'm dyin'?

MEG: It's a matter of opinion.

HARVE: Well, I ain't. But if the situation changes I'll make sure you're th'first to know.

SALLY: My address and phone number are taped to the refrigerator.

HARVE: Good. That way if it gets lost they'll know who to send it to.

SALLY: Don't forget!

HARVE: I'm not likely to forget anything as important as all that.

SALLY: I better get going. You ready, Aunt Meg?

MEG: I suppose.

(SALLY *and* MEG *rise.*)

SALLY: Harve, please take care of yourself.

(*She hugs him. He allows it for a few seconds, extricates himself, rises.*)

HARVE: Be a good girl.

(*He touches her cheek, then gives* MEG *a peck.*)

SALLY: I love you.

HARVE: You ought to.

(SALLY *and* MEG *turn to go.*)

MEG: You behave yourself, Harvey. I'll be up to visit.

HARVE: That's welcome news.

SALLY: Call me if you need anything.

HARVE: Goodbye, Sally.

(SALLY *and* MEG *exit.* HARVE *watches them go.*)

SALLY: (*Offstage*) Bye!

(HARVE *waves. We hear car doors slam, the sound of an engine starting, the horn beeping. Then, all is quiet except for the katydids.* HARVE *surveys the scene. Wearily, he crosses to the rocking chair. He sits down.*)

HARVE: Golly. I am bushed. I may sit in this chair till I die.

Fadeout

Scene Two

(*It is late morning.* HARVE *sits in the rocking chair. There is some trash on the porch now, and a couple of fishing poles. There is a shovel lying in the yard.*)

(*Lights up.* HARVE *is tying a hook and some leaders to the end of a fishing line. We hear songbirds and crickets. A hail comes from offstage right.*)

HERB: Hello Harvey!

HARVE: Who's that there? Is that you, Herb?

(HERB *and* HUEY *enter.* HERB *wears a baseball cap, a striped shirt, a checked tie, blue jeans, and boots.* HUEY *wears overalls and a flannel shirt.*)

HARVE: Well, look at you. What you doin' up here, Herb?

HERB: Came up ta see ya, Harve.

HARVE: I figured that much.

HERB: Place looks good.

HARVE: Good a you ta say so, Herb. 'Course I hain't been here long.

HERB: It shows.

HARVE: Who ya got there with ya?

HERB: It's Huey. (*He turns to* HUEY.) This is Mr. Sloth, Huey. He's the man I told you about. (*Back to* HARVE) Huey's here to apply for the job, Harve.

HARVE: What job's that?

HERB: I heard you wanted someone to shovel the shit in your stables.

HARVE: I wanted someone ta shovel the shit *out* of the stables, but I din't say I was takin' applications.

HERB: Huey's kind of a special case, Harve. (*He pushes* HUEY *forward.*) Say hello to the man, Huey.

HUEY: 'Lo, Mr. Sloth.

HARVE: Hello, Huey.

HERB: Tell him why you're here.

HUEY: I, I'm here be . . . because yuh yuh yuh need some one to do some work. I work g-g-g-good. I ain't stupid.

HARVE: I can tell you're sharp, Huey.

HERB: Huey needs a place to stay.

HARVE: You ever work a shovel, Huey?

HUEY: I know what a shovel is.

HARVE: That's good, Huey, cause you're standin' right next to one. What say you take that shovel, and go down to the barn. You ever been 'round horses, Huey?

HUEY: I like horses.

HARVE: You better. You go down to the barn there, Huey, with that shovel. There's some stables there, need cleanin'. You take the shovel, and you shovel all the horseshit . . . you know what horseshit is, Huey?

HUEY: Sure I do. I stepped in it before.

HARVE: You'll be wadin' in it, shortly. Now, Huey, you shovel all that horseshit out the back door of the barn. There's a good pile of it out there already. You put it in that pile. Think you can do that?

HUEY: I think so.

HARVE: Why don't you go get started.

HUEY: Okay, Mr. Sloth. I'll do it, yuh-yuh-you'll see.

HARVE: I'm sure you will.

(HUEY *picks up the shovel and exits.*)

HARVE: You figure I'll take that boy in, don't ya, Herb.

HERB: I know you, Harvey Sloth. Before long Huey'll be doin' a lot more 'round here beyond shovelin' shit.

HARVE: He's kinda dim, ain't he?

HERB: You could say that. He don't register much, far as I can tell. You know, he's like a cow. He shits and he eats. He walks around and he gets his share of air, but that's about it.

HARVE: Then again, there's not much else, is there?

HERB: Huey's mother and father claimed to be cousins. Most everybody knows they were brother and sister.

HARVE: 'Sthat right?

HERB: Moved here some time ago, from way upstate, one of those remote areas where your sister might be the only girl around, if ya know what I mean. Some a them trappers live so far away they forget what a Christian is.

HARVE: Ain't nobody about to go up there and tell them, neither.

HERB: Huey's good natured, though.

HARVE: Better to be stupid and good then stupid and bad.

HERB: I guess.

HARVE: I can't pay him nothin'.

HERB: Long as he's got a place to sleep.

HARVE: I s'pose he'll need to eat, too.

HERB: I s'pose he will.

(HARVE *considers it.*)

HARVE: I guess I could keep him occupied.

HERB: You could use the company.

HARVE: Never was real big on people.

HERB: How long you been without Sarah now, Harve?

HARVE: Don't know. Been some time.

HERB: How old was she when she died?

HARVE: Just forty-eight.

HERB: Cancer got her?

HARVE: Eyuh.

HERB: Been quite a long time, Harve.

HARVE: Not long enough. (*Pause*) I never expected to live this long myself.

HERB: You ain't so old.

HARVE: Older than you.

HERB: You don't talk about her much.

HARVE: I'm still mad at her for dyin' on me.

HERB: You never change. Ya know I ain't seen ya in over two years.

HARVE: Two years ain't but a pinch of my life, Herb.

HERB: So? Where ya been all this time?

HARVE: Been up ta Warner. Man I know there lost his wife 'bout three years ago. I needed somewhere to go and he needed company, so I went up there and stayed with him.

HERB: If he needed company, why the hell'd he ask you?

HARVE: He's a logger.

HERB: You work for him?

HARVE: More'n I wanted to. Worked our damn fool asses off. Then we'd go back to his place and idle ourselves into a somber mood. Golly, we were a somber pair.

HERB: Loggin' tends to put a kink in your gumption, don't it?

HARVE: Somethin' terrible. I don't drink and he drinks too much. When he drank he talked about his dead wife. Drove me crazy. I wouldn't talk about *my* dead wife and that drove *him* crazy. He'd drink himself to sleep and I'd sit up listenin' to him snore and gnash his molars. Either one of us could put just about anybody in a deadly depression.

HERB: Sounds dreadful, Harvey. What made you leave Manadonock in the first place?

HARVE: I warn't gettin' along with my son-in-law.

HERB: What brings you back?

HARVE: He's dead now.

HERB: That right? I had no idea.

HARVE: That ain't the bad news. Bad news is he took my daughter with him.

HERB: Jilly's gone too?

HARVE: Happened almost a year ago. Plane crash.

HERB: That's a terrible shame, 'bout Jill, I mean. Never did much care for her husband.

HARVE: Him there in that casket's the first time I ever went to see him voluntarily.

HERB: This place yours now?

HARVE: Nope. Sally's.

HERB: I guess it's better that way.

HARVE: I guess it is. Horses are mine.

HERB: That right? What you gonna do with 'em?

HARVE: Gonna set 'em loose in that pasture there and watch 'em run.

HERB: That's some lovely pasture.

HARVE: Yes, it is.

HERB: What you been doin' since your arrival, Harvey?

HARVE: As little as possible.

HERB: Been fishin'?

HARVE: I've tried, but I haven't been able ta reach the lake from this porch yet.

HERB: Ya might try walkin' down there.

HARVE: That's more bother than I care to go through.

HERB: Hain't you been doin' nothin', Harve?

HARVE: Why yes, Herb, I have. I been sittin' right here on this porch.

HERB: Who's been feedin' the horses?

HARVE: I fed 'em before I sat down.

HERB: Who's been feeding you?

HARVE: I can feed myself. I ain't lame.

(*Long pause*)

HERB: You got anything ta drink, Harve?

HARVE: I ain't looked. But I imagine there's some kinda liquor in there. Help yourself.

HERB: (*Crosses to the screen door.*) Get you anything?

HARVE: You know I don't drink.

(HERB *enters house.*)

HERB: Somethin' else, maybe.

HARVE: No thanks.

HERB: (*Inside house*) By Jesus, Harvey, this place looks wonderful. You ain't been in here at all, have you?

HARVE: 'Course I been in there.

HERB: Wouldn't know it from looking at it.

HARVE: You mind your manners, Herb McGoon.

HERB: Golly! Look at all this liquor!

(*We hear a crash.*)

HARVE: Them bottle's got tops on 'em, Herb. No need ta break into 'em.

HERB: It was one a them fancy brandy glasses, Harve. You don't use them, do ya?

HARVE: There's one less I'll use, anyway.

(HERB *emerges from the house.*)

HERB: You gonna let Huey sleep in there?

HARVE: Huey can sleep in the stables. That way he's bound ta keep 'em cleaner.

HERB: You gonna have him sleep in there through the winter?

HARVE: There's a room in there, with a stove.

HERB: Still . . .

HARVE: I'll just ask Huey if he minds, then. How 'bout that?

HERB: I think you ought to.

HARVE: What you drinkin' there, Herb?

HERB: (*He holds up a bottle of Pinch.*) Some kind a scotch whiskey.

HARVE: I imagine it's wasted on you.

HERB: I ain't about ta waste any of it. (*He takes a sinfully long drink from the bottle.*) Whew! I'll bet you could de-bark a tree with this stuff.

HARVE: You're supposed ta sip a whiskey like that.

HERB: I gave up sippin' a long time ago. (*He takes another long pull.*) Ha! That's better. Tell me, Harve. You had any visitors?

HARVE: Well, there's you. And there's Huey.

HERB: Nobody else, huh?

HARVE: Man from the phone company.

HERB: Came to fix the phone, did he?

HARVE: Came to put one in.

HERB: This house doesn't have a phone?

HARVE: Does now. I told him to leave it just inside the door.

HERB: But that phone ain't plugged in.

HARVE: No, it isn't.

HERB: Want me to plug it in for you?

HARVE: I'd rather you didn't.

HERB: That's what I figured.

HARVE: Charley Ruggles was up t'other day.

HERB: Charley? From the mill?

HARVE: That's right.

HERB: Up here?

HARVE: Just t'other day.

HERB: Charley Ruggles?

HARVE: I just said so, din't I?

HERB: Doesn't that beat all. What'd he want?

HARVE: He was hopin' to buy my car.

HERB: Again? What'd you tell him?

HARVE: I told him he could have it the minute I died.

HERB: You keep tellin' him that he's going to kill you.

HARVE: Wish he would. Save me the bother.

HERB: Meg been up?

HARVE: Once. She's threatened to come back, though.

HERB: I saw her, last week it was. She says you're bound ta ruin this place.

HARVE: She says that cause she ain't got it herself.

HERB: I din't know she wanted it.

HARVE: Meg's never changed. She doesn't want nothin' till I got it. Been like that since the day she was born.

HERB: Her husband still alive?

HARVE: Eyuh. He refuses to listen to reason and lay down and die.

HERB: You don't care for him, do you?

HARVE: I don't care for many people.

HERB: Always been a good friend to me, Harve.

HARVE: Eyuh.

HERB: Lots of people care about you.

HARVE: P'haps I been too nice to 'em.

HERB: You ain't as sour as you let on.

HARVE: Ain't I though?

HERB: When's Sally due back?

HARVE: She din't say.

HERB: You miss her?

HARVE: I missed her all my life.

HERB: She'll be back soon enough.

HARVE: I doubt it.

(*Long pause*)

HARVE: What kind a job you got, Herb?

HERB: I'm the road commissioner.

HARVE: That right? What a you do for a job like that?

HERB: I drive around and pick up hitch-hikers.

HARVE: S'that all?

HERB: Ain't been a new roadbed laid down in this county in over seven years. State takes care of the rest.

HARVE: Well, I guess you're performin' some kind of public service.

HERB: I guess I am.

HARVE: You still on the rescue squad?

HERB: Yes I am. Got one more year 'fore they retire me.

HARVE: How is the old squad?

HERB: You wouldn't recognize it. Most everybody you knew's gone.

HARVE: 'Cept for Sarah, that's the only thing I miss.

HERB: You were one good stretch of fireman in your time, Harvey.

HARVE: Still am. You remember that old hunting camp we saved?

HERB: Ya mean that chimney fire?

HARVE: Eyuh.

HERB: We brought a pumper but no tanker. Din't have no water.

HARVE: That's cause the owner put the fireplug on the path to the privy.

HERB: So people'd know where the privy was . . .

HARVE: And some damn fool radioed to the firehouse there was a hydrant on the property.

HERB: Place din't even have runnin' water, did it?

HARVE: No, it didn't. That chimney fire was workin' it's way up ta the roof, and all we had was hand pumps.

HERB: Warn't the well bout half a mile away?

HARVE: Up hill.

HERB: So you got your chainsaw out a the truck and cut the damn fire out.

HARVE: There warn't any other way, by Jesus.

HERB: I guess not. You saved the camp.

HARVE: I'll never forget the look on the owner's face when he saw me take that chainsaw to his wall.

HERB: I thought he might cry.

HARVE: Eyuh. We killed some fires in our time, din't we?

HERB: It ain't the same anymore.

HARVE: How's that?

HERB: Some body's been settin' fires on us.

HARVE: That right?

HERB: Been goin' on for a couple years now. Can't tell who's doin' it, but whoever it is knows what they're doin'.

HARVE: What makes ya say that, Herb?

HERB: S'always the same. Old houses, every one of 'em. Mostly owned by summer people. Hasn't been one yet where anybody was around ta get hurt.

HARVE: That's a blessing.

HERB: Hain't been one we been able ta save, neither.

HARVE: They all burned to the ground, did they?

HERB: Every one. Pretty to look at, but there's not much you can do.

HARVE: Old houses tend to go pretty fast.

HERB: Eyuh. (*Pause*) You know, Harve, somethin' like this happened once before. A long time ago.

HARVE: I don't remember.

HERB: It warn't exactly the same. It wasn't houses that were gettin' burned, just brushfires.

HARVE: Nope. I don't recall anythin' like that.

HERB: It was right after our Sarah died. You took some time off from the squad.

HARVE: That explains it.

HERB: It warn't natural. Piles of brush. They'd go up and they'd go out pretty fast. Out by the cemetery.

HARVE: They stopped though, din't they.

HERB: Yes, they did.

Harve: Maybe these house fires'll stop too.

Herb: Maybe they will.

Harve: Well, you be careful, Herb.

(Huey *enters. He is covered with manure.*)

Herb: By God, Huey!

Harve: Golly! I think you might gag a maggot.

Huey: I done the job, Mr. Sloth.

Harve: I can tell you have, Huey. How'd you like it?

Huey: I din't mind. The horses like me.

Harve: You give 'em fresh hay?

Huey: Yes sir.

Harve: It's no wonder they like you.

Herb: Would you like to work for Mr. Sloth, Huey?

Huey: I g-guess so.

Harve: Think you'd mind sleepin' out in the stables, there, Huey?

Huey: With the horses?

Harve: That's right.

Huey: I'd like that.

Harve: Tell you what, Huey. You clean those stables every day, and you feed and brush those horses, you can sleep in them stables as long as you like. You help yourself to any food you find around here. That sound 'bout right?

Huey: I guess so.

Herb: I think it sounds fine, Huey.

Huey: Okay.

Harve: Good boy. Now, why don't you take yourself down to the lake there and scrub the shit off your body. Mr. McGoon here will find you some clean clothes for when you get done.

Huey: T-Thanks, Mr. Sloth.

Harve: You got nothin' ta thank me for, Huey. Now go wash up.

Huey: Yes sir. (Huey *exits.*)

Herb: What you gonna feed that boy, Harve?

Harve: I got plenty a oats in the barn.

Blackout

Scene Three

(*It is late at night.* Harve *sits in the rocking chair. There is moonlight, but all we can see are Harve's legs. We hear katydids.*)

(*Moonlight fades in.* Harve *is rocking gently. Though we cannot see his face, we hear him bite into an apple. He continues rocking and chewing. A few beats pass. Lightning flashes, followed by distant thunder.* Harve *leans forward into the moonlight, his face a mask, his eyes on fire. He throws the remaining apple into the yard. He leans back out of the light. He appears to be bustling in the chair. Another flash of lightning.* Harve *leans into the light once more. He is holding a battered old fishing creel, one hand inside. We hear the thunder, less distant, and* Harve *leans back out of the light. He is still for a few beats. He lights a match; it illuminates his face.* Harve *stares at the flame until it threatens to burn his finger. With a puff, he blows it out. We hear distant thunder. A few beats pass. He lights another match, staring at the flame.* Harve *blows out the match. Blackout.*)

Scene Four

(*It is late afternoon.* Harve *sits in the rocking chair. There is more trash now, and many apple cores litter the yard. Things look as if they're deteriorating.*)

(*Lights come up.* Harve *is looking off, intently. He has a fishing pole clasped in his hands. The fishing line leads offstage.*)

Harve: Huey! Huey! You sure that hook ain't layin' on the bottom?

(Huey *runs onstage.*)

Huey: I don't think so, Mr. Sloth. I measured it like you said.

Harve: That bobber driftin' at all?

Huey: Yes, sir. It's driftin' towards the creek like you said.

Harve: I ain't had a nibble all day. Might have ta change the worm.

Huey: I changed the worm, Mr. Sloth.

Harve: Don't squabble with me, Hue. Change it again.

Huey: Yes, sir, Mr. Sloth.

(Huey *runs offstage. After a beat, we see the line pull and the pole bend from* Huey's *efforts.*)

HARVE: I don't think I can stand to eat another apple.

HUEY: (*Off*) I got more corn flakes, Mr. Sloth!

HARVE: I don't want none a that shit, Hue. I want fresh trout. (*Pause*) You got that worm yet?

HUEY: Nope!

HARVE: Take your time, Hue.

HUEY: There it is!

HARVE: Come on then. Throw it back in the lake.

(HUEY *runs back onstage.*)

HARVE: You clean the stables yet?

HUEY: Yes sir.

HARVE: Them horses get fresh hay?

HUEY: Yes, Mr. Sloth.

HARVE: Good boy. You din't forget ta brush 'em, did ya?

HUEY: No sir.

HARVE: You understand, Huey, them horses are Morgans. Ya got ta take good care of Morgans. That's a kind of horse that requires constant vigilance.

HUEY: I brush 'em every day, Mr. Sloth.

HARVE: Been givin' 'em the feed too, Huey? Like I told ya?

HUEY: Yes sir.

HARVE: Good boy. (*Pause*) How's your bed, Huey? You warm enough at night in that barn?

HUEY: I wish I could have a fire in the stove, Mr. Sloth.

HARVE: Gettin' cold, huh?

HUEY: I can see my breath.

HARVE: Person's got to know 'bout fires, Huey.

HUEY: I can set a fire.

HARVE: No doubt. What I'm concerned about is whether you can keep it in th'stove.

HUEY: I used to feed the stove at the gas station, Mr. Sloth.

HARVE: That right? (*Pause*) Well, if they'll trust you around gasoline, I'll trust you around hay. I guess.

HUEY: I'll be real careful.

HARVE: I don't know why they got a stove in there anyway. Silliest thing I ever seen. How the horses can stand it is beyond me.

HUEY: Please, Mr. Sloth.

HARVE: I'll let you try it, Hue. Long as you don't burn the place down. But you keep the door closed. I don't want you to upset them horses.

HUEY: Nope.

HARVE: I'm awful hungry. (*Pause*) I heard a people fishin' with dynamite. Light one stick and drop it right in the middle of the pond, kaboom! Then ya wait for the fish ta float up, and pick 'em off the water like change off the floor. (*Pause*) I wonder if we got any dynamite?

HUEY: You want me ta do anything else, Mr. Sloth?

HARVE: Yes, I do, Huey. I want you to go to my car, there, and look in the glove box. See if you can find my pistol.

HUEY: I don't like guns.

HARVE: I don't care 'bout that, Huey. Do what you're told.

HUEY: Yes sir. (*He crosses to the car.*)

HARVE: Bring any shells ya find, too, while you're at it.

(HUEY *removes a pistol and a shellbox from the car. He carries them gingerly to* HARVE.)

HARVE: Hain't loaded, Hue.

HUEY: I don't care.

(HARVE *takes the gun and shells. He puts the shellbox down and stares down the barrel of the gun.*)

HARVE: Looks clean enough. Ain't been fired in over a year.

(HARVE *points the gun indiscriminantly.* HUEY *ducks.*)

HARVE: I told you it hain't loaded. (*He looks out toward the lake.*) If I could see 'em from here I'd shoot 'em. (*He stares dolefully at the limp fishing line. He picks up the shellbox and loads the gun.*)

HUEY: Do you have to do that, Mr. Sloth?

HARVE: You seen anybody messin' 'round my car?

HUEY: I ain't seen nobody at all, Mr. Sloth.

HARVE: I'd hate ta lose that car. Best automobile I ever had.

HUEY: Why would anybody bother your car?

HARVE: 'Cause it's a damned fine piece a machinery, Hue.

HUEY: But there ain't nobody around here.

HARVE: Just the same. I don't want nobody to even try.

HUEY: How you gonna stop them, Mr. Sloth?

HARVE: I figure no fool's gonna steal a car with four flat tires.

HUEY: The tires ain't flat.

HARVE: I ain't started yet. (*He takes aim and fires. The front left tire blows out.*)

HUEY: Oh no, Mr. Sloth! Don't do that!

HARVE: Why the hell not?

HUEY: How will you get ta town?

HARVE: (*He aims and fires again. The front right tire blows out.*) I ain't goin' ta town. (*He fires again. He misses.*) Damn. (*He fires once more. The rear right tire blows out.*) I can't see the other tire.

(HUEY *cowers by the steps.*)

HARVE: I guess that'll have ta do.

HUEY: Now you're stuck here.

HARVE: Eyuh.

HUEY: Am I stuck here too?

HARVE: Hell, no, Huey. You can go any time you want. (*Pause*) You don't want to go, do ya?

HUEY: No sir.

HARVE: Good boy.

(*The fishing pole is jerked and almost flies off the porch.*)

HARVE: Good golly! We caught somethin'! (*He grabs the pole and gives it a jerk. The line is taut and the pole bends. He starts reeling in.*) Get the net, Hue! Quick! I got a monster here!

(HUEY *looks under some trash on the porch and finds the net. He stands ready, facing the oncoming catch.*)

HUEY: Is it a big one?

HARVE: Sure feels like it. Here she comes!

(HUEY *stands in awe as* HARVE *reels a large fish across the stage. The fish flaps around.* HARVE *stops reeling.*)

Catch it, Hue!

(HUEY *runs into the fishing line, jerks the pole out of* HARVE'S *hands.* HUEY *chases after the fish, clapping, kicking, and tripping. He falls in the dust, grapples with the slippery fish. It gets away.*)

HARVE: Get it, Hue!

HUEY: It's too big!

(HUEY *continues chasing the fish.* HARVE *is delighted with the struggle.*)

HARVE: Don't you let it get back to the lake!

(HUEY *stops for a second to rest. He stands between the fish and downstage right, guarding the pass.*)

HUEY: I can't seem to get it, Mr. Sloth.

HARVE: That fish is gettin' the better of ya, Hue.

HUEY: *I* know! (*He brightens and runs off stage.*)

HARVE: Where ya goin'?

HUEY: I'm goin' ta get my shovel!

HARVE: (*Laughing*) Good boy! You bop him once good, I'll bet he'll stay still long enough ta get him in the net. Make it snappy, Hue! (*He keeps his eye on the fish. He picks up his gun and aims at it. He fires two quick shots. Both miss.*) Damn it all to hell! (*He throws the empty gun at the fish. He reaches for the fishing pole but can't quite reach it from the chair. He starts to get up out of the chair.*) Hurry up, Hue! It's tryin' ta inch its way back to the water!

(HUEY *runs on with the shovel. He stalks the fish and then swings the shovel at it. He misses.*)

HARVE: By Jesus, Huey. Will you hit that thing!

(HUEY *smacks the fish with the shovel.*)

HUEY: Got 'em!

HARVE: I'll say you did. (*Chuckles*) You're all right, Huey.

(HUEY *kicks the fish into the net. He holds the net up triumphantly, grinning from ear to ear.*)

HUEY: It's a swell fish, Mr. Sloth.

HARVE: Ain't he just elegant, though. I been waitin' all my life ta catch a fish that big.

HUEY: What are we gonna do with him?

HARVE: Why, Huey. We're gonna eat him of course.

HUEY: We are?

HARVE: Just as soon as we get him cleaned, we're gonna start a fire and fry this old trout right up. Take the hook out of 'em, Hue.

HUEY: He might bite me.

HARVE: Not if you hit him hard enough he won't. From what I seen, you probably bashed the teeth right out of him.

HUEY: I don't want to touch him.

HARVE: Bring him up here, then.

(HUEY *takes the fish up to* HARVE.)

HARVE: This thing musta swim up river from Connecticut. It smells a the ocean, Hue. (*He grabs the fish and removes the hook. He holds the fish in front of* HUEY's *face.*) You ever clean a fish, Hue?

HUEY: (*Looking horrified*) I couldn't clean no fish.

HARVE: Time you learned. I ain't gonna be around forever ta do this for ya.

HUEY: Can't we cook it the way it is?

HARVE: No, we can't. Now you find me some newspaper. There's some inside.

(HUEY *goes into the house.*)

HARVE: I bet this trout's older than I am.

(HUEY *emerges with newspaper.*)

HARVE: Lay it down on that table, Hue. And drag the table over here.

(HUEY *does so.*)

HARVE: You got a jack-knife?

HUEY: No, sir. They wouldn't let me keep one.

HARVE: have ta use mine then. Hate ta get it all dirty. (*He removes a buck knife from the case on his belt.*) You watch this careful, now. I ain't gonna show ya again. (*He scales the fish. He lays the fish down and slits the belly open.*)

(HUEY *turns away.*)

HARVE: It's only a fish, Hue.

(HARVE *cuts away the fins and the head.* HUEY *covers his mouth.*)

HARVE: You'll get used to it, once you've cleaned a few yourself.

(HARVE *scrapes out the guts.* HUEY *gags.*)

HARVE: Christ, Huey! Lucky for you this ain't a bear. (*He lays the fish open and deftly removes the spine and connecting bones.*) This trout's spine's as big around as my finger! Pay attention now, Hue. This is the difficult part. (*He holds up the bones intact. He throws them off the side of the porch.*) Take a good look, Hue. It's no worse than what you see down that supermarket.

(HUEY *turns away.*)

HARVE: Won't that make a lovely meal.

HUEY: I don't think I want any, Mr. Sloth.

HARVE: Nonsense. Ain't ya hungry, Hue?

HUEY: I don't think so.

HARVE: You'll change your mind once you smell it cookin'. Why don't you show me how you make a fire.

HUEY: Can I?

HARVE: I just said so, din't I? Pick up some a the wood layin' round the yard.

(HUEY *gathers some wood.*)

HARVE: Don't take nothin' that's punky. You need a hot fire to cook a trout like this.

(HUEY *prepares the fire.*)

HARVE: You do know somethin' bout fires, don't ya?

(HUEY *finishes. He looks up at* HARVE.)

HARVE: There's some kitchen matches up above the stove.

(HUEY *runs inside for the matches. He returns on the run.*)

HUEY: Can I?

HARVE: I ain't gonna come down there ta strike a match for ya.

(HUEY *strikes a match. He stares at the flame. He lets it burn down, blows it out before it burns.*)

HARVE: Don't be wastin' them matches, Hue. That's all we got.

(HUEY *strikes another match, lights the fire.*)

Think she'll catch, Hue?

HUEY: Yes, sir.

HARVE: Good boy. That fire'll do fine. Go in the house there and find us a fryin' pan. A big one.

HUEY: I don't want any fish, Mr. Sloth.

HARVE: That won't make the fish any smaller. Now you go inside and find the biggest skillet we got.

(HUEY *runs inside the house.*)

HARVE: Bring me some lard, too. Some lard and some flour.

(HUEY *appears behind the screen door.*)

HUEY: What?

HARVE: After you find that skillet, you look on the back of the stove you'll see a coffee can. It's got some grease in it. You bring the can to me.

HUEY: Yes, sir, Mr. Sloth.

(HUEY *disappears for a few beats, runs out of the house with a large flat skillet. He hands the skillet to* HARVE, *runs back inside.*)

HARVE: Don't forget the flour!

(HUEY *appears behind the screen door.*)

HUEY: What?

HARVE: Never mind, Hue. Bring the grease.

(HUEY *disappears then reappears with the coffee can. Hands it up to* HARVE.)

HARVE: Good boy. Now I need some flour, Hue.

HUEY: I don't know where the flour is, Mr. Sloth.

HARVE: Did you look in the cupboard?

HUEY: No sir.

HARVE: Why don't you try that.

(HUEY *enters the house. He appears behind the screen door.*)

HUEY: I found it.

HARVE: Bring it out, then.

(HUEY *disappears for few beats, runs out with a bag.*)

HARVE: You din't happen ta see some cornmeal in there, did ya?

HUEY: I don't remember. I can't read so good.

HARVE: That why you brought me a bag of sugar?

HUEY: Golly, I'm sorry, Mr. Sloth.

HARVE: Never mind. Take this back inside and bring me some cornmeal instead. You know what corn looks like, Hue?

HUEY: I sure do.

HARVE: There'll be a picture of some corn on the package. Think you can find it?

HUEY: I'll try.

HARVE: Good boy.

(HUEY *goes back inside. He runs out, proudly holding up a bag of cornmeal.*)

HUEY: This is it, isn't it, Mr. Sloth?

HARVE: That's it, Hue. You're nobody's fool. Now go put the skillet on the fire and scoop some a this grease into it while I dust this trout.

HUEY: (*He takes the pan and coffee can and crosses to the fire.*) Why you got to dust the trout, Mr. Sloth? Din't you already clean it? (*He puts the pan in the fire and scoops a handful of grease into it. He wipes his hand on his pants.*)

HARVE: I'm gonna roll the fish in the cornmeal, Hue. Makes the skin nice and crispy. (*He lays the fish on some clean newspaper. He pours cornmeal over it, dusts both sides. The fat in the frying pan begins to spit.*)

HUEY: I don't think I want any.

(HARVE *holds up the finished product.*)

HARVE: There we go. Practically unrecognizable, Hue.

(HUEY *grimaces*.)

HARVE: Come on up here and get it.

(HUEY *hesitates*.)

Come on, son. *I* ain't gonna cook this fish.

(HUEY *goes up and takes the fish from* HARVE. *He holds it as far away from himself as he can. He brings it to the fire. He holds it up over the pan*.)

HARVE: What are you waitin' for? Drop it in the pan.

HUEY: I'm afraid to.

HARVE: It's too late to save that fish now, Huey. Drop it in there, skin side up.

(HUEY *slowly lowers the fish toward the pan*.)

HARVE: Don't lower it, Hue. Drop it!

(HUEY *drops it into the pan, skin side up. The fish sizzles*. HUEY *turns away*.)

HARVE: Got a light stomach, don't ya? I never seen nobody turn so green at the sight of raw flesh. Don't it smell heavenly, though! (*He takes a deep breath*.) Din't your father ever take you fishin'?

HUEY: I can't remember.

HARVE: Sure you can. Warn't that long ago.

HUEY: I don't remember!

HARVE: I guess not. It's doubtful though, isn't it. Last I heard, your father was a drunk.

HUEY: He din't like me much.

HARVE: Don't worry about it. He warn't a sensible man anyway. (*Pause*) I like you.

HUEY: You do?

HARVE: Sure I do. You're a good boy, Huey.

HUEY: I ain't really.

HARVE: If I say so ya are. Why don't you turn that fish over now.

HUEY: I don't know how.

HARVE: All you got to do is flip it. No. Never mind. I mean to eat that fish. Tell you what. You bring the pan up to me and I'll show you how.

(Huey *takes the pan off the fire and carries it gingerly up to* Harve.)

Harve: Watch me now. This'd be a good thing for you to learn.

(Harve *takes the pan and flips the fish into the air. It lands on the opposite side.*)

Harve: How 'bout that!

Huey: That was great, Mr. Sloth! Do it again!

Harve: We got ta cook this trout, Hue. (*He hands the pan back to* Huey.) Go on, get it back on the fire.

Huey: I wanna see it again.

Harve: Don't squabble with me, Hue.

(Huey *takes the pan back to the fire.*)

Huey: Can I try it the next time, Mr. Sloth?

Harve: 'Course you can. Din't you never cook nothin' before?

Huey: No sir.

Harve: What you been eatin' all these years?

Huey: There was stuff down at the gas station.

Harve: What stuff?

Huey: There was little cakes. And sodas.

Harve: You mean the stuff in them machines?

Huey: Uh huh.

Harve: That's what you been eatin' all these years?

Huey: My mother used to cook for me. But she's dead.

Harve: I heard. Well, Huey, you're lucky to be here with me and eatin' regular again.

Huey: I don't think I want any of the fish, Mr. Sloth.

Harve: Sure you do. Bring it back up here. We don't want to overcook it.

(Huey *takes the pan to* Harve. Harve *uses his knife to fork up a piece.*)

Harve: My, that's good! You ought to try some.

Huey: I don't want to.

Harve: Ain't you never had trout before?

HUEY: Not like that.

HARVE: It tastes best this way. Now you try yourself some.

(HARVE *spears a piece and holds it out to* HUEY. HUEY *turns away.*)

HARVE: Come on now, Hue.

HUEY: No! I said I don't want none!

HARVE: Take it easy. No need ta get desperate. I ain't gonna make you eat it.

HUEY: It's like it's still alive.

HARVE: It's deader 'n a stump, Hue. Never mind. Leaves more for me anyway. *I* like trout.

HUEY: I'm awful tired, Mr. Sloth. Can I go back to the barn?

HARVE: You clean up this pan tomorrow?

HUEY: Yes, sir.

HARVE: I spose so, then.

HUEY: Mr. Sloth?

HARVE: What is it, Hue?

HUEY: Can I make a fire in the stove?

HARVE: You sure that stove's all right?

HUEY: Looks okay.

HARVE: That don't tell me nothin'. You check them stove pipes?

HUEY: There ain't no holes.

HARVE: Well, you be mighty careful. You start them stables on fire I ain't comin' ta save you. And I expect them horses to stay quiet.

HUEY: I promise.

HARVE: You better.

HUEY: Can I take the matches?

HARVE: You can take one of 'em.

HUEY: But what if it goes out?

HARVE: You'll just have to come back and get another.

(HUEY *takes one match out of the box and sets the box on the edge of the porch.*)

HUEY: Night, Mr. Sloth.

HARVE: Night, Huey. (*Pause*) Sleep well, son.

Fadeout

Act Two

Scene One

(*The clutter in the yard and on the porch has grown alarmingly.* HARVEY *looks dirty, unkempt. It is midday.*)

(HARVE *sits alone on the porch in the rocking chair. He starts to doze, then looks up with a start.* SALLY *enters. She surveys the scene disapprovingly.*)

SALLY: My god, Harve. What have you done?

HARVE: Hello, Sally.

SALLY: I don't believe this.

HARVE: How have you been?

SALLY: Is there . . . someplace I can sit?

HARVE: You know how ta use a chair?

SALLY: If only I could find one.

HARVE: There's a couple up here if you like.

(SALLY *picks her way up onto the porch. She winces at* HARVEY'S *odor. She sits down somewhat reluctantly.*)

HARVE: Smell bother you?

SALLY: It's a bit of a shock.

HARVE: Keeps the mosquitos away. You'll get used to it.

SALLY: I'm not sure I want to. (*Pause*) You're going to ignore this, aren't you?

HARVE: If I'd a known you were comin', I'd have straightened things up.

SALLY: With what? A bulldozer?

HARVE: Now, Sally. It ain't that bad.

SALLY: It's awful. Aren't you even curious as to why I'm here?

HARVE: If I was curious, I'd a come to see you.

SALLY: I don't believe you. How could you allow this to happen?

HARVE: It takes some effort.

SALLY: You appear to be equal to the task.

HARVE: It's what I do best. Are you impressed?

SALLY: I'm overwhelmed.

(*They sit quietly for a few beats.*)

SALLY: I'm coming here to live.

HARVE: You don't mean it.

SALLY: Yes, I do.

HARVE: Why?

SALLY: Because it's all I got left.

HARVE: All you got left? I thought you had a mess a money.

SALLY: I did.

HARVE: You don't anymore.

SALLY: I invested it.

HARVE: You mean you spent it.

SALLY: There wasn't much to begin with. Daddy and Mum were living well above their means.

HARVE: I coulda told you that.

SALLY: This hasn't been easy for me, Harve.

HARVE: What about your job?

SALLY: I'm changing careers.

HARVE: Haven't you grown up yet?

SALLY: You told me to do what I want.

HARVE: I did, din't I. (*Pause*) Where'm I sposed to live?

SALLY: You can stay here with us.

HARVE: Us?

SALLY: I've got a partner, Harve. A woman. I had to sell half my share to this property.

HARVE: You din't.

SALLY: I did.

HARVE: Just what are you partners in?

SALLY: We have investments.

HARVE: Investments in what?

SALLY: Developments.

HARVE: You do tippy-toe around the point, don't ya.

SALLY: We mostly invest in real estate, and a few small companies.

HARVE: What kind a real estate.

SALLY: We have condominiums in Arizona.

HARVE: Condominiums, huh? Are they tasteful?

SALLY: Very.

HARVE: Thank God for that. So you don't own this property no more?

SALLY: My company owns it.

HARVE: I'm afraid to ask what your company plans to do with it.

SALLY: You don't want to know.

HARVE: Just how big is this company of yours?

SALLY: We employ about thirty-five people.

HARVE: Is this company comin' here with you, by any chance?

SALLY: 'Fraid so.

HARVE: Where are they gonna sleep?

SALLY: Oh, they won't be living here. Only working.

HARVE: What they gonna do? Cut the hay?

SALLY: They won't be doing much of anything until we get the offices built.

HARVE: You're gonna build offices here?

SALLY: We were hoping to convert the barn.

HARVE: Then where are the horses going to sleep?

SALLY: I'm afraid we may have to sell the horses, Grandpa.

HARVE: Sell the horses? You can't sell them horses. Them horses are mine.

SALLY: You can have the money.

HARVE: I don't want the money! I want the horses!

SALLY: What are you going to do with them?

HARVE: Whatever I want!

SALLY: I'm sorry, Harve.

HARVE: You ought to be. You're pullin' the rug right out from under me.

SALLY: It wasn't easy for me to make this choice, Harvey. But this property is mine to do with as I please. I need to settle down.

HARVE: 'Course you're right, Sal. Ain't mine ta get upset about.

SALLY: We mean to keep the place pretty much as it is.

HARVE: That'll be tough without the horses.

SALLY: Please, Harve. I'll need your support.

HARVE: I'd prefer it if you din't come at all.

SALLY: You don't mean that.

HARVE: No. No, I don't.

SALLY: I've been through a lot, Harve.

HARVE: You ain't half done yet.

SALLY: I thought you'd be glad to see me.

HARVE: I'm glad to see you, Sally. Don't get me wrong. But I'm an old man. I live in an old world. Ain't much a that world left for me.

SALLY: You'd still be in the woods.

HARVE: I guess.

SALLY: Maybe we can keep the horses somehow.

HARVE: Don't do me any favors.

SALLY: Damn it, Harve! I'm sorry! I really am. But it's already in motion. It's something I needed to do. We'll be moving here in a couple of weeks.

HARVE: That means I got a couple a weeks left to live.

SALLY: I wish you wouldn't talk that way. I don't have any more time to argue. I've got to catch a plane.

HARVE: I'd hate to make you late.

SALLY: I'll send somebody up here to help you get this place in order.

HARVE: I'll clear out this mess.

SALLY: By yourself?

HARVE: I made it myself, din't I?

SALLY: I don't know if I can do that.

HARVE: It's the only thing I'm gonna ask of you.

SALLY: Okay, Harve. But you better do it right away. I want it the way it was.

HARVE: I'll take care of it, don't you worry.

SALLY: I have a bad feeling about this.

HARVE: Your mother always trusted me.

SALLY: No she didn't.

HARVE: Your grandmother did.

SALLY: Okay, Grandpa. But I'm depending on you. (*She gets up to leave.*) I'll see you two weeks from now.

HARVE: You take care, Sally. (*Pause*) You know I love you, no matter what.

SALLY: Sure, Grandpa.

HARVE: You love me too, don't ya?

SALLY: I love you dearly.

HARVE: Good girl.

SALLY: Goodbye, Grandpa. (*She exits.*)

HARVE: Bye, Sal.

SALLY: (*Offstage*) Don't fuck up, Harvey!

Blackout

Scene Two

(*It is night.* HARVEY *is in the rocking chair, asleep. The interior lights of the house are on, and the porch light.*)

(*We see a flash of headlights across the porch, and the sound of a car. The headlights cut, the car stops. We hear the slam of a car door. Herb enters, unsteady in the dark.*)

HERB: Harve? (*He crosses cautiously to the porch. He peers around the yard, and into the distance.*) Harvey?

HARVE: What? (*He wakes with a jump.*) Might a known it was you.

HERB: I thought I'd check in with you.

HARVE: What time is it?

HERB: Nearly midnight.

HARVE: You mighta waited till mornin'.

HERB: I had the urge and here I am.

HARVE: I'm overjoyed ta see you, Herb.

HERB: What you doin' out on the porch?

HARVE: I'm nappin'. S'that all right with you?

HERB: I woulda thought there'd be beds in this house.

HARVE: Too hot ta sleep inside.

HERB: Too cold ta sleep outside.

HARVE: I ain't sleepin' anymore, am I?

HERB: Not if I can help it. Where's Huey?

HARVE: You wanna wake him up too?

HERB: Naw. I came ta see you. (*Pause*) How's he doin'?

HARVE: Well, he gets plenty of rest.

(HERB *starts up the steps but stops short.*)

HERB: Whew!

HARVE: Somethin' botherin' you?

HERB: When's the last time you bathed yourself, Harvey?

HARVE: I guess it musta been back in the spring. Fell through some thin ice.

HERB: Don't the smell bother you?

HARVE: After sixty-eight years I guess I'm used to it.

HERB: Well, it's a mighty assault on my senses.

HARVE: You gonna let a little odor come between two friends?

HERB: Don't know if I can wade through it, Harve.

HARVE: Ain't you stretchin this thing a bit far?

HERB: I'd hold my nose shut but I couldn't bear to have that air pass over my tongue.

HARVE: Whyn't you go inside and get yourself a bottle. Might make ya more neighborly.

HERB: Don't mind if I do.

HARVE: Try not to shatter anything this time, Herb.

(HERB *steps into the house.*)

HERB: I can tell you been in here, now. Place is startin' ta gather a clutter.

HARVE: Place ain't so bad.

HERB: (*He appears in the open doorway.*) No. It ain't. (*He comes out and sits on one of the chairs.*) So what you been up to, Harve? (*He opens a bottle of rye and takes a pull.*)

HARVE: Caught me a big ole trout just t'other day.

HERB: You don't mean it. Good eatin'?

HARVE: 'Bout the best trout I ever ate.

HERB: What'd you use?

HARVE: Worm on a bobber. (*Pause*) And a pistol.

HERB: A pistol?

HARVE: Caught him sittin' right here in this rocking chair.

HERB: The trout?

HARVE: No, ya dang fool. Me. I was sittin' in the chair when I caught him.

HERB: You mean to tell me you caught a trout from this porch?

HARVE: I just said so, din't I?

HERB: Harvey, you are the laziest man I ever known.

HARVE: It's the only thing I work at.

HERB: How'd you get the worm in the water?

HARVE: I cast it there myself.

HERB: You don't mean it.

HARVE: I'd swear on a stack of Bibles.

HERB: Din't Huey have a hand in all this?

HARVE: He cooked the fish.

HERB: That I believe. You give him some?

HARVE: I gave him more than he could eat. And that's the truth.

HERB: Awful big of ya, Harve.

HARVE: I'm lettin' him use the stove in the stables at night, too.

HERB: Is there still a stove in there?

HARVE: Eyuh. (*Pause*) Do you know why there's a stove in there?

HERB: Well, I guess I do.

HARVE: Mind tellin' me?

HERB: You don't know?

HARVE: No. I don't.

HERB: Well, before that was a stable, it was a sugar house.

HARVE: You don't mean it.

HERB: I'm surprised you din't know that.

HARVE: Doesn't look a'tall like a sugar house.

HERB: They built it up, of course.

HARVE: That right? (*Pause*) Thank you, Herb. You just cleared up one of the biggest mysteries of my life.

HERB: You know, Harve, looks to me as if your tires need air.

HARVE: I hadn't noticed.

HERB: Huey all right?

HARVE: Huey's fine, Herb.

HERB: Anything wrong with you, Harvey? You don't look as well as you might.

HARVE: I'm doin' fine.

HERB: You been gettin' enough to eat?

HARVE: Much as I want.

HERB: Got me a good garden this year, case ya need somethin'.

HARVE: What's behind all this concern for my welfare, Herb.

HERB: Just checkin' Harve. (*Pause*) You aren't gonna do nothin' stupid, are ya?

HARVE: I'm not gonna do nothin' at all.

HERB: You don't mind me comin' up here ta check onya, Harve?

HARVE: I don't mind you comin' up here to pay me a visit, Herb.

HERB: Eyuh. (*Pause*) You sure Huey's asleep?

HARVE: Saw his light go out couple hours ago. Why?

HERB: Nothin'. (*Pause*) You hear 'bout Percy Warner?

HARVE: No, Herb. I ain't heard about anything.

HERB: Percy mailed his pet rattlesnake to Whit Copperthwaite.

HARVE: He mailed a snake? Was't alive?

HERB: Oh, it was ever so alive.

HARVE: What brought that on?

HERB: Seems Whit sold Percy a rotten tractor. Thing up and seized second time out to pasture. Percy says it's still sittin' there. His cows think it's one of their own. He would like Mr. Copperthwaite to come remove it from his pasture.

HARVE: I imagine he'd like to get his money back.

HERB: Eyuh. But Whit says there warn't nothin' wrong with the tractor when he sold it and he already spent the money on a manure spreader. Percy says he'd take the manure spreader and a tow, but Whit says he ain't about to do that.

HARVE: I take it this dispute's been going on for some time.

HERB: Eyuh. Percy lost his patience and he took his pet rattlesnake and stuck it in Whit's mailbox.

HARVE: Did Whit find it all right?

HERB: I guess he did. Mr. Bonner, he's the mail carrier, he delivered the mail and says he never saw any snake. But Whit opened up his mailbox and the creature began to rattle. Almost got him.

HARVE: Is the snake still there?

HERB: Whit coaxed it out with a pitchfork.

HARVE: That's what I'd do.

HERB: Now Percy's twice as mad at him 'cause he killed the snake.

HARVE: Percy never did know how to behave.

HERB: He's a compulsive man.

(*Pause*)

HARVE: Those two fellas still holdin' that lawyer hostage?

HERB: It warn't a lawyer. It was one a them stockbrokers from New York.

HARVE: They let him go?

HERB: They're in the Albany jailhouse right now.

HARVE: Shoulda expected that.

HERB: Eyuh.

HARVE: What'd they have against him anyway?

HERB: It was Mel Collins' boys. The two of 'em put together ain't much better than half a wheel. Seems they met this fella downstate, and he told them about the stock market. The boys couldn't believe their ears. They could give this man a hundred dollars and he could turn it into a thousand. Sounded too good to be true. Turns out it was. They gave him five-hundred dollars and two weeks later he told them all they had left was fifty.

HARVE: You don't mean it.

HERB: Said if they waited a while it might make it up to a hundred. If they waited a while longer, they might get most of their money back. And if they waited till the turn of the century, they might make a profit.

HARVE: I'll bet they were pleased.

HERB: They took the man over t'the Mountain View Motel, rented a room, and tied him to the john. They fed him a couple a days and put the color TV in the doorway. Once they had him settled, they told him he could sit there until the stock went up, and how did *he* like waiting for their money to grow. Nobody found out about it for almost a month.

HARVE: Fella must a had some hellacious ring around his rear end.

HERB: I guess he did. Eventually the manager got suspicious.

HARVE: Eventually.

HERB: And he and the police convinced the boys to let the man go.

HARVE: I guess we're lucky to be livin' over here in Manadonock. Ain't such desperate characters around.

HERB: Don't know about that. We had two more fires last week.

HARVE: You don't mean it. Anybody hurt?

HERB: Not yet.

HARVE: Any idea who's doin' the damage?

HERB: Maybe. (*Pause*) We had a man from the FBI come 'round t'other day.

HARVE: What'n hell did he want?

HERB: 'Pears that arson is a federal crime. That makes it his business.

HARVE: I wasn't aware of that.

HERB: No sir, I wouldn't want to be in the arsonist's shoes.

HARVE: I suppose they'll catch him sooner or later.

HERB: They're bound to. I'll bet they're closin in on 'em right now.

HARVE: You think so, do ya?

HERB: They're gonna be watchin' the houses. Won't be so easy for him.

HARVE: Maybe he'll just stop doin' it.

HERB: I doubt it.

HARVE: Eyuh. I doubt it too.

(*Long pause*.)

HERB: Harve, there's somethin' I came over to tell you.

HARVE: You finally remember what it was?

HERB: Yes, I did.

HARVE: Good.

HERB: It's about Huey.

HARVE: What about Huey.

HERB: You sure he sleeps in them stables every night?

HARVE: What are ya gettin' at, Herb?

HERB: Huey was seen at the last fire we had. He was runnin' away from it.

HARVE: Makes good sense.

HERB: S'that all you got to say about it?

HARVE: Huey ain't startin' your fires.

HERB: Somebody saw him, Harve.

HARVE: What makes them think it was Huey?

HERB: You know that jacket of his, from the gas station, one that's got the name of the oil company on the back?

HARVE: It's hangin' on a peg inside the house there.

HERB: Whoever was running away from that fire was wearin' that jacket. That's Huey's jacket.

HARVE: Spose somebody else's got one like it.

HERB: You don't know for sure what Huey might do.

HARVE: I know he ain't startin' them fires.

HERB: How do you know?

HARVE: I just know, that's all. You'll have to take my word for it.

HERB: You know who *is* startin' the fires?

HARVE: Now, how would I know that?

HERB: Well, since your such an expert on this case . . .

HARVE: I'm no expert on the case! But I'll tell you for sure it ain't Huey.

HARVE: You holdin' out on me, Harve?

HARVE: There ain't nothin more to say about it.

(*Both men sit quietly.* HARVEY *closes his eyes.* HERB *looks over at him, he starts to speak, but then thinks better of it. He sits back, sighs, looks out toward the stables. A few beats pass.* HARVEY *begins to snore softly.* HERB *glances over at him, stands up, descends the stairs, stops, turns back to look at* HARVEY, *then exits. We hear a car door slam, and the engine start. The headlights flash across the porch and then the sound is gone.* HARVE *opens his eyes, leans forward with a pained look, sits back and shudders. Fadeout.*)

Scene Three

(*The clutter of the yard and porch continues to grow. The screen door is gone, leaving a gaping dark doorway.* HARVE *is dirty, unshaven, and sallow. There are piles of horseshit in the yard. It is afternoon.*)

(HARVEY *sits in the rocking chair, his eyes open, staring straight ahead. He could be dead.* HUEY *enters.*)

HUEY: (*Waving a pitchfork.*) I did it, Mr. Sloth!

(HARVE *just stares ahead.*)

HUEY: Mr. Sloth? (*He crosses and waves the pitchfork in* HARVE'S *face.*) Hey!

HARVE: No need ta yell, Hue. I ain't deaf.

HUEY: I did it, Mr. Sloth. Just like you said.

HARVE: What's that, Hue?

HUEY: The pitchfork. I took the handle off the hoe and put it in here. See?

HARVE: That's a fine job ya done there, Hue.

HUEY: It works, too. I already tried it once.

HARVE: I had a feelin' it would.

HUEY: Now I can take some a that hay down from the loft.

HARVE: Is there a lot of hay up there, Huey?

HUEY: There's lots of it still.

HARVE: What else you do today?

HUEY: Everything I was supposed to. And I changed the dressing on the mare.

HARVE: You already soak it?

HUEY: I did that this morning. You said I was sposed to do that first thing in the morning.

HARVE: That's right. I did. Have I seen that dressing, Hue?

HUEY: You said it looked fine.

HARVE: When's the last time I seen the mare?

HUEY: I brought her up here yesterday. Don't you remember?

HARVE: I'm just checkin' on ya, Hue.

HUEY: Oh.

HARVE: Don't want ya to forget nothin'.

HUEY: I won't.

HARVE: Good boy.

HUEY: Her leg seem to be better. She don't limp as much.

HARVE: It's only a touch of arthritis, Huey. Keep usin' that poultice like I said and she'll be at a gallop in a week or two.

HUEY: Are you a doctor, Mr. Sloth?

HARVE: No, Hue. I'm a trainer. You know what a trainer is?

HUEY: Maybe not.

HARVE: A trainer is somebody who keeps the horse just as healthy as he can. If he don't do his job right, and the horse gets sick, then you call the doctor.

HUEY: You did that?

HARVE: I done it all my life.

HUEY: How come you don't do it no more?

HARVE: I *am* doin' it. Right here on this farm. And you're doin' it too.

HUEY: I am?

HARVE: That's right, Hue.

HUEY: You mean I'm a trainer?

HARVE: Not yet you aren't. But you could be if you kept up at it. And don't forget nothin'.

HUEY: I could be a trainer?

HARVE: I just said so, din't I?

HUEY: Would they pay me?

HARVE: They might.

HUEY: I think I'd like that. (*Pause*) Where would I do it?

HARVE: Anywhere there's horses, Huey.

HUEY: Could I leave the state?

HARVE: Whatever would you want to do that for?

HUEY: 'Cause my mother said I should.

HARVE: Your mother might not a been quite lucid, Hue. There's nothin' better anywhere else.

HUEY: How do you know?

HARVE: 'Cause I been there.

HUEY: Where?

HARVE: Elsewhere.

HUEY: You been out a the state?

HARVE: That's right. I been to them Rocky Mountains out west.

HUEY: Wow! When did you go there?

HARVE: 'Fore I got married. Went to try my hand at horses in the wild.

HUEY: Wild horses! Wow! (*Pause*) Did you see any?

HARVE: Only 'bout several thousand.

HUEY: Golly! Did you really?

HARVE: That's right.

HUEY: Were you a cowboy?

HARVE: Please, Hue. Give me more credit'n that. I din't round 'em up or nothin'. I trained 'em.

HUEY: What for?

HARVE: Some fool got the notion they'd make good trotters.

HUEY: Did they?

HARVE: Not on your life. They ain't got the pace for it. Beautiful animals, though. 'Specially when a whole herd races across one a them parks they got out there.

HUEY: Parks?

HARVE: What they call a park out in the Rocky Mountains we'd call a state. Just as big as the Northeast Kingdom they are. And nothin' but grass and brush. Those wild horses'd run across one a them parks for the fun of it. Be like takin' a spin down to Boston. On a gallop. Beat up some cloud a dust, they did.

HUEY: Wow. Why din't you stay there?

HARVE: 'Cause it warn't home.

HUEY: You din't like it?

HARVE: Oh, it was terribly spectacular. I'll give it that. But folks out there ain't got a proper perspective on things.

HUEY: What's that?

HARVE: Everything's so big out there. And they got so much of everything. So much land. So many trees. Such big mountains and valleys. So many horses and so much cattle. They even got a lot more sky than we do. The only thing they don't got a lot of is people. And since there's so little people and so much a everything else, folks lose sight of the details, the small things.

HUEY: Is that what we got here?

HARVE: That's right. Out there you can go a hundred miles and see two different kinds a plants. You know they only got four trees to grow?

HUEY: Only four trees in all them mountains?

HARVE: They got a million trees out in them mountains, Hue. But only four kinds. They got their aspens, their cottonwoods, their firs, and their spruce. That's it. Now, don't that seem kinda repetitive to you?

HUEY: I don't know.

HARVE: Think about it, Hue. Now here you got your ash, your dogwood, your locust, your oak, your sycamore, your cherry, your walnut, your elm, your white birch, your silver birch, your red maple, your sugar maple, your birdseye maple, your curlyback maple . . . come ta think of it, we got more kinds a maple trees then they got trees. And that's just a few of the hardwoods, what you call your deciduous trees. Barely scratched the surface. I ain't even started on the conifers yet.

HUEY: I guess you're right.

HARVE: I know I'm right. They haven't come up with a tree that won't grow in New England. Not if it was worth a damn.

HUEY: Sounds simpler out there.

HARVE: 'Course it's simple. That's what's missin'. Do you know that folks out there burn pine in their stoves?

HUEY: No!

HARVE: I wouldn't burn pine in my stove if it was the last tree on the lot. 'Course they can't help it.

HUEY: Would you teach me about trees, Mr. Sloth?

HARVE: I think you better stick to horses, Hue.

HUEY: Please?

HARVE: Well, I'll do what I can from here.

HUEY: I'll try real hard to remember.

HARVE: I'm sure you will.

HUEY: What kind of tree is that, Mr. Sloth?

HARVE: That's an apple tree, Hue. Know how you can tell it's an apple tree?

HUEY: How?

HARVE: 'Sgot apples on it.

HUEY: Golly, you're right. What about that tree over there?

HARVE: You learned one tree today already, Hue. I'll teach you another tomorrow.

HUEY: Okay. (*Pause*) We gonna do any more fishin' Mr. Sloth?

HARVE: Not today.

HUEY: We haven't done any in a long time.

HARVE: Thought you din't like trout.

HUEY: You do.

HARVE: I can do without it.

HUEY: You don't eat enough, Mr. Sloth.

HARVE: Says who?

HUEY: My mother.

HARVE: Ain't your mother dead?

HUEY: Yeah.

HARVE: Shows ya how much she knows.

HUEY: She still tells me things.

HARVE: That right?

HUEY: Don't your mother still tell you things?

HARVE: No. (*Pause*) Sarah does.

HUEY: Who's Sarah?

HARVE: Sarah was my wife.

HUEY: That's right. You loved her a lot.

HARVE: I loved her very much.

HUEY: She's dead.

HARVE: Yes, she is.

HUEY: I guess we're both crazy.

HARVE: I guess we are. (*Pause*) You're all right, Huey.

Fadeout

Scene Four

(*The set is dark, bathed in pale light. The interior lights of the house are lit. The rocking chair is empty.*)

(HUEY *enters quickly, dressed in his long johns.*)

HUEY: Mr. Sloth! (*He runs up on the porch, surprised not to find* HARVEY *in the chair.*) Mr. Sloth? (*He heads for the door.*) I heard an awful noise. Woke me right up. Are you all right, Mr. Sloth? (*He enters the house. We hear his voice from within.*) Mr. Sloth? (*His voice trails off as he searches the house.*) Mr. Sloth? You awake? Mr. Sloth? (*He comes out of the house. He looks around desperately. He cups his hands around his mouth and yells.*) Harvey Sloth! (*He tilts his ear to the wind.*) Hello! (*He is getting scared now. He's not sure what to do. He notices something dropped on the porch steps. He picks it up. It is his jacket, and as he turns it over we see the oil company logo emblazoned on the back.* HUEY *fingers the jacket, looking off. Fadeout.*)

Act Three

Scene One

(*The set continues to deteriorate. In addition, there are several saddles lying in the yard, and other tack strewn on the porch. It is early evening.*)

(HARVE *sits in the rocking chair, sleeping, a newspaper over his face. He could be another pile of trash.* MEG *enters. She stops, surveys the scene, crosses to the steps, peers up at* HARVE.)

MEG: Is that you under there?

(HARVE *remains silent.*)

MEG: Harvey.

(*No answer.*)

MEG: You answer me. I know you're not dead. You smell like it, but I know you're not.

(*No answer.*)

MEG: Stop being a baby! Talk to me!

Harvey: That you, Meg?

Meg: Of course it's me.

Harve: (*He pulls the newspaper off his face.*) Meg. What a ticklish surprise.

Meg: Don't try and butter me up, Harvey. What the hell are you doing up here?

Harve: As little as possible.

Meg: I can see that. Sally called me. She's very upset, you know.

Harve: Is she?

Meg: You know she is.

Harve: She shoul'nt a come unannounced.

Meg: She was as upset about your condition as the condition of this farm. She said you looked terrible. She was right.

Harve: I'm gettin' awful tired a people comin' up here and jumpin' all over me. Whyn't you leave me alone?

Meg: We're concerned about you.

Harve: So? That mean you get ta take advantage of my good nature?

Meg: Good nature! You? You're nothin' but a sour old puss.

Harve: Look who's talkin'.

Meg: Harvey, what are you up to?

Harve: I ain't up to nothin'.

Meg: Yes, you are. I can tell.

Harve: You never could tell much.

Meg: You haven't done a thing around here.

Harve: Yes I have. Just t'other day I sat here and watched a leaf turn brown.

Meg: You smell like a dead skunk. Don't the flies bother you?

Harve: They know if they get too close I'll eat 'em.

Meg: Do you ever get out of that chair?

Harve: Last time it rained this porch developed a leak. Water dripped right on my head. It got pretty bothersome after a while. I almost got up then.

Meg: I don't believe a word you say, Harvey.

Harve: Suit yourself.

Meg: Have you made the effort to feed yourself?

Harve: Every once in a while, when the conditions are right, a car'll go by and run over a raccoon. If we're real lucky, just the head will be crushed and the rest of the meat'll be fine. We'll pick it off the road while it's still warm, and we'll tear into it like nothin' you ever saw. (*He looks up into the branches overhead.*) Most of the time I wait for one a them apples to fall in my lap.

Meg: Is that why you're not on the front porch? I figured I'd find you there, watchin' the cars go by.

Harve: I tried that. I sat there and watched them cars go by all day. I was exhausted. Got a stiff neck besides.

Meg: Oh, come on, Harvey.

Harve: I'd rather watch the horses anyway.

Meg: (*She turns to look.*) They look healthy enough.

Harve: Them horses are in perfect health. (*Pause*) They're mine now. Sally tell you that?

Meg: Sally told me you made a stink about sellin' em.

Harve: She only just gave 'em to me! Now she want to take 'em away? I waited all my life to have my own horses.

Meg: What would you do with them?

Harve: Why do I have to do somethin' with 'em? Gives me more pleasure than I've had in years just to know they're there.

Meg: Costs a lot of money to keep horses, Harve. You don't have any money.

Harve: Good Christ! Why do people die and leave ya things ya can't keep?

Meg: I'm sorry, Harvey.

Harve: It ain't fair, Meg.

Meg: Is it fair for you to let this place go to ruin? What the hell is going through your head? Someone should force you to bathe. I've never seen you this bad, Harvey. And your daughter's beautiful home is unrecognizable. I'm afraid to look inside.

Harve: It ain't so bad.

MEG: Says who? Says you, Harvey Sloth?

HARVE: Don't nag me, Meg. I'll do somethin' about this mess.

MEG: Sally will be here in less than a week. You promised to do it.

HARVE: That's more'n enough time.

MEG: I have to pick her up at the airport. She said she couldn't get a hold of you.

HARVE: Wouldn't matter if she could. You can see I got a flat tire.

MEG: You might fix it.

HARVE: Haven't got a spare.

MEG: Well, I don't mind doing it.

HARVE: You got a spare?

MEG: I'm not going to fix your tire! I'm just going to fetch Sally from the airport.

HARVE: Too bad. Thought I had me a deal goin' there.

MEG: You think you're real cute, don't you, Harvey. You sit there bein' nasty and foolish while everything around you goes to hell in a handbasket. I'm not going to let you get away with it. You know what I think?

HARVE: Do tell.

MEG: I think you're giving up. That's it, isn't it.

HARVE: Givin' up what?

MEG: Everything! You're gonna sit there and quit, aren't you?

HARVE: I'm tryin' ta come up with a solution.

MEG: Solution to what?

HARVE: Questions I got.

MEG: Like what? How to speed up the process?

HARVE: It does take some time.

MEG: See! You just said so, yourself!

HARVE: I ain't about to die.

MEG: It can't be that bad, Harve. You still got Sally.

HARVE: I never said it was bad. Maybe I'm tired is all.

MEG: Or maybe you're getting senile.

HARVE: Maybe I am.

MEG: Harve.

HARVE: Mind your own business, Meg!

MEG: I only mean to help!

HARVE: I know you're a decent woman.

MEG: What's wrong, Harvey?

HARVE: I don't know. There's been so much death, Meg. Too much. I hain't got time to mourn it all.

MEG: Then don't.

HARVE: How'm I sposed to stop? If people'd stop dyin' I'd stop mournin'.

MEG: People aren't going to stop dying, so you'd be better off to stop mourning.

HARVE: Herb always says a person oughta give death its due time.

MEG: It's terrible about Herb. It must have hit you hard.

HARVE: What about Herb?

MEG: Oh no. You didn't hear, Harvey?

HARVE: Hear what?

MEG: About Herb?

HARVE: I ain't heard nothin' 'bout Herb. Haven't seen him for days.

MEG: Oh dear.

HARVE: What are you talkin' about, Meg?

MEG: There was a fire two nights ago. Herb was the first to get there.

HARVE: You don't mean . . .

MEG: People who owned the place were out. But they left their dog in the house. You can imagine how it yelped. I guess Herb tried to save it.

HARVE: The dog?

MEG: He nearly got trapped inside. The roof fell in.

HARVE: Did he save the dog?

MEG: The other boys got there just as Herb was coming out.

HARVE: Did he save the dog, Meg?

Meg: The dog's fine, Harve!

Harve: Herb' dead.

Meg: Yes, he is.

Harve: (*He covers his face with his hand.*) 'F I believed in God, I'd curse him.

Meg: I'm sorry, Harve.

Harve: The dog! The damn dog.

Meg: The funeral was this morning. I thought you knew.

Harve: I wish you hadn't a told me that.

Meg: You'd have heard sooner or later.

Harve: Might a been later.

Meg: I don't like the look on you, Harvey. Scares me.

Harve: It ain't nothin' but a look a wonder, Meg.

Meg: You want a drink?

Harve: You know I don't drink.

Meg: There's always a first time. Might make you feel better.

Harve: If I started drinkin' now, I'd probably never stop.

Meg: I doubt that, Harvey.

Harve: I don't want anything to dull this pain I feel. I need to hurt for a while.

Meg: I'd tell you where Herb's buried, Harve, but I don't want you to do anything foolish.

Harve: What are you talkin' about?

Meg: When Sarah died, and you were lighting those brush fires near her grave?

Harve: I never did such a thing!

Meg: We always knew it was you, Harvey. That's why we were all set to convince you to join the rescue squad. We figured you'd stop setting fires once you got a taste of fighting them.

Harve: Meg, you've lost your mind.

Meg: Sure enough, once you got on that fire squad those fires stopped over in the cemetery. What made you do such a foolish thing, Harvey?

HARVE: I never did.

MEG: It's all right, now, Harvey. That was years ago. Everybody forgot about it. Nobody got hurt. (*Pause*) What were you thinking?

HARVE: A candle is a prayer.

MEG: Those weren't candles. Those were brush fires.

HARVE: They were bigger prayers.

MEG: Is that what you thought? Where did you ever pick up such a heathen attitude?

HARVE: From my heathen convictions.

MEG: Is that so? Well, you married a Christian woman, Harvey; you married her in a church. And you live in a Christian community. You ought to know better.

HARVE: I stopped doin' it.

MEG: Did you? I wonder.

HARVE: Meg, you don't think I'd actually set somebody's house on fire.

MEG: I'd hate to think you would!

HARVE: Come on, Meg.

MEG: No. I don't. But there's something about you that scares me.

HARVE: Don't matter.

MEG: You want me to help you get things in order, here?

HARVE: No.

MEG: No? (*She waits for him to say more.*) All right, Harvey. I'm leaving. I'll be back at the end of the week with Sally.

HARVE: Eyuh.

MEG: Let me know if you need anything.

HARVE: Uh huh.

MEG: Goodbye, Harvey.

HARVE: Bye, Meg.

(MEG *crosses. Her foot hits against the gun on the ground. She picks it up, turns to* HARVE.)

HARVE: I was fishin'.

Blackout

Scene Two

(*The porch and the yard are in a shambles. It is noontime.*)

(HARVE *is sitting in the rocking chair, the chair is turned 'round, and* HARVE *is facing the open of the house.* HUEY *enters, but stops short.*)

HARVE: Huey! I'm stuck, Huey! (*Pause*) I need a hand! (*Pause*) Damn. (*He rocks the chair, trying to turn it, but it only inches back toward the steps.*) Damn. (*He stops*) Huey!

(HUEY *waits, quietly watching* HARVE.)

HARVE: Damn it, Huey! I need a hand! (*He rocks the chair wildly, to no avail.*) Damn it to hell!

(*He stops.* HUEY *stirs.*)

HARVE: Is that you there, Hue?

HUEY: Yes, sir, Mr. Sloth.

HARVE: Din't ya hear me hollerin'?

HUEY: Yes, sir.

HARVE: What are you waiting for? Give me a hand.

HUEY: What do you want me to do?

HARVE: Turn me around, Hue. I can't stand to look at this wall for another minute.

HUEY: Yes, sir. (*He crosses up the steps, turns* HARVE *around.*)

HARVE: That a boy. What took you so long?

HUEY: Mr. Sloth?

HARVE: Uh huh.

HUEY: What're you doin'?

HARVE: What does it look like I'm doin'? I'm movin' the chair.

HUEY: How come.

HARVE: Thought I'd take it for a little ride down these steps.

HUEY: Wouldn't that be likely to break the chair all up?

HARVE: You know, you're probably right. Hadn't thought of that.

HUEY: I don't think I'd do it if I was you, Mr. Sloth.

HARVE: Too bad. I was looking forward to it.

HUEY: What's burning?

HARVE: Ain't nothin'.

HUEY: I smell something burning.

HARVE: I don't smell a thing.

(HUEY *turns toward the door. Smoke is drifting through the doorway.*)

HUEY: Fire! (*He runs into the house.*)

HARVE: Stay out a there, Hue!

(*We hear a crash of something falling.*)

HARVE: Huey!

(*A flaming chair flies out the door, followed by* HUEY. HUEY *kicks the chair down the steps and stomps the fire out. He turns to* HARVE.)

HARVE: Now look what ya done! Ya ruint that chair!

HUEY: I din't ruin it! You lit that chair on fire!

HARVE: What do you mean talkin' to me like that!

HUEY: I wasn't bein' disrespectful.

HARVE: Oh no? What was it then?

HUEY: I know you light fires, Mr. Sloth.

HARVE: There you go again! What kinda talk is that?

HUEY: It's the truth.

HARVE: Is it then? Spose I tell you people got their eyes on you. Spose I tell you people think you're the one's been settin' these fires.

HUEY: You know I din't do that, Mr. Sloth! You know!

HARVE: I don't know what you might do, Huey. Could be Herb was right about you.

HUEY: That ain't so!

HARVE: I never thought you'd turn against me, Hue. After all I done.

HUEY: You ain't right, Mr. Sloth.

HARVE: What you know 'bout what's right! You ain't nothin' but an in-bred moron yourself!

HUEY: Why do I gotta hear that?

HARVE: I was wrong to say that, Huey.

HUEY: All I ever seen you do was sit in that chair. I ain't never seen nobody sit in one place so long. It really made me wonder. Couple a nights ago I heard a terrible noise up here. Woke me up. I came up ta see if you were all right, but I couldn't find you. All I found was my jacket on the steps. Then I heard the horses. You was down by the barn saddlin' one of the horses. I was gonna shout for you but somethin' made me stop. I watched you ride off. That mare din't have no arthritis! She twisted her ankle when you was ridin' her. (*Pause*) I followed you the next night, Mr. Sloth. I saw what you did.

HARVE: What'd I do, Huey.

HUEY: You came ridin' out of that fire like the devil himself! Almost stopped my heart!

HARVE: I ought to whip you!

HUEY: Ya have ta get out a that chair to do it!

HARVE: Stand here at the bottom of the steps. I'll run ya down with this rocker!

(HUEY *crosses and stands up to* HARVE.)

HARVE: You don't think I'll do it, do ya?

HUEY: I don't care neither way!

HARVE: Damn you! (*Pause*) World's closin' in on us, Hue. Everything's catchin' up.

HUEY: I ain't gonna give up.

HARVE: Maybe you ought to! You could be in a flock a trouble.

HUEY: I ain't gonna sit down and die!

HARVE: You lettin' your fire out a the stove, Huey?

HARVE: I followed you there!

HARVE: I ain't been out a this chair in over a month.

HUEY: You get out of that chair every night!

HARVE: I ain't been out a this chair, Hue. I swear!

HUEY: I followed you!

HARVE: I ain't got the strength to go nowhere!

HUEY: Why do ya do it?

HARVE: I'm a dyin' man, Hue. I couldn't pin a rooster to the ground.

HUEY: You got to stop!

HARVE: I can't live with this world. It don't hold nothin' for me.

HUEY: You're sposed to teach me about the horses! And the trees!

HARVE: Everything I think's worth a damn can't be found no more.

HUEY: I ain't gonna let you do it, Mr. Sloth!

HARVE: Too late ta stop me, Hue.

HUEY: Get up! (*He grabs* HARVE, *tries to pull him up out of the chair.* HARVE *grips the arms.*)

HUEY: I know you can do it! (*He pulls harder but* HARVEY *resists.*) Get up old man! (*He loses his grip and falls backward down the steps.*)

HARVE: Don't look at me like that, Hue. I ain't evil, only twisted.

HUEY: What am I gonna do?

HARVE: Take care a them horses.

HUEY: You said Sally was going to sell the horses.

HARVE: You can go with 'em.

HUEY: No, I can't.

HARVE: Huey, I can't be your father anymore.

HUEY: You can't do nothin' for nobody, can you?

HARVE: Not even myself, Hue.

HUEY: You're a selfish old bastard.

HARVE: 'Bout time I was.

(*We hear frightened horses.* HUEY *turns to look toward the barn.*)

HUEY: Oh no!

HARVE: It's too late, Hue.

HUEY: You weren't even gonna tell me, were ya?

HARVE: Might as well sit up here and enjoy the spectacle.

HUEY: The horses! (*He exits on a run.*)

HARVE: It's too late, Hue! Watch her burn! (*Pause*) What a sight she is!

(*We hear the horses, more frightened, the crackle of flames.*)

HARVE: It's goin' fast, Huey! Ya better be quick! (*He leans forward rapturously.*) Hue! (*He rocks the chair forward and it plunges down the steps. Hitting the bottom it collapses and propels him on to his feet. He takes one shaky step.*) That a boy, Huey! (*He falls forward on to his face.*)

(*Blackout.*)

Scene Three

(*The yard and porch look like a war zone. There is charred debris and a blackened wood stove in the yard.* HARVE *is nowhere to be seen. It is morning.*)

(SALLY *and* MEG *enter.*)

SALLY: My God! What happened?

MEG: I knew he wasn't fit to be left alone.

SALLY: Gandpa? (*She runs into the house.*) Harve! (*She steps out on to the porch, surveys the scene.*) I knew the place might be a little worse for wear . . .

MEG: Never underestimate your grandfather.

SALLY: I wonder where he is?

MEG: I'm a little worried about that, Sally.

SALLY: Don't start. I don't care what kind of shape he's in. He's got some explaining to do.

MEG: We'll see.

SALLY: Oh no!

MEG: Good lord!

SALLY: What happened to the barn?

MEG: He burned it!

SALLY: What the hell . . . Grandpa!

MEG: Harvey, you show your face this instant!

SALLY: Aunt Meg, you don't think he was in the barn?

MEG: Let's pray he wasn't.

SALLY: But where . . .

MEG: He probably sat up here and watched it burn.

SALLY: Not now . . .

MEG: We'd better call the police.

SALLY: The phone doesn't work.

MEG: Then we'd better go somewhere and call them.

SALLY: I'll stay here. Harve might come back.

MEG: Come on, Sally.

SALLY: Harve! Grandpa, where are you?

MEG: Come on, Sally!

(MEG *pulls* SALLY *off. A few beats pass.* HUEY *enters, backing on, dragging* HARVE'S *limp body.* HUEY *drags* HARVE *to center and lets him fall.*)

HUEY: There we go! (*Pause*) You were right, Mr. Sloth. It's a beautiful thing to watch. Once I seen I couldn't do nothin' ta stop it, I just watched. Least I got the horses out. Don't know where the hell they are, but I s'pose they'll come back once they're hungry. He gathers the lighter pieces of trash from around the yard and lays them over HARVE'S *body*.) I feel pretty funny doin' this, Mr. Sloth. I ain't never done it before. (*Pause*) But even after what you done, I figure you deserve a decent buryin'. (*He examines his work.*) You need a marker. (*He looks around, spies a saddle, drags it over* HARVE'S *head.*) This ain't no good. The crows'll be after you in no time. I don't think I could watch that. Where'm I gonna find somethin' that smells worse'n you? (*Pause*) I know! (*He exits on a run. A few beats pass. A few more. He enters, pushing a wheelbarrow full of horseshit and carrying a shovel.*) I'll bet this'll keep the crows away. (*He dumps the shit on* HARVE, *evens it out with the shovel, exits for more.* HARVE *groans and stirs under the trash and shit.*)

HARVE: Can't see a damned thing. (*Pause*) Huey! (*He struggles, pushes the saddle away, and sits up.*)

HARVE: Good God. I think I might be dead. (*He examines the horseshit.*) Or reborn from a horse's ass! (*Pause*) Sure looks like Hell. (*Pause*) Damn! What if this is all there is? Din't know I was constructin' my own Purgatory. Guess I should have cleaned it up after all. (*Pause*) Din't have the courage ta kill myself. Thinkin' bout it scared the hell out a me. Thinkin' of not thinkin'. Not havin' that voice inside your head. Not bein' able ta see, or hear, or feel. Like turnin' off a light. (*Pause*) Not bein' able to draw a breath. (*Pause*) The horror!

(HUEY *enters, pushing the load of shit. He is pretty well covered in soot and manure—a frightful sight. He stops short when he sees* HARVE *sitting up.* HARVE *turns to look at* HUEY *and when their eyes meet they both scream.*)

Both: Aaahhh!

Huey: Mr. Sloth?

Harve: That you, Huey?

Huey: Yes, sir.

Harve: You about stopped my heart!

Huey: I thought you was dead!

Harve: Come to think of it ... so did I. (*Pause*) You been pilin' horseshit on me?

Huey: Yes, sir. Din't want the crows ta get ya.

Harve: What a silly old man. I really had myself goin' there. You been out there watchin' me make a fool a myself?

Huey: No, sir. I thought you was dead.

Harve: I was hopin' I was.

Huey: Well, ya ain't!

Harve: Seems like I been walkin' into a cold wind. A strong, bitter wind, pushin' me back, keepin' it hard. I waited for that wind to die, and when it din't I figured I'd give up myself. Death was all I had to look forward to. Worked hard all my life, all it got me was a routine. Got so I'd wake up, and I'd see a long line a days ahead a me, days just like the one before, and the one before that, and the one before that. I looked ahead a me and I looked behind me and every day looked the same. I was just ploddin' my way from back there to up ahead, without so much as a ripple, people I loved fallin' by the wayside, me gettin' lonelier and lonelier with each step, each day. And tired. Huey, I got so tired! (*Pause*) What for? What the hell for? (*Pause*) Only thing that gave me any pleasure was watchin' the fire. I got such a charge from the fire. It filled me up! Felt like I could stop everything. Like I could stay right there, the past frozen behind me, the future frozen ahead ... just me, and the fire. (*He closes his eyes in rapture.*) But it never lasted. The days behind would haunt me and the day ahead would demand me. They'd call out to me like an old nag. Make me move. Back to the routine. (*Pause*) Damn it, Hue! I never found any answers!

Huey: I ain't got but one answer, Mr. Sloth.

Harve: What's that, Hue?

Huey: You got to find the fire in somethin' else.

Harve: Is that so?

HUEY: You ain't like a crazy man, Mr. Sloth.

HARVE: Why not?

HUEY: You ain't got the juice for it. I'm just slow, myself, but I know crazy. My papa was crazy.

HARVE: Your papa was a drunk.

HUEY: He was crazy. You know how he died?

HARVE: Way I heard it, he passed out on the railroad tracks.

HUEY: He din't pass out. He stood up to that freight train. Stood right in the middle of the tracks, facin' the engine, yellin' "Come and get me you old fucker!", and BLAM!, it was all over.

HARVE: Is that true, Huey?

HUEY: I saw it happen!

HARVE: He *was* crazy.

HUEY: He was nuts, Mr. Sloth.

HARVE: Help me up, would ya, Hue?

(HUEY *crosses to* HARVE *and helps him up.* HARVE *stands shakily.*)

HARVE: Ya see that tree over there, Hue?

HUEY: The one that's burnin'?

HARVE: Eyuh. Know what kind a tree that is, Hue?

HUEY: A birch?

HARVE: Good boy! How do ya know it's a birch tree, Hue?

HUEY: Cause it's got birch bark on it.

HARVE: Always knew you were sharp.

HUEY: We gonna let that tree burn?

HARVE: Well, if we let that tree burn then most likely it'll catch fire to some a them other trees, and before ya know it the whole forest'll be ablaze. Don't know that I fancy that idea. (*Pause*) Woods're nice this time a year.

HUEY: Should I get a bucket?

HARVE: 'Smore'n we can handle, Hue. We'd better get some help. Tell you what. We'll go down and alert the populace and then you and I'll go somewhere and have ourselves a soda. What do ya say to that?

HUEY: Can we really?

HARVE: I just said so, din't I?

HUEY: I never done nothin' like that!

HARVE: I'm sure there's lots you haint done. C'mon, Hue, let's get old Betsy started up. I wonder where the keys are?

HUEY: They're in the ignition.

HARVE: Good place for 'em.

(HARVE *and* HUE *cross to the car and get inside,* HARVE *behind the wheel.*)

HARVE: One hell of an automobile. (*He turns the switch. The engine groans and sputters.*) Come on ole girl! (*He turns the key again. After a few coughs and sputters the engine roars to life.* HUEY *whoops.*) Ahah! Damn fine piece of machinery! (*He revs the engine, smiling broadly.*) Go on, Betsy! (*He lets the engine idle.*) Just listen to her hum.

HUEY: Mr. Sloth?

HARVE: Yeah?

HUEY: Would you teach me how to drive?

HARVE: Sure, Hue! I'll teach you how to drive. This here's the horn. (*He beeps the horn.*) This here's the blinkers. (*He hits the blinkers.*) This here's the lights. (*He turns on the lights.*) This here's the wipers! (*He turns on the wipers, beeps the horn again.*) You gettin' all this down, Huey?

HUEY: Yes, sir!

HARVE: Down hear you got your clutch pedal, and your brakes, and your . . .

HUEY: Mr. Sloth?

HARVE: What is it, Hue?

HUEY: How much you know about girls?

HARVE: Not much, Hue.

HUEY: More'n I do, huh?

HARVE: It's possible.

HUEY: I want you to tell me about girls.

HARVE: Aw, Hue, I can't go chasin' tail like some young bull. You're gonna have ta do that by yourself.

HUEY: I don't think I'd better.

HARVE: Maybe not. (*He fiddles with the radio. He finds a bluegrass station and lets it rest.*) Tell you what. I'll take ya to a square dance. I could do that. Might even be fun!

HUEY: There'd be girls there!

HARVE: Yes, there would!

HUEY: That's what I really want.

HARVE: Easy, Hue. Girls don't like to be pounced upon. You sit tight for now.

HUEY: What do girls like?

HARVE: I'll tell you later. We'd best go get our sodas before we burn down the whole state.

(HARVE *tries to back up and the car stalls. He and* HUEY *look out their windows at the flat tires.*)

HUEY: Looks like your tires need air.

(HARVE *laughs.*)

HARVE: You're all right, Huey.

(*A siren sounds in the distance and grows. Another joins it. Then another.* HUEY *and* HARVE *get out of the car and look off.*)

HARVE: I guess we're in a whole mess a trouble now, eh Hue?

HUEY: I guess.

Fadeout

David Scott Milton

Skin

D AVID S COTT M ILTON was an early member of the avant garde Theater Genesis, along with Sam Shepard, Leonard Melfi, and Murray Mednick. He has had more than a dozen plays performed Off-Off Broadway including *The Interrogation Room*, *Halloween Mask*, *The Metaphysical Cop*, and *Scraping Bottom*. *Scraping Bottom*, under the title of *Born to Win*, became the Czech director Ivan Passer's first American film and starred George Segal, Karen Black, and Paula Prentiss.

Milton's other plays include *Duet for Solo Voice* and *Bread* at the American Place Theater, and a revised version of *Duet for Solo Voice*, retitled *Duet*, on Broadway with Ben Gazzara.

Mr. Milton has had four novels published: *The Quarterback*, *Paradise Road*, *Kabbalah*, and *Skyline*. *Paradise Road* was given the *Mark Twain Journal* award "for significant contribution to American literature."

His adaptation of David Hare's *Knuckle* was seen on PBS television.

Skin, for which he won the Neil Simon Playwrights Award, was presented at The Odyssey Theater in Los Angeles.

For stock and amateur production rights, contact: Broadway Play Publishing, Inc., 357 West 20th Street, New York, NY 10011. For all other rights, contact: David Scott Milton, 1235 24th Street, #1, Santa Monica, CA 90404.

Characters
C HRISSIE
C ANTON
S AVAGE

Act One

(*Lights up. A beach house, sparsely furnished.* CANTON *enters with a young woman,* CHRISSIE.)

CHRISSIE: It was near the jetty where it broke down, my car. These two dudes pull over and offer to drive me to a phone. It had started—

CANTON: —to rain.

(CANTON *moves to the couch, takes up a peignoir from it, stashes it away.*)

CHRISSIE: So I get in with them and they begin to diddle around, feeding me *shit*, excuse my mouth. So I get their drift. So I say nothing doing. So they throw me out of the moving car.

CANTON: Some people are—

CHRISSIE: Animals.

(*She gazes at the room. There is a mirror, a hat rack, and a few knick-knacks.*)

CHRISSIE: It was so fabulous you picking me up like that. Perfect stranger.

CANTON: Ah.

CHRISSIE: With all the creeps and psychopaths out.

CANTON: Yes.

(CANTON *moves to the fireplace, lights a fire.*)

CHRISSIE: This is so—

CANTON: Yes?

CHRISSIE: Beachy.

CANTON: Hm.

CHRISSIE: Definitely I'm a beach person. Must cost—

CANTON: Well.

CHRISSIE: —more than a few bucks. The beach.

CANTON: You ought to get out of those clothes.

CHRISSIE: What do you have in mind?

CANTON: I was just thinking—

CHRISSIE: Uh huh?

CANTON: —you must be wet.

(*He moves behind her, his hand on the back of her jacket. She slips out of it. He places it in front of the fire to dry. Then he moves to a lamp, switches it on. It is a bright medical light. He turns her to him. The lamp hits her like a spotlight.*)

CANTON: Now let's take a look.

CHRISSIE: (*Pulling away*) You're being very aggressive.

CANTON: You've been in an accident. I'm a doctor. Strictly professional.

CHRISSIE: Oh, this is a new one. "Want to play doctor?" I haven't heard this one. (*Retreats*) Can I have something to drink? Coffee?

(CANTON *starts for the kitchen.*)

CHRISSIE: Cream, no—

CANTON: —sugar

(*She watches after him as he enters the kitchen. Then she moves to the phone, picks it up, dials. She holds the phone as it rings on the other end.*)

CHRISSIE: (*Into phone*) He's very pushy. There's something, well, psychopathic about him. (*Pause*) Don't come on to me like that, hard guy bullshit. Et cetera. (*Pause*) Listen to me. *Listen to me*, asshole. I'm not Diana Dunce. This man is *very dangerous.* (*Pause*) I feel the vibes. I'm a vibes person. (*Pause*) You're a person person, that's terrific. I'm a vibes person and my vibes tell me—*danger!* (*Pause*) Not the Colony Road. The other. You can't miss it, it's the rattiest house on the street. And, hey. This is going to take some doing so bring a weapon, one that can do some real damage.

(*She hangs up just as* CANTON *enters.* CHRISSIE *picks up a porcelain pillbox next to the phone.*)

CHRISSIE: Oh, look at this! Neato. (*Reads:*) "Love the giver." Neato bandito. This must hold very touching memories.

CANTON: Yes.

CHRISSIE: The giver was—?

(*No answer*)

CHRISSIE: You.

(CANTON *sets down the coffee tray. He takes the pillbox from her.*)

CHRISSIE: It's better to give than receive, the Bible says. Or was it Dr. Toni Grant? Do you ever listen to her? I heard this one time, this married couple? The husband takes their kid to the baby sitter. The baby sitter wants to make it with the husband. The wife wants a divorce. It was fabulous.

(*He turns off the medical lamp, snaps on a table lamp. It casts a soft glow over* CHRISSIE. *He adjusts the shade so that she is in half-shadow.*)

CHRISSIE: So you're a doctor? You're not a gynecologist, are you?

CANTON: (*Shakes his head*) I don't practice anymore.

CHRISSIE: Who wants a doctor who *practices*? I want someone who *knows* what they're doing.

(CHRISSIE *examines a small oriental bell.*)

CHRISSIE: Oh, look at this! Cute. One of those little bell things.

(*She rings it.* CANTON *watches her. He pushes the coffee and cookies toward her.*)

CANTON: Who were you talking to?

CHRISSIE: Talking?

CANTON: On the phone just before. You were talking—

CHRISSIE: Let me get the context here. Talking?

CANTON: —to someone.

CHRISSIE: Yes. Myself. I do that for a pick-me-up. "Hello, Chrissie, are you there?" "Yeah, I'm here." Reassuring.

(*In the half-light* CHRISSIE *appears as though she were made of porcelain.*)

CANTON: You have lovely skin.

CHRISSIE: Natural. No whatever. Lotions.

CANTON: Exquisite.

CHRISSIE: I prefer natural, don't you?

(*He does not answer. He continues to stare at her.*)

CHRISSIE: This coffee sucks, excuse my mouth. Do you have any wine?

(CANTON *moves to a bar area at one end of the room.*)

CHRISSIE: I our crowd we drink the most exceptional wines. (*Groping*) Chivas . . . ah . . .

CANTON: Regal?

CHRISSIE: *Mani*chivas. Fabulous.

(CANTON *is at the bar, checking.*)

CANTON: No wine. I have some—

CHRISSIE: No. I rarely touch alcoholic beverages. A little wine, though, is good for the digestion. Have you ever heard Dr. Rorsbach on the radio? He says that quail eggs are good for psoriasis.

(*Pause. He moves to her, studies her under the soft glow of the lamp. She grows uneasy.*)

CHRISSIE: So what do you do if you don't practice—?

CANTON: Work on myself.

CHRISSIE: Ah!

CANTON: When you work on yourself, the day never ends.

CHRISSIE: What do you do on yourself. I mean—what do you do?

CANTON: Study. the Tao, the I Ching—

CHRISSIE: Neato Frito.

CANTON: From morning to night my life is electric!

CHRISSIE: Tres interesting.

CANTON: Learning to open up, welcome my impulses.

(*He waves his arm as though welcoming* CHRISSIE *into the house. She does a little twirling dance around.*)

CHRISSIE: Ta dah!

CANTON: When I saw you on the road I had an impulse.

CHRISSIE: I knew it. I knew you did. I could see you did.

CANTON: I felt we connected.

CHRISSIE: Yes.

CANTON: Did you feel that, too?

CHRISSIE: Definitely.

CANTON: Yes.

CHRISSIE: Case closed.

CANTON: A year ago I would have never—And now I'm taking dancing lessons—

(*He does a quick dance step in front of the bar, continuing right on:*)

CANTON: —learning to tell a good joke. Oh, this is a good one. You'll like this one. The one about the Filipino thought he was a butterfly? *Funny.* No wait. Not a Filipino. *Malaysian.* Thought he was a *moth.* (*A sudden outburst*) *Damn!*

CHRISSIE: What's wrong?

CANTON: I just can't seem to—Damn! Damn!

(*He struggles to control himself.*)

CANTON: Forgive me. I have these—I get—I lose—

CHRISSIE: Well, just—

CANTON: I had this crisis, you see, spiritual crisis. Someone I—Well. Life changed drastically for me. And then—

(CANTON *gropes, hangs on.*)

CANTON: I had this collapse: I would get very verbose when I was by myself. With people I couldn't say a word. Now I just let it fly from the lips, blah, blah, blah—He was a Filipino. No, Malaysian. Korean! No.

(*He pauses.*)

CANTON: I'm sorry. Sometimes I lose—

CHRISSIE: —the train of your thought.

CANTON: I get these—

CHRISSIE: —lapses.

CANTON: Yes. Humpty-Dumpty sat on the wall. Humpty-Dumpty had a great—

CHRISSIE: Fall.

CANTON: Yes. Thank you. (*A beat*) You have lovely, lovely skin. (*Quickly*) It was a *Chinaman*, a Chinaman dreamed he was a butterfly. Stop me if you've heard it. He flitted about in the dream completely happy, never realizing he was actually a Chinaman. You know how that is in a dream? Then he woke up. His whole life after that was misery. He couldn't tell wether he was a Chinaman who once dreamed he was a butterfly or a butterfly now dreaming he was a—

CHRISSIE: —chink! That's neat.

(*Pause.*)

CANTON: There's Seagram's. Would you like—

CHRISSIE: Fabulous. In our crowd we drink *nothing* but Seagram's!

(*He moves back to the bar, finds the Seagram's, pours.*)

CHRISSIE: You'd like our crowd: they're neat people. We have such *fabulous* times! A drive down the freeway can be a rewarding experience. Just having coffee at a Bob's Big Boy. Now some people wouldn't think that's special but our crowd has a way of making it a fabulous occasion.

CANTON: How do you make having coffee at Bob's Big Boy a fabulous occasion?

CHRISSIE: It's the quality of conversation, what we talk about, our observations on life and death. You'd have to be there.

(*He hands her a drink, and seats himself opposite her.* CHRISSIE *toys with her drink and holds it up to the light.*)

CHRISSIE: I'm glad we connected. Canton.

(*Pause*)

CANTON: What?

CHRISSIE: I'm glad we—

CANTON: No, you called me—

CHRISSIE: Canton.

(CANTON *rises, moves close to her. He is standing above her now.*)

CANTON: How'd you know my name?

CHRISSIE: You told me.

CANTON: No.

CHRISSIE: You didn't mention it?

CANTON: No. I was just thinking: here we are like this and she doesn't even know my name.

CHRISSIE: I must have seen it on the door or the mailbox or something.

CANTON: No.

CHRISSIE: Oooooh, paranoia. Are you hiding something? You little devil, you. Not what you seem to be?

(*She finishes her drink. He takes her glass and pours her another.*)

CHRISSIE: You're trying to get me drunk! You want to get me drunk and diddle me! I know your type. Middle-age spiritual crisis. Humpty-dumpty, off the wall. You're not in the record business, are you?

CANTON: Why do you say that?

CHRISSIE: You look the type. Record executive.

CANTON: Really? In what way?

CHRISSIE: Smarmy, exploitative. You know.

CANTON: No. I don't know.

CHRISSIE: Well, think about it.

CANTON: I am—I was a doctor.

CHRISSIE: What were you doing in the Rainbow Bar tonight, if you're not in the record business?

CANTON: I like to look in their mirror. Stare at it long enough you start to resemble Mick Jagger.

(*He does a quick, grotesque imitation of Mick Jagger.*)

CHRISSIE: You went there to watch the young girls. Do you like watching young girls?

CANTON: How'd you know I was at the Rainbow?

(*She does not answer.*)

CANTON: You've been following me.

CHRISSIE: You've been following *me*. You picked me up, remember? Is that the way you do it, cruise the highways, pick up young girls in distress? Diddle them? Youse people think—

CANTON: Wait. Did you just say 'youse'? '*Youse*'!?

CHRISSIE: What's the matter with that?

CANTON: It's ugly, it's illiterate.

CHRISSIE: No one ever corrected me on that before. And I have some very educated friends. In our crowd, which is composed of many incredible and fabulous people, we say 'youse' all the time. I mean it's not like saying 'ain't'.

CANTON: Your crowd, then, is made up of morons—

CHRISSIE: You're not very open-minded—

CANTON: Pea-brained troglodytes!

CHRISSIE: Well, really. You know something? You're an incredibly tight-assed individual. You have built a defensive wall around you. You make judgments of people on a very superficial basis.

(CHRISSIE *goes to the window.*)

CHRISSIE: Oh, the ocean! What a magnificent sight!

CANTON: The waves—

CHRISSIE: Yes.

CANTON: —curling onto the beach.

CHRISSIE: Awesome.

CANTON: Yes.

CHRISSIE: I've never seen a beach so beautiful.

CANTON: Hm.

CHRISSIE: Makes you want to—take everything off! Swim for miles.

CANTON: The gravel might be a tad uncomfortable.

CHRISSIE: Gravel?

CANTON: That's the road. The ocean's in back.

CHRISSIE: I knew you were going to say that. I just knew it. I saw the ocean in my mind! You have no goddamn sensitivity or poetry. You're just a tight-assed, lame motherfucker, excuse my mouth, who will admit no one or nothing into his world.

CANTON: I picked you up, didn't I?

CHRISSIE: *Picked* me up? How do you mean that? You gave me a *ride*.

CANTON: Then what are you getting on my case about?

CHRISSIE: Mmm, that Seagram's. That's really terrific. I can feel it burning right down inside me.

(*She stretches out on the couch.*)

CHRISSIE: What do you want with me?

CANTON: I don't—

CHRISSIE: You picked me up, came here. Why?

CANTON: I *live* here.

CHRISSIE: You started down the Colony Road—

CANTON: Yes. In the rain—

CHRISSIE: You don't have a house in the Colony?

CANTON: No one lives there except—

CHRISSIE: Record producers, movie directors, oil millionaires. You're not any of these?

CANTON: I told you, I'm—

CHRISSIE: —a doctor.

CANTON: Yes.

(*A beat.*)

CHRISSIE: You're snowing me.

CANTON: You're snowing *me*.

CHRISSIE: Canton, we know all about you—

CANTON: We? Who's we?

CHRISSIE: —your *record* deals, relationships to certain *rock stars*—

CANTON: Please.

CHRISSIE: —monstro *dope* connections!

CANTON: Hah!

CHRISSIE: Hah, huh?

CANTON: I told you—I *was* a medical doctor—

CHRISSIE: Oh, come on!

CANTON: I gave it up—

CHRISSIE: Gave it—! *Fun-nee*!

CANTON: —because of basic ineffectuality.

(*He moves away.*)

CANTON: At one time I was interested in truth. The laminations of epithelial cells, their faceted symmetry, spell-binding exactitude. Dissectible truth. I gave it all up, went from science—

CHRISSIE: —to fantasy!

CANTON: Butterflies.

(CHRISSIE *smiles, twirls around.* CANTON *moves close to her.*)

CANTON: I had come to believe we have two souls—the real soul which dies and the dream soul which lives forever. (*Pause*) My life had become neon. Tzzzzzzzipppppop! Off-on! Gaps in my thinking, black holes in the brain. I couldn't make connections to people. I grew to detest the fact that I had to *touch* them. It's like being a keeper of reptiles in the zoo and you awake one day and loathe the feel of a snake.

CHRISSIE: What kind of doctor were you?

CANTON: Dermatologist.

CHRISSIE: Skin. (*She begins to laugh.*)

CANTON: What's so funny?

CHRISSIE: I was just thinking of my crowd. They'd find this—

CANTON: Funny?

CHRISSIE: Oh, definitely.

CANTON: Sitting at Bob's Big Boy—?

CHRISSIE: Right.

CANTON: —or zipping down the freeway, fast lane, that fabulous crowd of spectacular imbeciles, motorcycle morons, low-rider hydrocephalics? Neato-frito, neato-bandito!

CHRISSIE: Because your brain is turning to Swiss cheese, because people feel like snakes to you, because you are forced to seek out the company of women young enough to be your daughter, is no excuse to insult people of quality.

CANTON: You're right. Yes, yes—I'm sorry. I got—

CHRISSIE: —carried away.

CANTON: Yes.

CHRISSIE: What about your wife?

CANTON: What about her?

CHRISSIE: You tell me.

CANTON: What do you know about my wife?

CHRISSIE: Every doctor has a wife. Divorced? She take you over a barrel? Is that why you're living in this shack?

CANTON: My wife is dead.

CHRISSIE: Did you touch her? When she was alive?

CANTON: I don't want to talk about—
CHRISSIE: Did you touch her?

CANTON: I kept—

CHRISSIE: Missing?

CANTON: Yes. When she was dying, you see, it became very important—

CHRISSIE: —to touch her.

CANTON: Yes.

CHRISSIE: Especially then. Youse two probably—

CANTON: Don't say that.

CHRISSIE: What?

CANTON: 'Youse'.

CHRISSIE: I did not say that.

CANTON: You said, 'youse two probably—'

CHRISSIE: You really would like to make a moron out of me, wouldn't you? In our crowd we never say 'youse', we never say 'ain't'. We are a class crowd.

(CHRISSIE *moves to her jacket near the fire and puts it on. She prepares to leave.* CANTON *catches her with his voice.*)

CANTON: I had a dream about my wife the other night. (*Pause*) I called her on the phone. Long distance.

(CHRISSIE *turns to face him.*)

CHRISSIE: (*Smiles*) Hello.

CANTON: How are you?

CHRISSIE: Not well.

CANTON: You sound angry.

CHRISSIE: I'm just—busy. Is that the way it went?

(CANTON *turns away.*)

CANTON: Something like that.

CHRISSIE: Why did you desert me—is that what she said?

CANTON: No. I never. You left me.

CHRISSIE: You wouldn't talk to me. You wouldn't make love to me. You wouldn't touch me.

CANTON: You had not right—to leave me.

CHRISSIE: You treated me badly. Ignored me. Insulted me.

CANTON: I never. I was angry. You were retreating from me. Day by day—

CHRISSIE: I was dying.

CANTON: No right. No. No.

(*He walks to the window at the far end of the room, stares out.*)

CHRISSIE: That's the way it went.

CANTON: Something like that. She was peeved. In the dream I hung up and a cousin entered the room. His head was shaved.

(CHRISSIE *moves to coat rack near the door. A woman's straw hat hangs there. She take it up.*)

CHRISSIE: Oh, look.

(CANTON *turns from the window to face her.*)

CANTON: Put that down.

(CHRISSIE *places the hat on her head, admires herself in the mirror.*)

CHRISSIE: How adorable. Was it—?

CANTON: (*Advancing on her*) Put it down.

(CHRISSIE *stares at* CANTON *coldly.*)

CHRISSIE: Make me. You just make me.

CANTON: (*Pained*) You have no right—

CHRISSIE: You invited me in, remember?

CANTON: I never thought—I mean, these things get—

CHRISSIE: —out of control? How'd you like to hear an X-rated story?

(CANTON *turns away.*)

CANTON: You're really going too far.

CHRISSIE: Sexy.

CANTON: Pornography bores me. Ever see those films? Painful close-ups. Veins, folds of flesh, weird bumps, pimples. The topography of the human body was not meant to be observed from the vantage point of a pubic crab.

CHRISSIE: That's your opinion.

CANTON: Yes.

(CANTON *turns to her.*)

CANTON: What is it? The story?

CHRISSIE: Give me some money.

CANTON: Ah.

CHRISSIE: A dollar.

CANTON: I see. Ticky-tacky prostitution. The minor leagues. Porn for a dollar. If you need the money I'll give you some. I don't have much, but—

CHRISSIE: I've offended you.

CANTON: I thought you were something—else. I thought we were establishing something.

CHRISSIE: Pay my price. A dollar. It's not much.

(CANTON's *gaze is turned inward. Long pause. Then, softly:*)

CANTON: What's the story?

(CHRISSIE's *eyes are lit with a kind of ferocious passion.*)

CHRISSIE: How I climax myself. Do you want to hear it? For a dollar I tell the story, to watch me, it's five.

(CANTON *moves to her, gathering up her things.*)

CANTON: Doesn't interest me. Let's get out of here.

CHRISSIE: Where are we going?

CANTON: Just out. Anyplace. I'll take you wherever you want to go. I don't want to hear—you see, I don't want to hear—what you have to say. I dislike ugliness of that sort.

(CHRISSIE *pirouettes around.*)

CHRISSIE: But you like my hat?

(*She spins, admiring her reflection in the mirror.* CANTON *watches, transfixed by her image moving in and out of the light.*)

CANTON: Yes. I do. Could you wear it—on the side a little more?

(*She adjusts the hat.*)

CHRISSIE: Better?

CANTON: Yes.

CHRISSIE: And now—

(*She reaches into her canvas purse and pulls out a .32 snub-nosed revolver.*)

CHRISSIE: All your money.

(CANTON *stares, stunned, down at the revolver.*)

CHRISSIE: Cute, isn't it? Saturday Night Special. Your money.

CANTON: You disappoint me.

CHRISSIE: I've done my best. Your money.

CANTON: I'll give you everything I have. It's not much.

CHRISSIE: Now. But for my story you wouldn't give me a dime.

(CHRISSIE *aims the gun at his chest.*)

CHRISSIE: Where do you want it? The heart?

(*She lowers her aim.*)

CHRISSIE: Or—?

(CANTON *stares at the gun. His face suddenly becomes impassive, empty to all emotion.*)

(CHRISSIE's *finger tightens on the trigger. The gun fires: a weak, cap-gun sound.*)

(CHRISSIE *begins to laugh.*)

CANTON: A toy—?

CHRISSIE: —cap-pistol. Realistic, huh? I love to pull it on old men. Make them quake.

(*She moves to the stereo set.*)

CHRISSIE: Can I play some music?

(*He does not answer. She turns on the set. Willie Nelson, singing an old Lefty Frizzel song, "I Want To Be With You Always," comes on.* CHRISSIE *begins a slow dance to the music. She watches herself in the mirror.*)

CANTON: I mean that really is so shoddy. A cap pistol.

CHRISSIE: I didn't want to hurt you anybody. I just wanted to scare you a little.

CANTON: Well, you did. Yes.

CHRISSIE: I'm sorry. I don't know why I act so mean. What can I do to make it up?

(CANTON *comes up close behind her.*)

CANTON: I want to—

CHRISSIE: (*Moving to the music*)—touch my skin? Caress my skin?

(*She sways in front of* CANTON. *Her eyes never leave his. She runs her hands over her body.*)

CHRISSIE: Can you—climax me, do you think? Can you?

(CANTON, *watches her, mesmerized, pained.*)

CANTON: I want to hold you, reach you. I want to—

CHRISSIE: —touch me.

(*She is dancing close to* CANTON *now.*)

CHRISSIE: You want to examine my skin. Reach into my skin.

(*Slowly, she begins to disrobe.*)

CANTON: Yes.

(*She moves in and out of the light as her clothing falls away. The song ends. She stands there naked. The straw hat remains on her head.*)

(*She is in half-shadow now.* CANTON *watches the play of light across her skin.*)

(*At the front door, behind the glass, we see a shadow move, someone outside, watching.*)

(CANTON *moves toward* CHRISSIE, *then stops. He reaches his hand slowly, ever so slowly to touch her bare body.*)

(*The door bursts open. A man carrying a leather trumpet case strides into the room,* SAVAGE. CANTON *wheels to face him.* SAVAGE *swings out with the trumpet case. It catches* CANTON *on the side of the head and he goes down.* SAVAGE *kicks him and he rolls over.*)

SAVAGE: Where are the goods? Huh? The goods!

(*He walks away, rubbing his hands.*)

SAVAGE: Oh, we're really going to have us some fun now.

(CANTON *moans.* CHRISSIE *twirls around once.*)

(*Lights go to black.*)

Act Two

(CANTON *is seated in a chair. The medical lamp is on, shining white light into his face.* SAVAGE *stands above* CANTON, *behind the medical lamp.*

CHRISSIE *is at the bar, cutting slices of lemon peel. She is nude save for the straw hat and a transparent peignoir. When she moves it flares about her, flashing skin. In the shadows of the room, the peignoir, swirling from light to dark, appears like the wings of a butterfly.*)

SAVAGE: Freddie the Greek, Moustafa Gumshoe—

CANTON: I don't—

SAVAGE: Jerry. You know Jerry.

CANTON: Jerry? No.

SAVAGE: Freddie the Greek—

CANTON: The what?

SAVAGE: Mustafa Gumshoe.

CANTON: Mustafa who?

SAVAGE: The goods!

CANTON: I don't know what you're—

SAVAGE: Jerry, you know Jerry?

CANTON: I don't know any of these people. Who are you? Why are you doing this to me?

SAVAGE: We're going to get to the bottom of this if I have to tear your liver out!

(SAVAGE *walks away.*)

SAVAGE: You know Jerry, he came to me—

CANTON: I don't know Jerry.

SAVAGE: —broke flat as a clam's ass. Says to me, "Don't let them abuse me. Help me out." He was down on his hands and knees, pleading with me. "Give me my dignity!" Okay, I give him his dignity. But you knw how it goes with Jerry—

CANTON: No—

SAVAGE: An abrasive *punk*, loaded with wise-guy rationales why everybody is doing everything *wrong*. His point of view is, everybody got a dollar, give me the same.

CANTON: Who? What?

SAVAGE: Hey! Don't play Dickie the Dunce with me. I'm talking about Jerry! (*To* CHRISSIE) Fix me a drink. (*Back to* CANTON) The thing of it is,

Jerry and crime are the same: neither one pays. He gets out of the jackpot, starts promoting goods—

(*He mimes shoving something up his nose.*)

SAVAGE: So he has this wife, fabulous, a dream girl, looked like Tuesday Weld—

CHRISSIE: There's Seagram's, Wild Turkey.

SAVAGE: Tuesday Weld—some fine bitch. Yeah. Good. Seagram's.

CHRISSIE: Canton?

CANTON: What?

CHRISSIE: Drink?

CANTON: Seagram's.

SAVAGE: So I says to him, "Jerry, don't fuck me over, blah, blah blah." "Lenny" he says, "My word is gold." His problem was he was multi-levelled, but he always come up one level short.

CANTON: Some people—

SAVAGE: I don't want to know them! The thing of it is, I front him twenty-thousand dollars worth of goods, he sits half the day at La Scala impressing people, the other half tying up the office phone on calls that never go through.

(SAVAGE *moves to the door, locks it. He returns to the medical lamp, focuses it on* CANTON'S *eyes.*)

SAVAGE: So what's shaking, Bobby—and if it's bad news, I don't want to hear it.

(CHRISSIE *hands* SAVAGE *a drink, then one to* CANTON. SAVAGE *slaps* CANTON'S *drink away.*)

CANTON: Hey!

SAVAGE: My hand slipped, Bob. Sorry. (*Drinks deep*) Mmmmm. Only two times when I drink: when I'm alone or when I'm with somebody. Here's to your health. Where's your drink, Bob?

CANTON: It's—it's—you—

SAVAGE: (*To* CHRISSIE) Give him a drink. On the house.

(CHRISSIE *fetches the bottle.*)

SAVAGE: So here's the thing of it is, Jerry had this girl he's madly in love with—

(SAVAGE *takes the bottle. Grabs* CANTON *by the throat, pours liquor into his mouth. Keeps on pouring.* CANTON *sputters and gags.* SAVAGE *ignores him.*)

SAVAGE: —so ugly if she carried a broom you'd think a witch had crashed. He suspects she's promoting her crotch behind his back and so forth—

CANTON: (*Gagging on the booze.*) Arghhh, arghhhh—

SAVAGE: —who would fuck her, I say? You could walk her naked through Fort Pendleton, no one would lay a finger on her.

CANTON: Arghhhhhh.

SAVAGE: He has this wife looks like Tuesday Weld and he's goofy over some skank. Who can figure the human heart?

(*The bottle is empty;* SAVAGE *flings it to one side.* CANTON *attempts to rise; falls back on the seat of his pants.*)

CANTON: Who are you?

CHRISSIE: Bobby, don't get personal.

(CANTON *struggles to get up. He is drunk.*)

CANTON: What do you want here with me? What's in that case?

CHRISSIE: Bob, don't—

SAVAGE: My ax.

CHRISSIE: Musicians talk. Instrument.

CANTON: What kind of instrument?

SAVAGE: A Steinway piano. Now what's my drift here?

CHRISSIE: The phone.

SAVAGE: Right. The thing of it is, this is what he'd do. He'd ring the skank's number, put the phone on hold. I come into the office, the light is flashing all day. I say, "Jerry, what's with the phone?" "She come home," he says, "picks up the phone. I know what time she come in."

SAVAGE: (*Points to his head.*) Psychopathic. That was his problem. (*He rips the telephone cord from the wall.*)

CANTON: Hey!

SAVAGE: So I begin to get the picture here with Jerry. So I says to him, "Jerry, where's my money?" "I don't want to talk to you," he says. Hey! He doesn't want to talk to *me*? I'm the guy who put the bread on your table. Screw the world, but don't screw *me*. Not the guy who puts bread on your table. (*To* CHRISSIE) Why don't you put your clothes on?

CHRISSIE: Lenny—

SAVAGE: (*To* CANTON) A mental case.

CHRISSIE: I like to be comfortable.

SAVAGE: Out of my own pocket I fronted weight for this guy. And now it's "I don't want to talk to you"? "You motherfucker, I'll punch you from one end of the office to the other." He ate his shorts, believe me, cringed, pleaded.

CHRISSIE: Lenny, have you seen the view of the ocean? Fabulous. Let's go for a swim.

SAVAGE: So how's the record business, Bobby?

CANTON: I don't know anything about the record business.

CHRISSIE: God, I love the beach! Nude swimming. Invigorating.

SAVAGE: Yeah.

CHRISSIE: When I was a little girl I used to love to roam the neighborhood naked. Fabulous.

SAVAGE: Yeah.

CHRISSIE: If you express yourself physically, you won't get neurotic.

SAVAGE: Is that right?

CHRISSIE: My older sister, you know, Sarita?

SAVAGE: I've heard about her.

CHRISSIE: She's neurotic. Confused. She's a policewoman out in El Monte, you know?

SAVAGE: What's your point?

CHRISSIE: Once a month she flies up to Vegas and sells her body—prostitutes herself.

SAVAGE: That doesn't surprise me. That's what kind of society we're living in today. What's your point here? I mean, do you have a point?

CHRISSIE: I have a point.

SAVAGE: Bob and I have important matters to discuss here.

CANTON: Oh, you'll like this one! Hear about the Albanian thought he was a butterfly? No. *Armenian.*

CHRISSIE: I'm talking about my sister, Len. My *sister*.

SAVAGE: All right.

CANTON: Or maybe Lithuanian. *Lithuanian*.

CHRISSIE: I says to her, "Sarita, you're a policewoman sworn to uphold the law, you gave a sacred oath, and then you prostitute that oath. How do you justify that?" "Chrissie," she says, "I'm confused." If she'd just get rid of her inhibitions—

SAVAGE: A hooker policewoman, how many inhibitions can she have? Now put your clothes on—

CHRISSIE: (*Indicating the peignoir*) I *love* this! Your wife, Bob, was very chick. Did she get this at Fredericks of Hollywood? I saw one just like it—only it had big rid lips all over.

SAVAGE: See, Bob? All this talk about rape. Women walk around like that, everything hanging out, they wonder why there's rape in the world. If I didn't know her, I'd be tempted myself. Bob, there's nothing that'll cool down your sexual desire faster than knowing a person. We always want to possess what we don't know.

CHRISSIE: You're so cold-blooded, Len—

SAVAGE: Right.

CHRISSIE: —you don't even have compassion for yourself.

SAVAGE: Right. Okay. I'm strictly real people. Bob, what do you think of this one? I met a guy recently believed all death was psychosomatic. All, I says? You mean all the people who die every day, all the animals and things, all that is psychosomatic? The cow that gets slaughtered had a death wish?

CHRISSIE: What did he say?

SAVAGE: He had no answer to that one.

(SAVAGE *begins to fashion a noose from the telephone cord*.)

SAVAGE: So what's it going to be?

CANTON: What do you mean?

SAVAGE: The thing of it is, if I were you, I'd give up the goods. Everything you got. Gold records, diamond rings, stock certificates, negotiable bonds—

CANTON: I don't know what you're talking about. I'm a doctor.

SAVAGE: Witch doctor?

CANTON: What?

SAVAGE: *Witch*? Halloween.

CANTON: Medical.

SAVAGE: Where's your waiting room, X-ray machine?

CANTON: I've relinquished my practice.

CHRISSIE: Another drink, Len?

SAVAGE: Not so much ice this time.

CHRISSIE: Drink, Bob?

(CANTON *rises unsteadily*.)

CANTON: No. No more booze. The bar is closed.

SAVAGE: Pour him a drink and make it a tall one.

CANTON: No!

SAVAGE: Don't rile me, Bobby.

CANTON: Don't call me Bobby. My name is Robert. Or Bob.

SAVAGE: Picky-picky. Give him a drink.

CANTON: No.

SAVAGE: Put it on my tab.

(CHRISSIE *passes* SAVAGE *another bottle. He forces it into* CANTON'S *mouth*.)

CANTON: Please—Arrrgggh. (*Coming up for air*) You have to start treating me with respect—Arggggh.

SAVAGE: You have to earn respect, Bobby.

CANTON: I don't have to earn anything from you. Come in here, try to terrorize me. Arggggh.

(SAVAGE *flings the bottle away*. CANTON *manages to get to his feet*.)

CANTON: You don't know who or what I am.

SAVAGE: A man with a severe drinking problem, the way I see it.

CANTON: You have this all wrong—

SAVAGE: All wrong? I come in here, find you with my wife in a compromising situation—

CHRISSIE: I'm not his wife, Bob.

SAVAGE: In a manner of speaking. Don't rile me. (*To* CANTON) Jerry fronted the goods with my money. He got his, you got yours. Now I want mine. If I have to rip your tongue out, I'm going to get it.

CANTON: Don't mess with me—

SAVAGE: I'm going to mess with you a lot.

CANTON: You might get more than you bargained for.

SAVAGE: I'll take my chances. On the highway of life—

CANTON: You have to take your chances. Yes!

(SAVAGE *advances on* CANTON.)

SAVAGE: On that highway you know what you are? A broken down jalopy.

CANTON: You're trying to panic me. Well, I don't know the meaning of the word. Cool as a cucumber. Look at that hand—

(*He holds out his hand. It is shaking violently.*)

CANTON: So just stand back. Don't push me. Broken down jalopy? Oh, no. Cadillac Eldorado!

CHRISSIE: You're drunk, Bob.

CANTON: I'm not drunk. I'm angry. I always look like this when I'm angry. Just back off.

SAVAGE: If you're a Cadillac, I'm a Rolls Royce.

CHRISSIE: Rolls Royce! Ooooooooo-wheeeeee.

SAVAGE: You don't think I'm a Rolls? What am I, then? A Chevy? Is that what you think I am? A Chevy? Go on, say it. A Chevy?

CHRISSIE: All right. A Chevy.

SAVAGE: Call me a Chevy! How about I call you a self-centered, acid-brain freak?

CHRISSIE: If that's that way you feel.

SAVAGE: That's right.

(CHRISSIE *sinks down onto a chair and begins to weep.*)

CHRISSIE: You cruel fucker. You have no right saying things like that to me. I'm a sensitive human being.

SAVAGE: And what am I?

CHRISSIE: An animal, a killer and a brute.

SAVAGE: That's the superficial side of me. I have a sensitive side, too.

(CHRISSIE *takes up her canvas purse. She starts for the door.*)

CHRISSIE: I'm getting out of here.

(SAVAGE *grabs at her. She pulls away.*)

CHRISSIE: Don't you touch me.

(*During the ruckus,* CANTON *has moved to the sideboard. He is now edging open one of the drawers.*)

SAVAGE: Go on, walk bare-assed back to town. Flaunt your privates for the world to see! That's always been your main ambition in life.

(*As* CHRISSIE *starts for the door,* CANTON *yanks open the bottom drawer of the sideboard.*)

CANTON: Wait. I have something here.

SAVAGE: Hey!

(SAVAGE *rushes toward* CANTON. CANTON *swings around with what appears to be two pistols in his hands.* SAVAGE *dives for cover behind the couch.*)

SAVAGE: What do you have there, Bob?

(CANTON *is holding a pair of gold shoes.*)

CHRISSIE: Oh, cute.

CANTON: Try them on.

(CHRISSIE *moves to* CANTON.)

SAVAGE: What are you doing there?

(CANTON *places the shoes on* CHRISSIE.)

CHRISSIE: (*Admiring the shoes*) Gold.

(*She stands, moves around in the shoes.*)

CHRISSIE: I always wanted gold shoes.

CANTON: (*To* SAVAGE) Don't underestimate me. Shy? Withdrawn? That's a *subterfuge.* I'm breaking out, becoming a fun guy! So just watch yourself.

SAVAGE: (*To* CHRISSIE) Take them off. They look ridiculous.

CHRISSIE: Lenny, make up your mind. Do you want me dressed or undressed?

CANTON: I've been taking dancing lessons, learning how to tell jokes. Ever hear the one about the Iranian thought he was a locust? Let's see—how does it go?

CHRISSIE: You don't know how to communicate to people, Len. That's your problem.

SAVAGE: Walk around half-naked? Call that communication? Give me a break.

CANTON: There was this Iranian. No, maybe he was a Filipino. I'll get it. Let me just think about it for a minute—

SAVAGE: (*To* CHRISSIE) Take everything off.

(SAVAGE *grabs at* CHRISSIE. *She dances away from him.*)

CHRISSIE: See, see, Bobby—

CANTON: Bob!

CHRISSIE: —he's a dangerous man. Everything has to be his own way.

SAVAGE: The shoes, the hat, the nightie. Everything.

CHRISSIE: You're just like my father, Len. What's your sign?

SAVAGE: Off!

CHRISSIE: Virgo? Are you a Virgo? Hypercritical, demands perfection? Why don't you take off your belt and beat me? I got scars from beatings.

SAVAGE: Where? Let's see.

(SAVAGE *pulls at her peignoir.*)

CHRISSIE: I don't see any scars. Do you see any scars, Bobby?

CANTON: Bob.

SAVAGE: Bob. I don't see any scars.

CHRISSIE: Inside, you motherfucker. Excuse my mouth, Bobby.

CANTON: *Bob*! (*To* SAVAGE) Look, you have this all confused. You came here for—(*Gropes*)—goods. I don't have any. I don't know what goods you're talking about.

SAVAGE: The goods from Jerry. You met with Jerry's wife, then with a guy they call Freddie the Greek, then with the A-rab, Mustafa Gumshoe—

CANTON: The only person I met was her. I met her and I helped her. We connected.

SAVAGE: She can't connect her head to her neck.

CHRISSIE: We connected, Len.

CANTON: See? She said we connected. Don't you trust her?

SAVAGE: I trust her. Why shouldn't I trust her?

(SAVAGE'S *eyes narrow. He looks from* CANTON *to* CHRISSIE.)

SAVAGE: (*To* CHRISSIE) What have youse two been cooking up behind my back?

CHRISSIE: Don't say *youse*, Len. It's illiterate.

SAVAGE: What is this connection?

CHRISSIE: Conversations. We had some fabulous conversations.

SAVAGE: What were you talking about?

CHRISSIE: Don't you trust me?

SAVAGE: Trust is my middle name. What were you talking about?

CANTON: The Tao. The I Ching. We've had—

CHRISSIE: —some fabulous conversations.

CANTON: Fabulous.

(CANTON *and* CHRISSIE *stand together.* SAVAGE *is isolated.*)

CHRISSIE: Remember that conversation we had at Bob's Big Boy?

SAVAGE: I remember. We talked about car mufflers.

CHRISSIE: Oh, Len, you don't remember. We talked about more than that. Much more.

SAVAGE: What?

CHRISSIE: You don't remember?

SAVAGE: I remember everything. I had the superburger with cheese, french fries, ketchup on the side. You had the Big Boy Special, an order of onion rings, and sliced tomatoes. We talked about car mufflers. What did you talk about?

CANTON: Life and death.

SAVAGE: That's no big deal. The thing of it is, anybody can talk about that. With car mufflers you gotta have the facts.

CANTON: Did you ever meet someone, a very special someone, who had a special meaning for you? Where everything was exactly right?

Where every word you said, every gesture you made, meshed with incredible, extraordinary precision and rightness?

Chrissie: You never met anybody like that, Len.

Canton: Where the quality of conversation, the things you talked about, the observations on life and death—

Chrissie: I knew you were going to say that! Isn't that remarkable? That's it, Len. The observations on life and death.

Savage: (*To* Canton) Look, you're trying to mess me around. (*To* Chrissie) Don't you see what he's trying to do?

Chrissie: You have to have some trust in this life, Len.

Savage: I told you, trust is my middle name. But there are other things to consider. We came here to do a piece of work. Nothing is going to stop me from that. Now we get down to business or I start to chop you into little pieces.

Canton: Chop me into little pieces? You're not serious.

Savage: Is a heart attack serious, Bob?

Canton: I see a woman in distress, pick her up—

Savage: Did the lady ask to be picked up? This is a fact of law here, a question of abduction.

Canton: Oh, come on!

Savage: *Did she ask to be picked up*? The thing of it is, in California, for your information, there's what they call the Little Lindbergh Law where you transport a lady someplace to interfere with her sexual privacy—that's a capital offense. There was this fellow, Caryl Chessman, maybe you remember him? Well, Mr. Chessman is no longer around and you may well ask him why except that he can't tell you cause they gave him the *gas chamber*, but it was a similar situation and so forth so I'm well within my legal rights here, fella.

Canton: Oh, please. Please! I pick up a lady in distress, try to help her, find myself cornered, badgered, intimidated. Well, it doesn't work. You don't know who you're dealing with. This is a karate expert here, master juggler, super magician, bon vivant, fun guy.

Savage: Give me a break.

Canton: I can rumba, cha-cha-cha, do the bump, the grind, the fish—

(*Drunkenly, awkwardly,* Canton *begins to demonstrate his various talents.*)

CHRISSIE: That's cute, Bob.

CANTON: Languages. Move my lips—the most miraculous foreign languages come out! Bon soir, comment-allez-vous, eintz, tzvei, drei, feir, blah, blah—

SAVAGE: Blah!

CANTON: I've had cocktails with world leaders, danced with ladies so dazzling they'd blind you with their beauty. (*He takes a silk scarf from the sideboard.*)

CANTON: (*To* CHRISSIE) Madame, for you. A gift.

(SAVAGE *is warily circling the room.*)

SAVAGE: I know what you're doing. I know.

(CANTON *approaches* CHRISSIE.)

SAVAGE: What are you doing there?

(CANTON *puts the scarf around* CHRISSIE's *neck.*)

SAVAGE: Don't do that—

CANTON: I don't think you want to mess with me.

CHRISSIE: (*Toys with the scarf.*) Silk! Oh, how lovely!

(SAVAGE *grabs at the scarf.*)

SAVAGE: Give me that.

CHRISSIE: No.

(SAVAGE *tears the scarf from her, throws it to one side. Advances on* CANTON.)

SAVAGE: My tail's in a knot now! My ass is *red.* (*To himself*) All right, calm down. (*To* CANTON) I got a *murderous* temper.

CANTON: Just calm down.

(SAVAGE *swallows. Takes a deep breath.*)

SAVAGE: All right. (*Brightly*) Hear the story about the lark and the buzzard, Bob?

CANTON: No, I—ah—

SAVAGE: You'll like this one. Thing of it is, little philosophy here. Buzzard's flying around looking to eat him a lark. Get the picture?

CANTON: All right.

SAVAGE: Lark sees a hole in the ground, hides. Cow comes along and performs a defecation on the lark. After a while the lark pokes his head out, doesn't see the buzzard, and begins to sing—

CANTON: (*Forced laugh*) This is good. I like this.

SAVAGE: —whereupon the buzzard swoops down, lifts him out of the shit, and bites the fucker's head off.

CANTON: (*Shakes his head*) Ferocious.

SAVAGE: Three lessons to be learned here, Bob. (*Holds up one finger.*) Sometimes it's not so bad to be shit on. (*Two fingers*) When you're up to your neck in shit, sometimes it's not so good to sing. (*Three fingers*) Finally: not everyone who lifts you out of shit is trying to do you a good turn.

(SAVAGE *moves to* CANTON, *his manner soft now, buddy-buddy.*)

SAVAGE: Do you get my point here, Bob?

CANTON: Well.

SAVAGE: I figure you're the type likes a good philosophical story.

CANTON: Oh, yes.

SAVAGE: Look, I'm a bottom-line guy. Let's get to the bottom line. Bob.

CANTON: I'm a bottom-line guy myself. Len.

SAVAGE: Give it to me: what's your bottom line? Bob.

CANTON: What's yours? Len.

SAVAGE: Who paid off Freddie the Greek? Fronted the money to Moustafa Gumshoe?

CANTON: I don't know. I—

SAVAGE: Stroked Freddie, greased the A-rab?

CANTON: *Greased*? Now just wait a minute—

SAVAGE: (*Poking* CANTON'S *chest*) Let's not be *obtuse* here, Bob. There were deals cut and the thing of it is a deal is a deal in my book.

CANTON: Greased? *Stroked*? No. I mean—you don't know what the situation is. The situation is—

CHRISSIE: Complex.

CANTON: Complex.

SAVAGE: Enlighten me.

(CANTON *moves to* CHRISSIE'S *side*.)

CANTON: I picked this woman up out of humanitarian principles, an act of kindness. I saw in her an immense potential, what you might call *star quality*—

SAVAGE: Don't let that fool you, Bob.

(CANTON *moves around* CHRISSIE, *molding the air about her*.)

CANTON: She's a butterfly, don't you see that?

SAVAGE: I don't see that.

CANTON: She can soar, she can sing. Poetry in motion.

SAVAGE: Frankly, I don't see that.

CANTON: You see the caterpillar—

SAVAGE: That's right.

CANTON: But she's so much more. Perfection! Put her in the right light—

(CANTON *adjusts the floor lamp. The lamp on* CHRISSIE *creates an extraordinary sculpture of light and shadow*.)

CANTON: —magic! I've gone through rough times—

CHRISSIE: You hear this, Len?

CANTON: She can change all that.

(CANTON *moves swiftly about the room, seized with a surge of energy*.)

CANTON: I'm ready to bust loose, join the crowd, zip down the freeway with the best of them.

(SAVAGE *watches* CANTON *warily, clocking his manic energy*. CANTON *is at the back door now*.)

CANTON: I'm a little shaky. Okay. That's readjustment. Opening up my personality. Busting loose!

(*Suddenly* CANTON *flings open the back door and yells out:*)

CANTON: AAAAAAAaaaaaaaaaaaaaaa!

(*Screaming at the top of his lungs*, CANTON *rushes out into the night*. SAVAGE *scurries after him*.)

(*We hear from outside the house:*)

CANTON: HELP! HELP! AAAAAHHHHHHHHHHHHHHH!

(*Now* CANTON *reappears being dragged into the room by Savage, who has a choke-hold around his neck.*)

CANTON: That's my voice exercises. Just move the lips, let it come out, blah, blah, blah.

(SAVAGE *throws him to the floor. While* CANTON *gasps for breath,* SAVAGE *sets about tearing the room apart, opening cupboards and drawers, flinging dishes, silverware, assorted tools all about.*)

(CHRISSIE *watches with a sly smile, enjoying the whole thing.*)

(CANTON *sprawls on the floor, panting. He waves his arm in a weak gesture toward* CHRISSIE.)

CANTON: Reach out. Reach. Touch someone. Connect. She has youth, life. She can illuminate the dark, banish loneliness.

(*He rises shakily to his feet.*)

CANTON: Look at her! Magical, magical lady.

(SAVAGE *has found what he is looking for: a hammer and nails.*)

CANTON: What are you going to do there?

SAVAGE: Crucify you.

(CANTON *pales, gazes down at the palms of his hands.*)

CANTON: Crucify—?

(SAVAGE *brandishes the hammer and nails.*)

SAVAGE: I warned you not to get my ass red!

(SAVAGE *begins to nail shut the rear door.* CANTON *darts toward* SAVAGE, *crazed, desperate.*)

CANTON: You don't scare me. I can deal with you like that!

(*He snaps his fingers ineffectively.* SAVAGE *continues to nail up the door.*)

CANTON: You don't know who or what I am. You see me now, here, like this—but I'm so much more. There are things about me you could never imagine. Never. You see a husk, dried, empty—

(SAVAGE *has completed nailing the door shut. He turns his attention once more to* CANTON.)

SAVAGE: All right. Husk. Yeah?

(CANTON *backs off a step or two.*)

CANTON: There's more. Much more. I've done things, life and death things. I know all about that. Life and death. Remember the Korean War?

Savage: Do you got a point here?

Canton: I'm a trained killer. Lasers. Listen. Elite unit. Five thousand men. *Lasers*. Get the picture?

Savage: Fill me in.

Canton: Holograph army. Human wave. Lasers. You can't kill 'em, can't even hit 'em. Check my files. Captain Canton, Laser Master. I could have wiped whole nations from the face of the earth. Humanitarian principles, however, prevailed. Nevertheless, certain hostile armies were obliterated. We're getting to the nitty-gritty now, so just back off. The laser master made his mark. Check with the war department.

(Canton *is hanging on the brink of hysteria now, nine-tenths bonkers.*)

Savage: Kill some gooks, huh, Bob? Well, I'm no gook.

Canton: You can't scare me and you can't hurt me. I just snap my finger and you're finito!

Chrissie: You're drunk, Bob.

Canton: I'm not drunk!

Chrissie: What are you barking at me for? I called you *Bob*, didn't I?

Canton: Yes, yes. I don't blame you. You're—very special to me. Yes. Very special.

Savage: I've been trying to be nice with you, Canton. I tried to be a gentleman.

Canton: You've violated my world—

Savage: Violated?

Canton: Barging in here, swaggering around.

Savage: Swaggering? Have I been swaggering? That's my normal walk.

Canton: I don't like it.

Savage: You don't like my walk?

Canton: You walk like a monkey—

Savage: Hey, Bob. You're coming on pretty strong.

(Canton *snatches up two more silk scarves from the sideboard. He brings them to* Chrissie, *begins to arrange them on her.*)

Chrissie: Beautiful.

SAVAGE: I see what you're doing.

CANTON: Blah, blah, blah.

SAVAGE: You can't buy her cheaply. Trinkets. She wants the real stuff.

CANTON: Real stuff? Ha!

SAVAGE: Gold. Diamonds. Kilos of snow.

CANTON: Ha. Ha. Ha.

(SAVAGE *moves to the trumpet case, handling it with businesslike dispatch. He lifts it to his lap, toys with the catch.*)

SAVAGE: I don't want to hear whining, pleading, excuses. Everything you got.

(SAVAGE *opens the case.* CANTON *moves toward* SAVAGE, *straining to see what's inside.*)

CANTON: You don't scare me. What are you going to do?

(SAVAGE *fingers something in the case.* CANTON *moves even closer.*)

CANTON: What? What are you going to do? What do you have in there? Huh, Shorty? What are you going to do? Huh?

(SAVAGE *looks up from the case, incredulous.*)

SAVAGE: *Shorty*? Did you just call me Shorty?

CANTON: That's right. Shorty.

(SAVAGE *glowers, anger rising, approaching murderous rage.*)

SAVAGE: No one calls me Shorty. I'll bite your neck off, call me Shorty.

(CANTON *dances forward, then back.*)

CANTON: Shorty. Shorty. Shorty.

SAVAGE: (*Beside himself*) You're being very hostile, Bob.

CANTON: (*Having immense fun now*) You're damn right I am.

SAVAGE: Size is a point of view, what's the big deal? Napoleon—how tall do you think he was? The late Alan Ladd, James Cagney—

CHRISSIE: Toulouse Lautrec—

SAVAGE: Who's talking about that freak, there were others. Size is over-rated and I'm just not talking sex here.

CANTON: You're dealing with the wrong guy. I don't have to take this abuse, understand? I have never taken abuse. And that's what you're dishing out. And if you persist—

(SAVAGE *runs his hands over something inside the case.*)

SAVAGE: Yeah?

CANTON: If you persist—

(SAVAGE *weighs something in the case.*)

SAVAGE: Right?

CANTON: —you're doing it at your own risk, because I can be, in your venacular, a mean *motherfucker*, if I have to—

CHRISSIE: Excuse your mouth, Bob.

CANTON: I can be very, very mean.

SAVAGE: Okay.

(*A smile comes over* SAVAGE's *face. He continues to run his hand over something inside the trumpet case.*)

SAVAGE: Be mean. Let's see it. Let's see you be mean.

CANTON: You know what you're asking for? Meanness.

SAVAGE: Right.

CANTON: The real thing.

SAVAGE: Yeah. Yeah. Let's see it. Let's see how *mean* you can be.

CANTON: All right.

SAVAGE: Okay.

(*A beat. Then:* CANTON, *lets out a horrible, banshee scream. Leaps into an oriental martial position. Berserk, bounds into Samurai dance, sweeps in a frenzy around the room. Waving an imaginary sword, glowers, moans, grows more and more frantic, vanquishes imaginary enemy hordes.*)

(*Howls.*)

(*Then sinks sobbing to the floor.*)

(CHRISSIE *and* SAVAGE *stare at him, amazed. Slowly they approach him.*)

CHRISSIE: Bob? Bob? Hey, Bob . . .

SAVAGE: Get a grip on yourself, Bob.

(CANTON *looks up, dazed.*)

CANTON: I'm sorry. My mind missed a connection there, short circuit. Oh, God.

SAVAGE: He's drunk.

CANTON: How embarrassing.

CHRISSIE: Take it easy, Bob. Get a—

SAVAGE: —grip, Bob. Grip.

CANTON: Humpty Dumpty sat on a wall, Humpty Dumpty had a great—had a great—What? What?

CHRISSIE: Fall.

CANTON: Gap in my mind. Where was I? I was listening to music. I was talking to you. I was—Oh, God. My wife—

CHRISSIE: Yes?

(CHRISSIE *and* SAVAGE *have moved away from him. He stands in the center of the room, isolated in a circle of soft lamplight.*)

CANTON: My wife was dying. She lay there comatose.

CHRISSIE: Dying.

CANTON: And the sound from her lips—wishh, wishhh, over and over again, hour after hour—

(CHRISSIE *and* SAVAGE *in shadow.*)

CHRISSIE: Wishhhhhhhhhhh—

(CANTON *holds his hands over his ears.*)

CANTON: I left her for a while. The sound continued.

CHRISSIE: Wishhhhhhhhhhh—

CANTON: The ocean—

CHRISSIE: Wishhhhhhhhhhhh—

CANTON: The nurse.

CHRISSIE: Yes?

CANTON: Came to me.

CHRISSIE: The nurse came to you—

CANTON: 'Dr. Canton, you better hurry to her,' she said. 'Hurry to her. I think you better. I think.'

(*We see* CHRISSIE *in the mirror behind* CANTON. *He plays to her reflection.*)

Chrissie: You better hurry.

Savage: Hurry.

Canton: I entered the room, stood at the foot of the bed. She lay there on her stomach, her face buried in the pillow. Clock on the night table: *tick-tick-tick-tick-tick*. Half empty glass of water. Over there, little porcelain pill box with the words—

Chrissie: —"Love the giver"—

Canton: —on it. I turned her over. Her eyes were milky. Her face, like parchment. Her skin—you could see through it, see the stillness beneath it. No movement, not a shimmer of life. (*Calls*) 'Sarita'—

Chrissie: Sarita. Her name—

Canton: (*Softly*) Sarita.

Chrissie: Yes?

Canton: (*Softer yet*) Sarita.

Chrissie: What?

(Canton *appears isolated in his circle of light.*)

Canton: I hugged her to me. Tried to press my life into her. I could not—the skin, you see, thin as it is, forms an impenetrable wall. Here is life. Here is death. That thin tissue between. And you cannot break through. Thin as it is, you cannot force life through. After that, a while after that—

Savage: Yes? A while—

Canton: After that I saw myself in a different context. Looked at myself clearly. I was nothing. Nothing I had ever done was worthy of the designation, human. It had all been busy work.

Savage: Busy work is very human.

(Chrissie *sits on the couch,* Savage *on a chair. Both are in half-shadow.* Canton *addresses them, pleading as though he were a defendant before his judges.*)

Canton: I felt appalled to be human in that sense. I had had a concept of myself, you see, as a man of some accomplishment. Doctor Canton. I knew skin, its breathtaking intricacy, beauty. You could apprehend the skeleton through the skin; could palpate configurations, veins, arteries, pulse beats. Humanity stirred there, awakened at my touch, moved toward me, merged with me, melted the ice-block of solitude in which I existed. I was alive because skin was warm and sweaty between us. And then you died—

CHRISSIE: Who?

CANTON: She. She. My wife. No more. Cold skin. Cold. Cold. I stared at my life as though through a narrowing tube, everything small, so small. Miniaturized. Life of the ant. And great black holes in the brain began to spread. (*To* SAVAGE) She's exquisite, isn't she?

(CANTON *moves to the sideboard, takes out a delicately crocheted shawl. Hands it to* CHRISSIE.)

CHRISSIE: How beautiful. Soft.

CANTON: Soft, yes. Warm.

CHRISSIE: Soft and warm.

(SAVAGE *rises, moves to* CHRISSIE.)

SAVAGE: Take it off. We didn't come here for that.

CHRISSIE: What did we come here for?

SAVAGE: You know!

CHRISSIE: I seem to have—

CANTON: —forgotten.

CHRISSIE: Yes.

SAVAGE: Does this help you remember?

(SAVAGE *flips open his case. A short ax gleams inside.* SAVAGE *lifts the ax out of the case. The blade catches the light, glints with it.*)

CANTON: That doesn't frighten me.

SAVAGE: No.

(*He passes the ax from hand to hand over his head, does tricks with it, slicing the air. The blade whistles, gleams.*)

SAVAGE: You're a juggler, right? I'll chop off your ears, that'll give you something to juggle.

CANTON: Come on. Do it. *Come on.*

(SAVAGE *advances, swishing the ax over his head.*)

SAVAGE: The goods—where are they? Where are they?

CANTON: What *goods*?

(CANTON *skips and dodges away.* SAVAGE *comes after him, slicing the air with the ax, narrowly missing.*)

CHRISSIE: Please, Bob, please. Give him what he wants.

CANTON: I don't know what he wants. Goods? There's nothing here. Don't you see that?

(SAVAGE *lunges at* CANTON.)

CHRISSIE: (*Screams*) Look out, Len! He knows karate!

(CANTON *sidesteps him;* SAVAGE *trips and goes sprawling. The ax flies from his hand.* CANTON *and* SAVAGE *grapple for it.* CANTON *comes up with it.*)

SAVAGE: No fair. You used karate. In a fair fight I'd take you any day.

CANTON: Now what do you want from me? Huh? Huh?

SAVAGE: Easy, Bob. Don't take this so personal.

CANTON: I do take it personal. I take it very personal.

(CANTON *starts for the telephone.*)

CHRISSIE: What are you going to do?

(CANTON *at the phone lifts the receiver.*)

CANTON: How'd you like jail, Len? Meet a lot of class people. Your *crowd.*

(*He dials.*)

CANTON: Hello, connect me to the sheriff's—hello. (*He realizes the phone cord has been yanked.*)

CANTON: Shit.

SAVAGE: (*Advancing*) Give me the ax, Bob.

CANTON: Come close, you'll get it in your head. If I were you, I'd jump into my Rolls Royce or whatever the hell you have, and get out of here fast.

SAVAGE: I'm not going anywhere. Give me that ax.

CANTON: Come and get it.

SAVAGE: You'll never use it.

CANTON: Try me.

(SAVAGE *starts toward* CANTON *who brandishes the ax.*)

CANTON: I mean it. I'll brain you.

(SAVAGE *moves nearer.*)

SAVAGE: Let's see you, let's see you—

CHRISSIE: Bob, no!

CANTON: Don't—

SAVAGE: Give it here.

(SAVAGE *leaps toward* CANTON. CANTON *brings the ax hard down on* SAVAGE'S *shoulder, then whacks him across the chest.* CHRISSIE *screams.*)

(SAVAGE, *apparently mortally wounded, totters, begins to fall.* CANTON *looks on, appalled.*)

(*Then:* SAVAGE *suddenly leaps up straight, laughing wildly.* CANTON *examines the ax, tests the blade. It bends.*)

CANTON: Oh, come on. Come on.

SAVAGE: (*Grinning*) What's the problem, Bobby?

CANTON: It's rubber. It's goddamn rubber. *Rubber.*

CHRISSIE: Oh, Len. Now that's not funny. That's not funny at all.

SAVAGE: Hey, a real ax, someone could get hurt.

CHRISSIE: There's a time and a place. Do you know what you did to my nerves there? Look at my hands. Look at them. (*She holds out her hands.*)

CANTON: You people are mickey-mouse. Mickey-*mouse.* Toy pistol. Rubber ax. I've had it with you two. You have no style.

SAVAGE: Now wait a minute, Bob—

CHRISSIE: Anybody have a valium? My nerves—

CANTON: I mean, come in here, terrorize me with mickey-mouse weapons. Call that style? Jesus.

SAVAGE: What are you complaining about, Bob? No one got hurt did they? What are you, a violence freak? All people want these days—blood and guts.

(CANTON *and* SAVAGE *sit opposite each other.* CHRISSIE *moves to the bar.*)

CHRISSIE: Drink, Len?

SAVAGE: Drink'd be nice.

(*She attempts to pour some Seagram's. The bottle is empty.*)

CHRISSIE: All we got is Wild Turkey.

SAVAGE: Yeah, that's fine.

Chrissie: Bob?

Canton: What? Oh. Yes.

(*She pours the drinks.*)

(Canton *sits on the couch, stares at the floor, looking lost, alone.*)

Canton: I mean, here I am looking forward to a quiet evening. A drink or two, a reminiscent song on the stereo. In the background the ocean rolling, the crash of waves—

Chrissie: Crashhhhhh.

Canton: Wind off the water, moan and creak of roofbeams—

Chrissie: Ooooooooooooooooooooh, krikkkkkkkkkkkk.

Canton: Later perhaps I set up my projector, home movies. I like those nights. You upgrade the quality of the inner being. Conjure up the past, anticipate the future.

Savage: Yes.

Chrissie: A quiet evening.

Canton: Then this.

Savage: We've had a few laughs, haven't we, Bob?

Canton: Well. Laughs.

Savage: The night's early. There'll be more.

(Chrissie, *serving the drinks:*)

Chrissie: Rubber-fucking-ax. You're too much.

Savage: You had your toy pistol. Why can't I have my little joke?

Canton: Yet even in our fantasies—

(Chrissie *hands him his drink.*)

Chrissie: Cheers, Bob.

(*He accepts it without looking at her.*)

Canton: —we lack control. They erupt in tawdry ways, never seem to pan out. Have to get my act together. I seem never to leave the house, stay drunk for days.

Chrissie: Bottoms up, Bobby.

(*She drinks deeply.* Savage *rises, paces briskly.*)

Savage: Forget the past. Let's get your act—

CANTON: —together.

SAVAGE: Get down to facts. Hard facts. What about all them goods?

CANTON: I told you—I have nothing. No goods. I don't want to talk about goods! Jeez.

SAVAGE: The gold records, the diamonds—

CANTON: Nothing. I don't know where you got such a silly, stupid idea.

(SAVAGE *stands as though struck by lightning. Long pause.*)

SAVAGE: Well, what the hell am I doing here, then? Freddie the Greek? Moustafa Gumshoe?

CANTON: Moustafa Gumshoe! Do I look like a man who would know anyone called *Moustafa Gumshoe?*

SAVAGE: It's possible . . .

CANTON: No, it's not. It's very unlikely. None of it fits! I mean you say I'm a dope-dealing record producer. I mean, look at this house. *It's not on the Colony Road.* I mean it's absurd!

SAVAGE: You know what I think? I made a mistake here! I can't believe it. How? How can this be? Jesus, fella, I owe you an apology—

CANTON: Well—

SAVAGE: I know how it goes. The way of the world. The thing of it is, she promises you the sun, moon, and stars, and you negotiate down from there. Stick to car mufflers, Bob. Her body—

(CHRISSIE *twirls around.*)

CHRISSIE: Ta dah!

CANTON: —is a dangerous weapon. I get the picture. She's the one to blame.

CHRISSIE: Hey wait a minute. When I talked to you on the phone—

SAVAGE: Don't put it on me. I'm tired of taking the rap for you. Con-fucking-artist, come to me with these intricate rip-offs. I'm getting heated. I can't help it. Give me some more of that Wild Turkey.

(CHRISSIE *moves to the bar, pours out more drinks.*)

CHRISSIE: Gobble, gobble, gobble . . .

SAVAGE: Okay, Bob, you want the bottom line, I'm going to give you the bottom line. This is the way it went here, on my mother's grave. I was on the beach somewheres, Redondo, Huntington—

CHRISSIE: —Venice.

SAVAGE: Down by the beach. You'll appreciate this. And I meet her, this one, Chrissie—

CANTON: Ah.

SAVAGE: She had her clothes on, then. Looked like class. Who knew she was an exhibitionist?

(CHRISSIE *returns from the bar with the drinks, passes them out, then flops down on the couch.*)

CHRISSIE: Looked like class? I am fucking class.

SAVAGE: Yeah. Life in the fast lane, she says. Doesn't even own a car. Bob, take it from me, never get involved with a psychopath. Listen to this scheme: "You know so-and-so?" she says. "I know him. The worst. You know him?"

CHRISSIE: "The worst."

SAVAGE: "You know such-and-such bar?"

CHRISSIE: "The Rainbow, in Hollywood."

SAVAGE: "This lame motherfucker comes in there, big record producer."

CHRISSIE: "Likes young girls."

SAVAGE: "I know the one."

CHRISSIE: That's just the way it went.

SAVAGE: That's just the way I said it. This is the way it went, Bob. "The man owns eight record companies, he's the wealthiest man in this town, I've had dinners with him. It's nothing for him to spend 400 dollars."

CHRISSIE: I never—

SAVAGE: Pathological liar! You said you'd love to kill him. Has gold records all over the place, money stacked on the mantle piece, ash trays filled with ace-high blow. Murderous cunt. Kill him, you said, it'd teach him a lesson.

CANTON: Kill me? She really said that?'

SAVAGE: This is the way it went, on my mother's grave, Bob. Death is psychosomatic, that kind of thing.

CHRISSIE: Life in the fast lane.

SAVAGE: Give me a break. I eat my lunch in the fast lane. My world is the fast lane.

CHRISSIE: Why didn't you kill him, then? You're such a tough guy. You've killed this one, you killed that. You've killed shit.

SAVAGE: Don't tell me what I've killed. I know what I've killed.

CHRISSIE: Bull-*shit*, excuse my mouth.

SAVAGE: You think it's so easy to kill a man? You got flesh to go through and muscle and fucking bone. It's hard work and it's dirty. And you get a lot of screaming and crying. Don't tell me about killing. Who needs it? Can't sleep at night. People look at you funny. Sometimes you even get arrested, go to fucking jail. No one likes a killer.

CHRISSIE: But they respect a killer.

SAVAGE: Who needs that kind of respect? You don't get love.

CHRISSIE: Respect is better than love. Love is fantasy, respect has substance. You hear this, Canton? This is the kind of discussions our crowd has all the time—

CANTON: Hmmm.

SAVAGE: I'll do anything for a cunt. Act the big shot, demean myself. What for? She wanted me to kill you, hear that? That's a woman for you. Blood and guts, they get off on it.

CHRISSIE: I didn't want you to kill him.

SAVAGE: What did you say before?

CHRISSIE: I never said that.

SAVAGE: What did you say? I got a photographic memory so don't fuck me around. What did you say?

CHRISSIE: There's no talking to you. You're very hard and excitable., Isn't our crowd fabulous, Bob?

CANTON: Well. Your crowd? Yes. A fun crowd.

SAVAGE: I have a sense of responsibility, you said. When I commit, I commit. This is facts, this is word for word.

CHRISSIE: You're twisting everything.

SAVAGE: In school for me, Bob, history was a snap. Names, dates, facts. Ask me anything of a historical nature.

CANTON: Magna Carta.

SAVAGE: What?

CANTON: Date. Magna Carta.

SAVAGE: American history, Bob.

CHRISSIE: Look, I didn't want you to *kill* him, understand? I just wanted to know you were capable.

SAVAGE: I am capable. I am.

CHRISSIE: Rubber ax?

SAVAGE: You're getting me fucking angry. I am fucking angry now. I am an-gry.

(SAVAGE *leaps up and grabs a chair; raises it above* CANTON.)

SAVAGE: You don't think I'd kill him? You don't think so?

CANTON: Hey, wait a second here—

SAVAGE: Well, I'll tell you something. I could—but I won't. I won't do that. Just because you're goading. (*To* CANTON) Bob, really. I meant American history. Like the War of 1812. Dates like that. Go on, ask me anything.

CHRISSIE: Didn't you hear what he called you before? Mickey-mouse! That's what the world thinks of you. Mickey-mickey-mouse!

SAVAGE: I'm getting upset. Now I'm getting upset. Okay, let me cool down. The thing of it is, Bob, to get back to my drift, some people think death is psychosomatic. What's your opinion—as a medical man?

CANTON: It's not black and white.

SAVAGE: It's not black and white. You hear that now?

CHRISSIE: I never said it was.

SAVAGE: Just listen to the man, you'll learn something.

CANTON: In the case of my wife death started very small. A spot, a mole. I recognized it, diagnosed it.

SAVAGE: Yeah.

CANTON: Melanoma. Cancer. Skin.

SAVAGE: Right. I'm following you.

CANTON: Nothing could be done.

SAVAGE: Nothing could be done. That's a rough one.

Canton: The mole, you see, is malignant, cancer originating in primitive pigment cells. Spreads like fire into the skin, through the blood stream. My wife—

Chrissie: Yes—

Canton: —was consumed.

(Savage *leans forward toward* Canton.)

Savage: Did you love her? Or was it a marriage of convenience?

Canton: Love her?

Savage: Bottom line.

Canton: Yes, I believe I loved her.

Savage: You believe—

Canton: I loved her very much.

Savage: Tough.

Canton: Well.

(Chrissie *begins to weep.*)

Chrissie: Jeez, that's—that's—I'm very touched by all this.

Canton: (*Brightly*) We're having a fun time, aren't we?

Savage: This is what I would call a broadening experience of confrontation and revelation.

Canton: Fabulous.

Savage: (*To* Chrissie) Come over here.

Chrissie: I like it here.

Savage: Come here!

(*She does not move.*)

Canton: All right. What I'd like to show—

Savage: What is it, Bob?

Canton: Well—

Savage: Touching love letters from the little lady? A flower petal preserved in the pages of a book of poetry?

Canton: Yes, well. I mean, no—it's some film I took.

(Canton *rises and moves to the dresser. There is a movie projector on top.* Canton *begins to set it up.*)

CANTON: When she was dying, my wife—I bought this camera, Super 8, sound. I was certain I wouldn't have her very long, and I didn't—trust my memory. I had begun forgetting things. A kind of madness was burrowing in. There had been holes, terrifying gaps in my thought—

SAVAGE: That camera, that Super 8? You like it?

(CANTON *is trying, without much success, to thread the projector.*)

CANTON: Oh, yes. Fine. Fine.

SAVAGE: I thought about getting one, you know? Handy for picnics. You know, preserve things that touch one deeply. Childhood, the halcyon days. Family gatherings. Nice on Super 8. How you doing there, Bob?

(*He is hopelessly tangled in film.*)

CANTON: I'm doing fine. I'm a fun guy. Olė!

CHRISSIE: This film, Bob, it's not sexy, is it?

CANTON: Sexy? No. No.

SAVAGE: See what you're faced with, Bob? If you don't give 'em tits and ass they're disappointed.

(CANTON *snaps on the projector. Against the rear wall, the film comes on, upside down and backward.* SAVAGE *watches with interest.*)

SAVAGE: What's this, an art film, Bob?

(CANTON *realizes the film has been threaded wrong. He turns off the projector and begins to rethread it.*)

CHRISSIE: There's nothing wrong with sex. When it's an expression of love.

SAVAGE: In its place. Between strangers. Don't flaunt it. Save it for the back rooms. Lonely nights. My mother was a woman of dubious reputation; she'd give herself for the amenities: the butcher, the druggist. She wanted shoes for us, there'd be a shoe salesman. She's whisk me away, 'go play with your yo-yo, Little Lenny.' I cried: "My yo-yo's falling apart', so she humped a Filipino named Carlos and I had me a Super Spinner with iridescent spool. Like that.

CHRISSIE: Oh, Len, that's so sad.

SAVAGE: What sad? Look at me: that woman made me what I am today, which is pretty terrific. (*A beat*) Excuse me, I get all choked up when I think about dear old Mom. That bitch!

(CANTON *turns on the projector again. The film plays on the rear wall. A dying woman lies in bed. The woman looks very much like* CHRISSIE. *She is staring at the camera.*)

(CHRISSIE *watches, bored. She does not notice the resemblance.*)

WOMAN: (*In the film*) "What is it, hon?"

CANTON'S VOICE: (*Off camera, in film*) "I just want to—"

WOMAN: "I look awful."

(CANTON *is staring at* CHRISSIE. *She stifles a yawn.*)

CANTON'S VOICE: (*In film*) "You look fine."

WOMAN: "I saw myself in the mirror this morning. I'm becoming a skull."

CANTON'S VOICE: "No—"

(*We hear* CANTON *in the film sobbing off camera.*)

WOMAN: "Don't do that, honey. Please. Don't do that."

(CANTON *watches* CHRISSIE *intently. She is bored, restless. She glances at her wrist watch.* SAVAGE *is totally absorbed in the film.*)

CANTON'S VOICE: (*In film, stifled*) "I can't help it. Oh, God."

WOMAN: "Please."

(*The sobbing increases. The room in the film goes every which-way as the camera, still running, falls to the bed. In the film we see* CANTON *embrace his wife. The film ends.*)

(CANTON *snaps off the projector, begins to take the film off the reel.* CHRISSIE *stands, visibly peeved.*)

CHRISSIE: Why show that? It's *ugly*.

CANTON: No, no—it's a fun film. You're not looking at it in the proper perspective—

CHRISSIE: Films shouldn't be ugly. There should be romance and flowers. Pretty people doing pretty things.

CANTON: (*To* SAVAGE) There's a resemblance. Did you notice?

SAVAGE: Resemblance?

CANTON: A cetain-resemblance.

CHRISSIE: Oh, please. (*She stretches and yawns.*)

CHRISSIE: Well, nothing moving but the clock.

(*She starts toward the back room.* SAVAGE *moves to block her way.*)

SAVAGE: Where are you going?

CHRISSIE: To get dressed. Isn't that what you've been yelling about?

SAVAGE: Your clothes are right there.

CHRISSIE: Those aren't my clothes.

(*She moves for the back room door.*)

SAVAGE: Don't go in there.

(CHRISSIE *hesitates, turns back to* SAVAGE, *then continues to the door.*)

SAVAGE: I said don't go in there!

(CHRISSIE *stops in front of the door, turns to face* SAVAGE.)

SAVAGE: Get over here. Did you hear me? *Get over here.*

(CHRISSIE *does not move.*)

SAVAGE: Over here. Over. Get—get—

(CHRISSIE *stares at him impassively.* SAVAGE *has become like a small child.*)

SAVAGE: Please.

CHRISSIE: Sometime's it's easier to die than to earn a buck.

(*She enters the back room.* SAVAGE *sinks down into a chair, staring off.* CANTON *moves to him.*)

CANTON: Len?

SAVAGE: What does she know about love? What do I have now? Without her? I was set up, conned.

(*He rises and begins to move about the room, straightening up. He picks up an empty bottle, some glasses, takes them to the bar.* CANTON *watches.*)

SAVAGE: I was already wearing those diamond rings, plastering my walls with gold records. When you live life in the fast lane you got to keep up appearances. And now—

CANTON: —it's all fading—

(CANTON *moves to the window, stares out. He turns to the room.*)

CANTON: Sometimes when it's quiet out here, in the black heart of the night, I permit her to walk into my life again. You adjust the light, get it at a certain angle—

(CANTON *moves to the lamp, turns it down. The room is almost dark now, just a small area of light.* SAVAGE *is in shadow.*)

Canton: I play out whole scenes with her. I capture her again. I study her skin. I try to come to terms with her death.

Savage: (*His voice is very quiet now; we can barely see him.*) As a doctor, you must know—

Canton: Doctor?

Savage: —nothing fits the way you imagine it.

Canton: Doctor.

Savage: And that's the way of the world.

(Savage *is barely visible in the dark.*)

Savage: Well. I'll be going now, Bob.

(*He picks up the rubber ax. Holds it up. Its silhouette casts an ominous shadow. He returns it to its case.*)

Canton: (*Talking to* Savage's *dark form.*) You can stay with me.

Savage: I have people waiting. My crowd. You know, from where I live, the whole world appears like a jeweler's tray, the sky all stars, the city lights, clotted diamonds spilling into the ocean. The nights are cool, an icy edge. You look down the hillside behind you, you can see the freeway—

Canton: You can stay, Len. If you want—

(*A beat.* Savage *comes out of the darkness into the light.*)

Savage: She's yours, doctor. Don't turn your back, though. She'll knife you in a second.

(Canton *turns from* Savage *to the window.*)

Savage: You'll have to come visit up at the house, Doc.

(Canton *does not answer.* Savage *returns to shadow, moves to the front door.*)

Savage: (*Quieter*) Doctor? Doctor Canton . . .

(Savage *exits.* Canton *continues to stare out the window.* Chrissie *enters the room dressed not in her own clothes, but in something pale, demure. She is transformed. She sits on the couch.*)

Chrissie: (*Her voice is quiet, refined*) Darling, would you fix me a drink? You know the way I like it.

(Canton *moves to the liquor cart. He does not take his eyes from her.*)

CHRISSIE: And turn on some music.

(CANTON *snaps on the stereo. Willie Nelson singing, "I Want To Be With You Always," comes on.*)

CHRISSIE: How was your day?

(CANTON *does not answer.*)

CHRISSIE: Darling?

(*He does not answer.*)

CHRISSIE: The lab report—did you see it?

(*He does not answer.*)

CHRISSIE: What did it say?

(*He does not answer. He has poured her drink. He moves to her with it. He hands it to her. She is staring at him with a look of infinite sadness.*)

END

Mac Wellman

Energumen

MAC WELLMAN's first plays were commissioned and produced by K.R.O. Radio in The Netherlands. One of these, *Fama Combinatoria*, was subsequently staged at the Theatre "De Brakke Grond" in Amsterdam in 1975, and later performed in ten other Dutch cities and in Belgium. In 1976 his play *The Memory Theatre of Giordano Bruno* was produced at the W.P.A. in Washington, D.C. A K.R.O. version of the piece, completed in 1979, was selected to represent The Netherlands at the Prix d'Italia competition for radio-drama. In the same year his play *Starluster* was staged at the American Place Theatre, and later published in the *Performing Arts Journal's Wordplays* anthology. In 1982 his one-act *The Self-Begotten* appeared in the Ensemble Studio Theatre's Marathon. As Playwright-in-Residence at the Bay Area Playwrights Festival in 1983 he worked on the *Phantomnation* collaboration.

Wellman's most recent productions include *The Professional Frenchman* at the Brass Tacks Theatre in Minneapolis, as well as *Energumen* at the Soho Rep. As Playwright-in-Residence at NYU he adapted Lope de Vega's *Dog in the Manger*. He edited *Breathing Space*, a collection of sound-text art, for *Black Box*, a literary magazine on cassette tape. Wellman also has edited an anthology of new American drama entitled *Theatre of Wonders*, forthcoming from Sun & Moon Press. His poetry, plays, and articles have appeared in many publications. Wellman's books of poetry include *In Praise of Secrecy* (1977), *Satires* (1984), and the forthcoming *Art of the Apostrophe*. His play *Harm's Way* is published by Broadway Play Publishing, and his *No Smoking Piece* and *The Porcupine Man* (with music by Michael S. Roth) appear in Broadway Play Publishing's *Short Pieces from The New Dramatists*.

For stock and amateur production rights, contact: Broadway Play Publishing, Inc., 357 West 20th Street, New York, NY 10011. For all other rights, contact: Helen Merrill, 337 West 22nd Street, New York, NY 10011.

Persons of the Play

MEGAN FEATHER, a young person

JACQUES PETIT, a "Professional Frenchman"

DEBORAH MARTIN, a deprogrammer

MR. FEATHER, a concerned parent

SAMUEL NUTLEY, a deprogrammer

THE MASTER OF MANY PERFECTIONS, alias John Sleight

And various WAITERS, SANTAS, and DISCIPLES at the "Seat of Bliss and Perfect Understanding".

Energumen is the first in a series of five plays that take place at various locations in Washington, D.C. and other capitals of the Free World. The others are, in order of composition: *Diseases of the Well-Dressed*; *The Professional Frenchman*; *The Self-Begotten*; and *The Bad Infinity*.

As mentioned above, the action of *Energumen* occurs at various locations in the D.C. area, during the Christmas season.

MEGAN and JACQUES are in their late 20s; DEBORAH and SAM, in their 30s; THE MASTER OF MANY PERFECTIONS is about 45; and FEATHER is older, perhaps 65. All are elegantly dressed throughout.

Energumen is a toy of figments.

The play is for Yolanda.

Scene One

(*An elegant private club.* DEBORAH *sits knitting.* SAM *enters and sits down. A* SANTA *stands by a Christmas tree upstage at the street entrance.*)

SAM: Can I borrow some money?

DEBORAH: I had to borrow myself.

(*Pause*)

SAM:
Feng, at the laundry, is restive.
Threatens to burn my shirts.
I'm going to lunch with old man Feather.
Look at these shoes.

DEBORAH: She was just here.

SAM: That was silly of you.

DEBORAH: She came on her own.

SAM: What are you knitting?

DEBORAH: You still owe me for the last job, bucko.

SAM: You knit horribly, bucko.

DEBORAH: Nope.

SAM:
Look, I'm very sure the old man'll
give me a check as an advance.

DEBORAH:
I do believe our little disciple
has shown her hand.

SAM: Howso?

DEBORAH: Never you mind. Just yet.

SAM:
Has she mentioned
"The Master of Many Perfections" and
"The Seat of Bliss and Perfect Understanding"?

DEBORAH: What makes you think she mixed up with that?

Sam:
You don't think she's fallen in with ordinary
Jesus freaks!? She's too well-bred for that.

Deborah: She makes up fake dreams to confuse her shrink.

Sam: How could you tell?

Deborah: When she was a child she dyed pigeons different colors.

Sam:
I would have expected some kind
of political mania, but then
you and I have no common
ground as far as that goes,
do we? Someone has the hook
in her. Up to the elbow.

Deborah: Your metaphor's atrocious.

Sam:
One cannot be witty and think
at the same time. That desperate
again? I see "law school" written
all over your face.

Deborah:
I'll hang around long enough to
watch you make a fool of yourself
again. Look, I'm broke.

(*Pause*)

Sam: Hooks can have elbows.

Deborah: Where will you lunch?

Sam: I have no idea.

Deborah: You see that man?

Sam: You mean Santa Claus?

Deborah: He's been watching us again.

Sam:
In that case I'm going across the street
for a pack of cigarettes. And a shoe shine.

(*He gets up to go. She holds up a ten-dollar bill. He snatches it and
strides out. Pause.*)

Scene Two

(*The Club.* DEBORAH *and* MR. FEATHER *are talking while seated on a sofa. The* SANTA *stands by a Christmas tree near the entrance. Next to him is a kettle, suspended from a tripod, for charitable donations.*)

FEATHER:
. . . bloated, horribly bloated.
I had no idea Mr. Nutley and
I belong to the same club.

DEBORAH: He doesn't. I do.

FEATHER: Oh.

(*Pause*)

We old fossils have fixed ideas
in some respects. Very fixed.

DEBORAH: Yes, I am told that.

FEATHER:
Of course you realize that until five
years ago this was a men's club,
exclusively.

DEBORAH: Would you like to see the contract?

FEATHER:
The one thing you must promise is
absolute secrecy. In Sophy's state
Megan's departure was quite a shock.
For me as well. My attorney
is a horse's ass, and I don't know
that I should trust you, but I do.
Mr. Nutley is a story, hasn't he?

DEBORAH: He's a walking comic book.

(*Pause*)

FEATHER:
I like women who knit. It seems
like a restful activity. Will
Mr. Nutley be here soon?

DEBORAH: Will you sign?

FEATHER: What is it?

DEBORAH: I beg your pardon?

FEATHER: What exactly are you knitting?

DEBORAH: I wonder where he is?

FEATHER: For someone special?

DEBORAH: For whomever it fits.

FEATHER:
You have no idea how badly
this has affected poor Sophy
with her continual swelling.
It is a mistake to suppose that a young
person possesses any more of innocence
than one would find in a young animal.
Mischievousness, yes; innocence, no.
When I was a child I was fully
aware of what I was doing
as I manipulated my parents,
for I knew exactly how to
wheedle and whine my way
into their good graces. So that
I could get whatever I wanted.

(*Pause*)

I am not a proud man, but I am careful.

DEBORAH:
Perfection of the human spirit is not
what we promise. Only a little improvement
of the ratiocinative faculty, in the reality-
testing area.

FEATHER:
Needless to say I did not get everything
I wanted. One never does. Rarely.
What I am trying to express is my concern
that this hated energumen be plucked
from her brain.

(SAM *enters. He spits in* SANTA'S *face, vaults that sofa, and ends sitting next to the astonished* FEATHER.)

SAM: My name is Samuel Nutley.

FEATHER: Where on Earth did you come from?

SAM: Miss Martin, may I see the affadavits?

DEBORAH: Of course, Mr. Nutley.

FEATHER: My word, he appeared so suddenly . . .

(*Pause*)
My daughter is of the changeable
sort. She tottered on the brink of faith
early, but then for no apparent reason . . .

(*Pause*)

But let me begin at the beginning.

(*Pause*)

She went to the Beauvoir School at Washington Cathedral.
Acquired a few felicities of proper decorum. Went on
to Vassar and studied the sciences. That I opposed.
Physics smacks of wizardry nowadays. Who can control
a child who refutes straight lines and who tell you
that if you walk out the front door and continue walking
in a googolplex of centuries you are bound to enter the
same room by the back door? It's absurd and undisciplined.
And then there was sex and drugs.

(*Pause*)

Her mother's strange illness began then.

SANTA:
Hey you, motherfuck! are you going to
fork over the goods or what!? Well?
Your fucking heart is made of fucking stone,
I'll bet! You got no feelings of charity,
I'll bet! You spit right in Santa's face,
man, and that is downright bush league.

(*A* GUARD *pulls him away.*)

SAM: Go on.

FEATHER: Was that man addressing us?

DEBORAH:
The most terrible, or rather, one of the most
terrible aspects of this kind of phenomenon
is the guilt aroused often unjustifiably
in the parent.

FEATHER:
But Miss Martin I have no feelings
of that sort altogether. It's rather
shocking how lighthearted I feel.

Sam:
You have offices in Washington, New York, Richmond,
Indianapolis, Sapporo, and Curaçao?

Feather:
You are curious why we do not
contemplate a move?

Sam: Precisely.

Feather:
I am an old man. My wife is ill.
Our lobbying efforts, which are critical
for the well-being of the firm, positively
demand close, continual attention . . .

Deborah: Mr. Nutley is not trying to pry.

Feather:
Sorry if I seem fractious. After Iran
I'm afraid I see ghouls of antibusiness
everywhere. Even in the service professions.

Sam: Words are wonderful! I am fascinated
by a word you used, Mister Feather.
The word *energumen*. It is a favorite
of mine also:
"If then this Energumenus
hath a thousand lengths
and breadths that are so
many crosses against her."
Words are indeed wonderful.
If you engage in billing and cooing
in English it may be assumed that
among other things some rubbing
of noses, or bills, takes place.
In Dutch the word *bill* signifies one
of one's posterior cheeks, or buns, as
they are commonly known. The word *koe* [*Pronounced*: "coo"]
means cow. Moo. So that in the Netherlandish
language billing and cooing might have a
startling set of associations. For a Dutchman.

(*Pause*)

Let it pass. But the really curious
fact about the word energumen
is that it signifies both the possessed

person proper and the demonic agent.
Both possessor and possessee are, in fact,
energumen. What do you think of that?

(*Pause*)

FEATHER: Mister Nutley, I'm afraid I don't follow.

DEBORAH: Mister Nutley is fond of cryptic parables.

SAM:
Now Mister Feather, is it not a fact that
Mrs. Feather and the Secretary of State share
the same astrologer?

FEATHER: Good gracious! How did you know that?

SAM: No matter. Let it pass.

FEATHER:
Mister Nutley, I'm afraid I don't see the point
of any of this.

SAM:
Getting back to the word *bill*: I am afraid,
in this instance, I shall be forced to double
my fee.

(*Pause*)

FEATHER:
Mister Nutley, if you save my daughter
you may triple it.

Scene Three

(MEGAN *and three* SANTAS *in the back room of La Belle Epoque, each with a music stand.* MEGAN *is leading them in a choral version of the* Internationale. *She is disappointed with their performance.*)

MEGAN:
Gentlemen.
You have to be more precise.
There's simply no excuse
for this kind of sloppy work.

(*They suffle about.*)

FIRST SANTA: Rome wasn't built in a day, Miss Feather.

MEGAN:
Mister Claus,
We are not building Rome.

We are tearing it down.
From the top.

(*They sing*)

Scene Four

(DEBORAH *and* FEATHER *chatting at The Club. The* SANTA *is absent.*)

FEATHER:
You interest me, Sam. These days
failure and adversity and hardship
tend to dispirit people. Everyone
wants more money, of course, but
very few men are willing to do
what's required to keep it. You,
on the other hand, seem to thrive
on adversity. I like that.

SAM: A patchwork is what I am, sir, I'm afraid.

FEATHER: Nothing wrong with that.

SAM: In that sense, there's nothing wrong with
anything.

FEATHER:
But you know it. That's the thing, Sam.
It frees you.

(*Pause*)

I had words with her mother
last night. It appears the child
is absolutely dead set on pursuing
the object of her enthusiasm.

SAM: How is Mrs. Feather?

FEATHER:
Bad, badly. The swelling has gone down
appreciably, but what with all this . . .
I shouldn't wonder if we'll have a new
round of punctures and drainings.

SAM: I seem to have misplaced my watch.

(*Pause*)

What time do you have? She will
be joining us in about five minutes.

FEATHER:
As you can imagine I had quite
a spell of time to mull things over, to sort
out difficulties and to assess, as best I could,
the positive and negative elephants of life, my life,
when I was in jail.

SAM: (*Looking for the watch.*) Now isn't that funny? Oh, sorry.

FEATHER:
If you look in the mirror over the fireplace
you can see, as though it were a picture,
the front door. Ah, and old Saint Nick . . .
The Senator proved very helpful once
I got out, you know. A very loyal man,
the Senator, and a credit to our party,
and to the country.
When Megan began going through her "radical"
phase, he scotched some rather nasty charges
a lot of Dupont Circle shopkeepers had
got up against her, Jews the lot of them.
She had been banging up windows with her
friends, perfectly harmless stuff. But the
Senator saved Sophy and I considerable embarrassment
I assure you . . .

(*Pause*)

As for my conviction

(*Pause*)

I wear it like a badge of honor.

(*Pause*)

And, of course, when I got out six months
later he introduced me to representatives of the
Intertop Corporation, and everything has proceeded
very nicely since then. I rather like Switzerland,
in fact. Going freelance is risky, Sam, very risky.
That's the main thing I've learned.

SAM:
It's very difficult, sir. But I'm afraid
I will need money, sir, in order to proceed
with the affair.

FEATHER: Why didn't you say so, Sam? Hell.

(*Hands him an envelope.*)

Sam: Thank you, sir.

Feather: (*Hands* Sam *the missing watch.*)
And this, I bet you never noticed, didn't you?
You should be more careful, my boy! Just
one of the things I picked up *inside.*

Sam: You must have wonderful reflexes, sir.

Feather:
Like a man of thirty, Sam. It's all up here.
Ah, there she is!

(Deborah *enters.*)

Scene Five

(*The Club.* Deborah, Sam, *and* Feather, *who is dressed as a* Santa. *There is Christmas music. They sit by the fire, chatting.*)

Sam:
I have this friend. He's an old
Washingtonian. That means he's
been here maybe fifteen years, a
real lowlife type, but hardworking,
a bartender, cab driver, gambling
man out of Detroit. No,
he saw the way things were
headed and went off to
the Berlitz School . . .

(*Pause*)

Not to learn French, but to
acquire a real French accent.
He and his friends now own
an extremely chic place "La Belle Epoque",
on Pennsylvania Avenue. Oh, there's an
American bar down the road a bit . . .
And he goes there and I go there and
we all kid him about it.
His name's Jacques Petit now,
but he's got money in the bank.
We call him "The Professional
Frenchman" . . . Food's not bad.

(*Pause*)

Feather:
Miss Martin, I like Mr. Nutley.
I like the way his mind works.

You know what it is, Sam?
It's the law of mimicry.

DEBORAH:
You shouldn't go around
spitting in people's faces, Sam.

SAM: Whatever are you talking about?

DEBORAH: That Santa the other day was the real thing.

(*Pause*)

FEATHER: It's "protective coloring". I like both of you.

Scene Six

(*La Belle Epoque. After hours.* MEGAN *performs for* JACQUES, *who sits with his back to the audience.*)

MEGAN:
Such a nice time we are having! Now you're
upset! Your moods change so rapidly it's
quite hard to figure you out. But I shall
try. Would you like to hear a story? I tell
stories. The kind few people have the patience
to listen to. At the "Seat of Bliss" they think
I'm a kind of enlightened seeress. I can speak in
tongues. Once upon a time there was a
tongue. It rode lazily downstream in a
canoe until it came to a place where the river
forked. It decided it would grow onto a
human being. It wanted to say something
so it could make up its mind which way to go.
It couldn't make up its mind without speaking
but it couldn't speak. The tongue thought it
might turn into a snake with a forked tongue.
Then it could take both paths, I mean streams.
But in order to do that it would have to tell lies,
and our precious little tongue didn't want to.
George Washington Tongue.
Well it got so frustrated it turned into a
penis. *Moi, je deteste les penises.*
You think I'm crazy, don't you?
My parents' expensive shrink
says I'm a chronic hysteric.
I think I'm a heavenly being.
What do you think about that, mon?

(*Pause*)

I'M A TERRIBLE FEROCIOUS MONSTER
AND I EAT UP LITTLE BOYS LIKE YOU.

(*Pause*)

JACQUES: Can't you make it a little more convincing,
you know, heartfelt?

MEGAN: (*Looks puzzled*)
So you don't think he'll go for it?

JACQUES:
Remember how it was in acting class?
You've got to connect with the material.
Sincere.

Scene Seven

(SAM, *disguised, applies for disciplehood at the Seat of Bliss and Perfect Understanding, which occupies a grand old house in Washington, D.C. SAM kneels facing THE MASTER OF MANY PERFECTIONS, who also kneels. The scene begins with a long pause.*)

MASTER: Tell me, my son, why have you come?

SAM: I am seeking enlightenment.

MASTER: There are many paths.

SAM: There is only one way.

(*Pause*)

MASTER: It is a hard thing to deny the craving for the world.

SAM: The world is veil, master. I seek release.

MASTER:
We live for one another within the ashram.
There is no "mine" or "yours". All that
is a fading of light into darkness.

SAM:
All I have, master, is a Rolex watch.
But it is a new one.

MASTER: May I see the watch, my son.

(*He takes the watch and examines it.*)

You are heavy with sin, my son.
Your spirit creeps.

SAM: All the days of my life are an unspoken anguish.

MASTER: Here is your watch, my son.

SAM: Please accept the watch as a gift.

(*Pause*)

MASTER:
Time is not a proper gift from one free man
to another.

SAM: Time is dust. We exist in time.

MASTER: We exist to die in time. And to awake in eternity.

(*Pause*)

I will accept the watch.

SAM: What instruction will you give me?

MASTER:
I have no instruction. That is my instruction.
There is only endless renunciation.

SAM:
I am nothing,
spun out of nothing,
as a cloak to nothing,
speaking nothingnesses.

(*Pause*)

MASTER:
You are full of the world's cunning yet.
We shall beat that out of you.

(*Pause*)

Now go.

SAM: Thank you, master.

(*He gets up.*)

MASTER:
The watch is not enough.
We must have money.
We must have money.
The raiment of existence
must be soiled. So that
eternity's flame shines
all the brighter.
Bring money.

(*Pause*)

It *is* you.

Sam: Yes, John.

(*Pause*)

Master:
I am not concerned
with you purpose,
only your presence, Sam.
Bring money next time.

Sam: Yes, Master.

Scene Eight

(*The basement of the Seat of Bliss. Sam and two Women, one of whom is
Megan, toiling over identical washtubs doing laundry. Behind them the
usual Christmas tree and an ominous Santa. Indonesian music. Sam is
obviously troubled by the Santa.*)

Megan:
He will often say things which
upon first hearing sound quite
stupid and boring, but upon
further reflection sprout into
meaning. Like bean shoots.

Woman: How wisely you speak.

Megan:
Selflessness has been a hard
achievement for me, sister.

Sam:
Ah, do you think we could perhaps
send that man . . . away? (*Meaning the Santa.*)

Woman: Hush, new disciples are not allowed to talk.

(*Pause*)

I maintain a profitable law practice
on the outside. One must struggle
to sustain distance from the life
of sorrowfulness. My astrologer
once told me I was fated to be
a singer of songs in an unknown
language. And then, I have always
wanted to write short stories

MEGAN: You too! And I thought I was alone!

WOMAN: Oh, sister, what a joy it is to unburden the heart.

MEGAN: The new disciple is a man.

WOMAN: Yes, he appears to be one.

MEGAN: Oh, I did not mean to suggest . . .

WOMAN: You still carry freight from the other world, sister.

MEGAN:
Yes, I am afraid. I am continually
tormented by a curious mind.

WOMAN: That is the worst temptation.

MEGAN:
I have always had a great difficulty in
not thinking.

WOMAN: Pray for release, sister.

(*The* SANTA *sneers at* SAM.)

Scene Nine

(*The Seat of Bliss. There is a telephone on the table. The Christmas tree
has fallen across the floor.* SAM *looks around and, ascertaining that he
is alone, moves to the phone and dials. Several disciples enter and see
the tree. They puzzle over it, then restore it to upright position.* SAM *ignores them as he talks. They pay no attention to him.*)

SAM:
Energumen two this is energumen one . . .
Nothing startling to report here. The holiday
season proceeds along its dismal course.
I want to poke around here a little
before deciding on a course of action.
Of course, Debbie, of course . . .
No kidding! What about the
Cleveland-Pittsburg game?
Well, look at the sports page.

(*The* MASTER *enters.*)

MEGAN: Idle talk is spiritual flatulence, my son.

SAM: Yes, Master.

(*He hangs up. The* MASTER *departs. He dials again. Pause.*)

SAM:
I would like to start a subscription
to the *Post*. That's right. The address is
twenty-four hundred Que Street Northwest. Right.
Que as in *quodlibet*. Que as in queer. Right.
Troll is the name. T-R-O-L-L. Yes . . .
A. Troll. Ah, there is no mailbox at
that address. No. As a matter of fact
there is no house there either. No,
it's not exactly an apartment
building. It's more like a bridge.
Just tell the carrier to throw the
paper over the bridge. That's right.
I live underneath the bridge. Yes.
Sunday and daily both. Thank you.

(*Hangs up and dials again. A recorded voice is heard.*)

VOICE:
Hello, Scorpio, this is your D.C. Sun-Scope Forecast.
It's better not to count on travel to bring about
tremendous progess just now. The best route to
financial reward would seem to be a good consistent
effort and reliance on the facts. If you are
thinking of making an investment be sure that
the project is quite sound. Avoid gambling
just now.

(*He hangs up.*)

Scene Ten

(*Same as before. The* MASTER *and two* DISCIPLES *masked, one of whom is* SAM. *The latter kneel facing each other. The* MASTER *carries a riding crop, and slowly walks round them asking questions.*)

MASTER: What is more real. Money or the lack of it?

SAM: Money . . .

DISCIPLE: The lack of it . . .

MASTER: You first.

DISCIPLE:
The lack of money is more real because . . .
because it is the soil out of which
spiritual growth . . . grows.

Master: Interesting . . .

Sam: He's wrong. Money is more real.

Master: Why.

Sam:
Because
with it all things may be acquired.
Including a lack of money.

Master:
Of what use for the soul
are the instrumentalities
of power?

Disciple: None whatsoever.

Sam:
They are the interface
between the soul and its
objects.

Master: You first.

Disciple:
The utility of things weighs down the
soul.

Sam:
Wrong again. The information
a soul gathers constitutes its only
effective existence. A thing that
has no use is without substance.

Master: Interesting . . .

(*Pause*)

Which of the perfections of the soul
is highest?

Disciple: The harmonious bliss that comes of self
transcendence.

(*Pause*)

Master: What do you think?

Sam: Death is the only perfection of the soul.

Master: And why do you say that?

Sam:
Death is the only perfection. It is
the only product of a living being
which contains all of the exigent
forces within it, and expresses them.
It is the only effect which contains
all of its causes . . .

Disciple: How dare you speak these blasphemies!

Master: My child, please leave us.

(*Pause*)

Disciple: Yes, master.

(*He goes. Pause.*)

Master:
I am not sure I understand why
you are here. Who is it you wish to
pluck this time?

Sam: The woman, Megan Feather.

Master: You may take her. She is free to go. We are all free.

Sam: She will not leave voluntarily.

Master: Oh, and why is that, Sam? Have I cast some spell on her?

Sam: Yes, you have.

(*Pause*)

Master:
I have read in the newspapers that you are being sued
by several of your ex-clients.

Sam:
I am going to destroy you, if it takes me a hundred
years. I promise.

Master: My spirit is light. My spirit dances.

Sam:
Cleveland beat Pittsburgh thirty-eight to nothing,
you motherfucker. Thirty-eight to nothing. Times
are changing.

Master:
You may not have her.

I would have given her to you
if you had asked but you did not ask.

SAM: You asshole.

(*Pause*)

MASTER:
Your anger has made you a small-minded person, you should
learn to empty yourself; that way you could become
large-spirited like I am.

(*Pause*)

But I am wise; I feel no negative
emotion. That is my weapon. Not to feel
that which I do not wish to feel. You,
Sam, are made weak by what you hate.

SAM: You are a demon.

MASTER: Yes, I suppose I am.

SAM: (*Getting up to go.*)
Thirty-eight to nothing. Remember
that, John. Times are a-changing . . .

(*He goes out. The* MASTER *calls after.*)

MASTER: You may not have her!

(*He gives the finger to the departing* SAM.)

Scene Eleven

(*The Club.* TWO DISCIPLES *carry in* THE MASTER OF MANY PERFECTIONS *on
a sedan chair. He is formally attired.* SAM *and* DEBORAH *sit on the sofa
downstage. In front of the sofa is a low table. On the table are a brandy
decanter and a bowl of fruit. He greets* SAM *loudly and with great
warmth.*)

MASTER:
Hello, Sam, hello!
It's good to see you
My God, it's been a
long time! Must be
about a hundred
years! You look
well! Yes, very, very
well! As you see
I'm doing all right!

So this is your
club! A lot of
powerful men are
members, I suppose!
You know, my
club is not nearly
so exclusive, Sam!
It's so good to see you!

(*Pause*)

SAM: Oh sorry. This is Deborah Martin.

(*They nod.*)

SAM:
And this is . . .
The Master of Many Perfections.

MASTER:
Oh, I don't stand on protocol,
you know that. John Sleight's
the name.

SAM: Shall we sit down.

DEBORAH: I'd like a brandy.

MASTER: Not a bad idea.

(DEBORAH *pours three brandies.*)

MASTER:
Your secretary is very
pretty, Sam.

SAM: She's my partner.

MASTER:
One must be careful about these things
nowadays, eh Sam?!

(*Pause*)

DEBORAH: Mr. Feather has hired us to . . .

MASTER:
Please, Miss Martin, we'll get down
to business before long. Sam and I
haven't seen each other in years.
Why not try to enjoy the moment?
Business is so tiresome.

(*Pause. They drink.*)

MASTER:
I'm organizing a Congress on Spirit
at the Sheridan Park. We lucked out
this year and received a large grant
from the Intertop Foundation.
You know them!
And so, what with the matching
Funds from the government
we're in a position to
hold a really nice little
symposium . . .

(*Reaches into his pocket and produces a swichblade knife which he
opens. He stabs a piece of fruit, begins peeling, cutting, and eating it.*)

On the ramifications of spirit.
To find the burr. You've got to think
through all the possible design sticks
past stupor. Wrench off the warlock's hat
and sing like hot coals! Schemes, schemes
like rats' bellies. It's a nearly decomposable
system scratching your eyes out, Sam.
From the inside. The design logic of
pillar of salt organizes so much memory
into a block of sooty smoke. I am being
a beak, Sam. Those burrs under my skull
there's no program for, Sam.
I'm hot as an oven door.
I'm hot as an oven door
and I itch horribly.
So I scratch.
When I conjure pure apples and pears
of artificial memory I grow as cold
as a flow chart for a dead brain wave
on a piece of empty graph paper . . .
It's the burr. Up here. In my head, Sam.
Cold as an icicle on Buddha's nose.
You understand, Sam.

(*Pause*)

So that I'm glad to see you.

(*Pause*)

In fact, this may seem odd . . .

(*Pause*)

I'd like to ask you to lead a
seminar. Oh, the subject's open.
You could talk about
deprogramming.

(*The all laugh, then frown.*)

Master: A bad joke, I guess.

Deborah: You really are the . . .

Master:
Energumen, my dear?
Yes, I am he.

Deborah:
Pardon me, I am going to go.
You two are simply incredible.
Or perhaps you have both
forgotten that the consciousness
of a living person is at stake.

(*Pause*)

No response? So be it. Bye bye.

(*She leaves.*)

Master: Very emotional. Wonderful eyes.

(*Pause*)

Is she passionate? Very nice body.

(*Pause*)

Do you fuck her with conviction, Sam?

(*Pause*)

You never do anything with conviction, Sam.

Sam: I'll be back at the Seat of Bliss tonight.

Master:
Senator Armitrage is going to set up an
investigation of you, Sam.

Sam: I know.

Master: Join me.

Sam: NO.

MASTER: We could be rich.

SAM: Nope.

MASTER: I won't let her go.

SAM: We'll see about that.

MASTER: Tell me, Sam. What makes you tick?

(*Pause*)

No? Nothing?

(*He gets up to go.*)

Be seeing you. Oh, one last thing. If you return,
no more sneaking out to read the newspapers.

(*Pause*)

We have friends in the trees.

SAM: I only read the sports page.

MASTER: A man like you?

SAM: It has the virtue of being real.

MASTER: Whatever. It must stop.

(*Begins to go.*)

SAM: Don't give me orders, John.

MASTER:
You bore from within.
But I am Proteus . . .

(*He goes.*)

Scene Twelve

(*The Seat of Bliss. Night.* SAM *on the phone. Outside the window a* SANTA
peers in. SAM *doesn't see him.*)

SAM:
Energumen one this is energumen two . . .
For Christ-sake! I haven't got all day.
The "Master of Many Perfections" has
taken it into his head to call for a
month-long retreat: that means no
contact with the outside world.
I've got a plan, but I haven't

got the time to explain. This place
is driving me crazy. No, no, no!
Just turn to the sports page and
read me some scores. ANY SCORES!

Scene Thirteen

(The Seat of Bliss. Sam sits in a chair, reading. Megan storms in.)

Megan:
Look, you, I don't know
what your game is, but
I'm not having any
of it, you understand?
I am here of my own
free will, and no one
can make me go away.

(Pause)

My parents sent you
didn't they? They just
never give up. What
kind of fool do you
take me for, anyway!?

(Pause)

I do not choose to belong to
the world of rough calculation
and petty-minded little buyers and
sellers of established middle-class
bullshit America . . . no more . . .

(Pause)

You people think you own everything.

(Pause)

Who are you anyway?

(Pause)

You look like something out of the
Junior League Cotillion.

Sam: Sam Nutley is the name.

(Pause)

Cigarette?

MEGAN: You can't smoke in here.

(*He eats the cigarette.*)

SAM: Candy.

(*Pause*)

MEGAN: Who sent you?

SAM: Your parents.

MEGAN: I thought so.

(*Pause*)

Well, you can tell them from me
that I have had enough of
their manipulation and pressure
and disapproval. I am sick
and tired of having to live up
to their antiquated set of
expectations, of having to
endure their endless and in-
sufferable mediocrity; I am
completely fed up with it.

(*Pause*)

Are you listening?

SAM: Yes.

MEGAN:
You look quite stupid,
you know, sitting there.

SAM: It's not nice to call people names.

MEGAN:
I am determined that I shall be
Free. F-R-E-E. That is all
that matters to me anymore.
The Master of Many Perfections
has given me the strength to
be free precisely because he
has seen with great clarity
the human soul and the universe
are of an identical configuration.
One logic enmeshes all. It is
so simple a child could understand.

SAM: I don't understand.

MEGAN:
Do you have a background in
theoretical physics? What
is your background in?

SAM: I thought you said a child could understand.

MEGAN: Understanding and explanation are two different things.

SAM: Indeed they are. Want a cigarette?

MEGAN: Good god, no.

(*Pause*)

SAM:
Go on. Please explain.
I'm listening. Really.

(*He eats another cigarette.*)

MEGAN:
Thought reigns supreme because
everything that is not an illusion
is a thought of god's . . .

(*Pause*)

I am necessary for god as a thinker of his thought,
a dancer of his dance, a singer of his song . . .

(*Pause*)

The Master has transcended his actualized self . . .

(*Pause*)

You know, he can look at a shoal of minnows
and tell what direction they will all turn,
when they turn and flash as one . . .

(*Pause*)

I've seen him do the same with a flock of birds.

(*Pause*)

SAM:
I would never say that John Sleight
did not possess a remarkable intuition.

MEGAN: How did you know his name?

(*Pause*)

SAM: Anyway the thing is your parents are quite ill.

MEGAN: Father, sick? I don't believe it.

SAM: Both.

MEGAN: I don't believe you.

SAM: The disease is called Murphy's Crud.

MEGAN:
What kind of joke is this?

SAM:
The unfortunate victim of Murphy's
crud becomes subject to fits of
logorrhea, and will ramble on incoherently for hours on almost any
subject without paying the slightest
attention to what's really happening.
Even talking about the disease is a
danger.

(*Pause*)

It is surprisingly common in the more
prosperous sections of town.

MEGAN:
I don't find this the least
bit amusing. Really not.

SAM: Why don't you call your parents?

MEGAN:
I plan to do just that.
Anyway they are nothing to me.

(*Pause*)

SAM: Want to go out for dinner?

MEGAN: WHAT!?

SAM:
I said do you want to go out for dinner.
You know. Eat.

(*Pause*)

Or have you transcended
your alimentary tract?

MEGAN: You must be crazy.

SAM:
Well the month of seclusion is coming up
and I thought it might be nice to go out
to a really nice French restaurant and have
a really nice elegant meal before the
bread and water days begin.
What do you think?

(*Pause*)

I've made a reservation for next Thursday.
For two. At La Belle Epoque. Eight sharp.
It's right next to the old Circle Theatre.
If you remember where that is.

MEGAN: I won't go.

SAM: I'll meet you there.

MEGAN:
Such a nice time we are having! Now you're
upset. Your moods change so rapidly it's
quite hard to figure you out. But I shall
try. Would you like to hear a story?

Scene Fourteen

(MEGAN *and* DEBORAH *at a luxury shooting range, shooting. Both wear ear guards. As they fire there are bright flashes, but no noise. As the scene begins they are both reloading.*)

DEBORAH: I used to do quite wicked things.

MEGAN:
I am unpredictable, but basically I'm into forming
easy, liberated, free-floating sexual attachments.
With no strings.

(DEBORAH *steps forward.*)

I am definite about that.

(DEBORAH *shoots. Steps back.*)

I can't handle cloying relationships.

(MEGAN *steps forward and shoots.*)

DEBORAH: I used to get drunk at parties . . .

(MEGAN *shoots again.*)

MEGAN: Most of the men I know are creeps.

(*Steps back.* DEBORAH *steps up and shoots.*)

DEBORAH: I'd find the ugliest man at the party and go home with him.

(*She shoots again.*)

I can be very disgusting.

(*She steps back.* MEGAN *steps up.*)

MEGAN:
My new boyfriend is French. He's not like these asshole
American men. Money means nothing to him.

(*She shoots.*)

He's very cute.

(*They both reload. Pause.*)

DEBORAH:
I only do that sort of thing when I'm feeling
very wild.

MEGAN:
His name is Jacques. He runs a place called
"La Belle Epoque".

DEBORAH:
Afterwards I don't remember a
thing.

(*She steps up and takes aim.*)

Scene Fifteen

(*The Club.* MEGAN *and* DEBORAH *are talking.* SANTA *is in the back, by his
Christmas tree.* FEATHER *appears at the door, looking around as if for*
DEBORAH. *She sees him in the mirror and slides down in the sofa. He
chats briefly with* SANTA *before spotting the pair.*)

MEGAN:
Have you ever lost a sock
in the washing machine? I mean
you put two socks in and only one comes out?

(*Pause*)

It's matter becoming spirit.

DEBORAH: (*Seeing* FEATHER.)
That's intriguing.

MEGAN: You're so easily surprised by me.

DEBORAH: I am very interested in wild people.

MEGAN:
Is something wrong, Debby? You seem frightened
by something. You're so quiet.

DEBORAH: I'm just tired.

FEATHER: (*Approaching*)
Ah, there you are! Deborah, may I have
a word with you alone. Who's your
young friend?

DEBORAH: A friend.

(*She goes off arm-in-arm with* FEATHER *quickly.*)

Scene Sixteen

(*The Club.* DEBORAH *seated;* SAM *walks in, looking angry.*)

DEBORAH: Don't go back please.

SAM: Dead battery, Deb.

DEBORAH: Something is wrong.

SAM: What's bothering you?

DEBORAH:
Something's wrong. Feather surprised Megan and me
today. I was, as usual, being an ear.

SAM: Wish I could've seen that. I need a wrench.

DEBORAH: They didn't recognize each other.

SAM: Uh-huh . . . (*Sits down. Pause.*)

DEBORAH: The situation is far more complex than I thought.

SAM: Complexity is a state of mind.

DEBORAH: She's been acting, but I don't know why.

SAM: If her father's not her father, who is he?

DEBORAH:
There is a long, thin wire that runs
through all their heads.
We've got to tap that line.
Tap, top, Intertop.

SAM:
I've got a dead battery.

(*He gets up.*)

It's late. I'm tired.

(*Pause*)

Then why is he paying us!?

DEBORAH: I have something to say.

SAM: But why us?

DEBORAH: It's pretty important.

SAM: Cold as hell out there.

DEBORAH:
If you go back to that place I'll quit.
I'll call the police. I'll do anything
I can to sabotage the job. I'm afraid.

SAM:
People know who we are. Why!?
They didn't recognize each other.
Don't stand there looking darts at me.
Use your brain. Think.

DEBORAH: Somebody is after John Sleight.

(*He sits down again.*)

SAM: Aside from us.

DEBORAH:
She has no family in the area.
I checked. They'll all dead.
In college. Or back in Grosse Pointe.
Where they come from.

SAM:
She's an innocent.

(*Pause*)

And the "Master of Many Perfections"
is just the kind of demon that presides
over a traditional slaughter of innocents.

DEBORAH:
If you screw her, I'll kill you.
If you screw her, I'll kill you both.
Just remember that.

(*She gets up. He picks up the phone and dials.*)

DEBORAH:
I'm going back to Law School, Sam.
If you can't beat 'em, join 'em.

(*She rushes out.*)

SAM:
I'd like a number on the Hill.
For Senator Armitrage's office.

(*He writes down the number.*)

Thanks.

(*He hangs up.* DEBORAH *enters.*)

DEBORAH: I was going to steal your car, but the battery's dead.

SAM:
Wonder what they'll think on the Hill
when they find out Feather isn't Feather.
Sure, I'll drop the case.

DEBORAH: I don't believe you.

Scene Seventeen

(*The Seat of Bliss late at night. Both the* MASTER *and* SAM *are hidden, crouched on the floor. If anything, they mimic furniture. The* MASTER *is not aware of* SAM'S *presence.* DEBORAH *enters, looks around, and stops in her tracks. Long pause.*)

MASTER:
King Amanullah, of the Patzinaks,
said, after shooting off a cannon:
"I feel just like an Englishman."

DEBORAH: You frightened me.

MASTER:
Allow the fear to flow
through you, my dear.
That way it can
find its way out.

(*Pause*)

DEBORAH: Well. I'm here.

MASTER:
It is difficult
to put into words.

(*Pause*)

DEBORAH:
Let me hazard
a guess . . .

MASTER:
But if you allow me,
I shall try.

(*Pause*)

For your own sake.
Stop Sam.

DEBORAH: Why? Why me?

MASTER:
Lubricities of the soul do
not quench the body,
its incurable heats and
lust.

DEBORAH: This is crazy.

(*She moves to go.*)

MASTER:
Stop.
Hear me out.

DEBORAH:
Hand her over and
we'll be off your back
pronto.

MASTER:
There is an oil painting hanging on the
wall of your club. It depicts the feral
joys of some soldiers and sailors on leave.
The Secretary of War, a disciple of mine also
in his dotage, had the painting removed
from the War Department. It seemed to show
our stalwart young soldiery in a bad light.
Much drink, crowds of loose women, the wet
out and in of flesh. Pay strict heed, Deborah.

Megan is lewd. Megan's whole nebulous
lewdness is focussed, I fear, on Sam. I know
her: she'll drag him down.

DEBORAH:
Unbelievable
you are.

MASTER:
Make him stop.
For yourself.
It's all I want.

(SAM *stands up*.)

MASTER: Ah, hello, Sam.

SAM:
I arrived a little
before you.

MASTER: We are talking . . .

DEBORAH:
We are talking
about art.

SAM:
All I wanted to say is that
I've decided to drop the Feather case.
You win, John.

(*Pause*)

Cat got your tongue?
I said we are out of the case
as of now.

DEBORAH: What are you talking about?

MASTER:
Don't believe him.

(*Pause*)

It surprises me to hear this.

DEBORAH:
I am fucking
stunned.

SAM:
I should hope so. You see
Feather is a false Feather.

Whoever it was hired me
hired him first. You've been set up.

(*Pause*)

So
no need to worry about my putative lust.

MASTER:
Senator Armitrage's
put me up for membership in the club.
I feel like half an Englishman already.

Scene Eighteen

(*Three* SANTAS *at the back room of La Belle Epoque. One of them is* JAC-
QUES. *And* MEGAN. *The phone rings. A* SANTA *answers it and passes it to
another, who offers it to her. She refuses.* JACQUES *take the phone and
performs.*)

JACQUES:
Yes, this is Senator Armitrage . . .
What? Who says so?

(*He stands up.*)

Oh no . . .

(*He sits down.*)

Who do they think I am?
Nothing doing. I'm not
risking twenty years
of seniority for the
sake of some Holy Roller
who put his money
on the wrong horse.
Commodity futures is a tricky game
in that part of the world. Me?

(*Pause*)

It's a private matter. I don't like
to be called at this number. I don't
care what they said at the Agency.
Fuck him. Fuck the Patzinaks.
We have a reputation to maintain
in that part of the world.
That's final.

(*He hangs up.*)

Who do they think I am?

Scene Nineteen

(*Three* Santas *leapfrog across an empty stage. Blackout.*)

Scene Twenty

(*An elegant bar-restaurant with a panorama view of Washington. The whole restaurant slowly rotates atop its tower so that the view sweeps by. The place is empty except for* Megan *and the* Master. *He stands by the window.*)

Master:
The world.
Megan . . .
The world will stare.

Megan: You don't understand.

Master:
I've got it under control.
Another drink?

Megan:
I have to have that money back.
Tell me, is there such a thing as Murphy's Crud?

Master:
Linkage failure in the subsystem
governing appetition. We need an
absolute truth-vectoring device
for suppressing hunger. The two of them,
Sam and what's-her-name. I've been set up.

Megan: I can't disappoint Intertop. You owe.

Master: (*Pacing*) Commerce bores me.

Megan: We seem to have an impasse.

(*Pause*)

Master: They appear to have dropped the case, Megan.

Megan: That's odd.

Master: It seems Feather is not Feather.

Megan: I told them I was self-begotten.

MASTER:
Evidently.
Without that microchip plant
I'm wiped out. You know that.

MEGAN: "Those agile, Asian fingers."

MASTER: I'm begging you.

MEGAN:
Sorry.
My lawyers insist I wind up the business.

MASTER: What about my lawyers?

MEGAN: You have wonderful lawyers, John.

MASTER: What about the way?

MEGAN: Which way is that?

MASTER: Our way. The way of spirit.

MEGAN: Spirit's fine in its place.

MASTER: (*Musing*)
There are, of course, many ways . . .
From point to point
the connections are all
clear, but they don't add up.
It's like a bunch of children
playing leap-frog. Look,
I'm broke.

MEGAN: I can't disappoint the Senator.

MASTER:
I told you.
The Patzinaks have expropriated my lands.
Where was the Agency? You promised.

MEGAN:
Neither the Agency, nor the Senator,
nor Intertop, can save bunglers.
Why did you try that coup, behind our backs?
You know the Senator. You should've
gone to him before it was too late.
Honestly, what do you think I am?

MASTER:
Santa Claus.

(*Pause*)

You are Santa Claus.

MEGAN:
I've asked my lawyers
to draw up a schedule of
payments. Here.

(*Hands it to him.*)

Sam said he knew you. Before. At M.I.T.
Sam said you invented a computer language.
You're not an innocent.

MASTER:
I told you. We don't talk about what
happened before. It's all erased.
I told you.

MEGAN: He said you were considered a genius

MASTER:
Me? From point to point, but
it didn't add up. The copula's missing.
It's not enough. Copula. *Copulavit* . . .
Not enough. You need glue. Glee. One must
all stick. Be gripping power. It must learn
to bite and hold. With one's teeth. Sharpen
them on sticks, rocks, axeheads, grindstones.
You know what holds all the elements in the starry
fields of heaven? Together? Charm . . .
They're all concatenated on a
spidery silken fine-woven web of charm.
Charm, Megan. But it would all fall
apart. It would not cohere.
It must. It's got to be. So
when I was gleaming one day
I caught fire and poured out silky
waves . . . of charm.
Who is this Jacques?
You're fucking some Jacques . . .

MEGAN: Don't hate me for my choices, John.

MASTER:
Giordano
Bruno thought if you memoried symbols
of power you created vast flowers of charm.

Bite; bite. I can see your heart beating.
You have a long hatpin next to your
heart and you plan to stick me, you
and your filthy red Santas. You don't trust me.
It doesn't hold together. Because the language
of nature's an unspeakable horror! Unspeakable.

(*Pause*)

That's why I changed into what I am.
You set me up didn't you? It was you.
Why?

(*Pause*)

Because I see you through a spider's eye.
There're thousands upon thousands of you.
And each one is different. It doesn't hold.
Because . . . oh, how I worshipped you!

(*He approaches her.*)

MEGAN:
Sorry, John.
I'm into a new kind of thing called
"managed revolution". That takes lots of money.
So, you see I'm an innocent still.

(MASTER *takes out his switchblade and slowly approaches.*)

MASTER: Demon.

(*A crowd of demon* SANTAS *appears.* MEGAN *pulls out a long hatpin and impales him as he lunges at her. He slumps to the floor, dead.* JACQUES *emerges from the demon machinery, takes off his beard and hat. All the* SANTAS *stare at the corpse.*)

JACQUES: I thought you were only going to scare him.

MEGAN: He frightened me. Jesus Christ. He's dead.

(*They all leave except for one* SANTA. *Pause. He removes beard and hat. It is* SAM.)

Scene Twenty-One

(*The rotating bar-restaurant again.* SAM *is disguised as a* SANTA. *Next to him is the tripod-and-kettle affair from earlier scenes at the club. He rings a bell.* DEBORAH *sits at the bar.*)

DEBORAH:
It's all over the papers.
You're finished, Sam.
Oh, why did you do it?

SAM: Ho, ho, ho.

DEBORAH: Laugh . . .

SAM: I am.

(*Pause*)

DEBORAH: I'm going to Law School.

SAM: You'll be a credit to your profession.

DEBORAH:
I have so many debts.
Inflation's wiping me out.
I need to make a lot of money.

SAM:
She's gone to Mexico
on a travel-study grant.
Guess I wasn't quick enough.

DEBORAH: Take off the costume or I'll cry. Please.

(*He takes off the hat and beard.*)

SAM:
Maybe there're deprogramming grants. Ho, ho, ho.

(*Pause*)

In case you're interested I didn't kill him.
But I would have. You don't believe me.

DEBORAH:
It's too much. I'm
an ordinary person
with ordinary hopes.

SAM:
You remember our friend
"The Professional Frenchman"?
He was in on it.

DEBORAH: I can't stand your friends. You know that.

SAM: It's like figuring out a chess problem.

DEBORAH: You were in love with her. You were sleeping with her.

Sam:
Who the devil told you that?

(*Rings his bell.*)

Ho, ho, ho!

(*Pause*)

Deborah: Anyway, I'm not going with you. I mean it . . .

Sam: You'll make a fine lawyer.

Deborah: What exactly did you tell Senator Armitrage?

Sam:
Never got through to him. Bastard. So I called up
the Master. Told him about Jacques and Megan.
It didn't seem to get to him.

Deborah: I told you not to go back.

Sam: I blew it.

Deborah:
I have to take care of myself.
I want you to know how much
it matters to me that you see that.

Sam: There's no future in rationality.

Deborah:
And don't lay a guilt trip on me.
I won't tell them I've seen you.

Sam: Thanks.

Deborah: Don't be so manipulative.

Sam: What?! What the hell do you mean?

Deborah:
Oh, forget it. I shouldn't have come.
This is a waste of time.
You're such a romantic.

Sam:
Romantic my ass! Look, there was a woman I know
had a child, a real nice little kid, with a
kinda square head, real eyes that open and shut.
See? Now the mother was a kook. She'd get saved,
reborn, rolfed, flushed out with carrot juice,

stuffed full of megavitamins. You name it,
she'd just naturally go for it. She'd fly
from the asshole of one salvation into the mouth
of the next.

(*Pause*)

I just figured she was excessively spiritual—
which by the way is not the problem with people
that get sucked into these things. Anyhow, she
joined the group, a very bad group, called the
"Dance of Purity". You may have read about them.
The big guru got it into his head that she

(*Pause*)

had been defiled by the devil and had borne
the devil's child, you follow what I'm saying?
She threw the kid out of the
out of the fucking window. Fourteen stories down.
Bang! Just like that. *You are the devil's child* she
said before she did it. If I had been there you know
what I would have done? I would have thrown the
mother out of the motherfucking window, because
if that kid was the devil's kid
that makes me the devil.

(*Pause. She laughs.*)

DEBORAH: You're a terrible liar.

(*Pause*)

Good bye.

(*She starts to leave. Pause.*)

And what makes you think
you embody rationality,
you prig?

(*Pause*)

The lady in question's a not very
nice person. She's playing revolution
just like she was playing religion.
It's all interchangeable in her mind.
But rational you won't be disabused
of your fantasy of saving the saved.
You never asked one goddamn thing

about me. You never needed
what I could've told you a long time ago.
Sky's crashing down on us, but you,
you don't get it. You just don't get it.

(*Pause*)

Keep warm with this.

(*Throws her knitting at him and starts to leave.*)

SAM: You'll be back.

(*She stops and turns.*)

DEBORAH: No, I won't.

(*She leaves.*)

Scene Twenty-Two

(*La Belle Epoque. Closing time. The "Professional Frenchman" is clearing up.* FEATHER *enters. The* WAITER *tries to stop him, but he rushes past.*)

WAITER: But monsieur!

FEATHER: Damn you, man, get out of my way!

WAITER: Jacques, he demand to see you.

FEATHER: Are you Jacques Petit?

JACQUES: Monsieur, I am sorry. We are closed.

FEATHER: I know your name is Rusty Sadler.

JACQUES:
Monsieur, I am, as you say, Jacques Petit.
But we are closed. You must go.

FEATHER:
You don't understand.
I know. I know it all.

JACQUES:
Monsieur, I have no idea of what
you are talking.

(*Pause*)

FEATHER:
No, don't play dumb. You've got
to know about it. It's in the papers.

He's dead. The Master is dead. She
killed him. Nobody knows. Except
me. But she was trying to pin it
on them. On Sam and Debbie, oh,
Debbie. My sweet. My undoing . . .
Done. They pick you up and
throw you down, these
fastidious fuckers. It's true.
You don't think I don't know about
you and Megan? I know. I know
all about you. You're no Frenchman.

Waiter: Il est fou.

Jacques: La Police.

Waiter: Oui.

(*He goes to phone.*)

Feather:
You're from Detroit, Michigan.
You're a Communist Revolutionary.
You're Megan Feather's lover. You
are the only one left and you
are going to pay me because they
all flew the coop. All of them.
She hired me. You can play dumb
all you want. It won't help you.
I'll take you to court. I'll sue.
I am owed five thousand dollars
for my impersonation of her father.
It worked. It was flawless. It was
absolute perfection. A work of art.
But she didn't know I worked for the
Agency. But they double-crossed me too.
That's why I'm here. I won't leave.
I know you know me. I know it . . .

Jacques:
Monsieur. I do not know you
if you are dipped in Bechamel.

Waiter: Il est trop fou.

Jacques: Mondieu! Mondieu!

Feather:
One of 'em is going to pay me.
One of 'em. I don't care who.

But one of 'em. And she, the
other, it's sickening, she didn't
even recognize me after our
intimacy, she pretended not
to know . . . to know me, oh,
I had to pretend too, I was
being paid, but Jesus Christ,
I am a human being, I have
feelings too! They fuck
you and flee in this damn
town, but I am a person of
considerable importance. I was on
the Secretary's blue-ribbon committee
before we caught the flack for that
damnable turnabout in Somalia . . .
They had to have a scapegoat,
Don't you see? Tell me the truth.

JACQUES: Monsieur, we have called the police.

FEATHER:
A cool one you are . . . Look, Jacques,
I AM THE POLICE, THE BIG POLICE!
No, don't go away, I'm not
through, I see it now, she
wanted a cover for her Commie
plot to . . . You can't fool me,
you're an American. But it's
Debbie, she's the one, you know
she didn't even recognize me.
She acted like it didn't
ever happen.

(End of play)

Michael Wolk

Femme Fatale

As a novelist, Mr. Wolk is the author of the mystery thriller, *The Big Picture* (Signet), and the forthcoming *The Nose On Broadway*. For the stage he has recently completed *Heartstopper*, a suspense comedy set in Times Square.

Femme Fatale was presented as a staged reading at Playwrights Horizons, New York City, in October 1983. It was produced by Andre Bishop and directed by James Peskin, with the following cast:

JOSH . . . . Steven Marcus
MICHELE . . . . Paula Mann

It was subsequently produced at the Raft Theatre in New York during February 1984. James Peskin was the producer, and directed the following cast:

JOSH . . . . Jed Cooper
MICHELE . . . . Lisa Waltz

A revised version of *Femme Fatale* was produced at The Cast at the Circle in Los Angeles in April 1985. It was produced by John Wells of Appian Way Productions and Ted Schmitt for the Cast Theatre. James Roach directed the following cast:

HAL . . . . Gregg Henry
MICHELE . . . . Lisa James

This play is for Susan.

For stock and amateur production rights, contact: Broadway Play Publishing, Inc., 357 West 20th Street, New York, NY 10011. For all other rights, contact: Mary McAllister Literary Agency, P.O. Box 692, Cooper Station, New York, NY 10276.

Characters
HAL GAINES, age 30
MICHELE LARSON, age 22
Setting
New York City. Fall is in the air.

1. Goddam mysterious

(HAL *and* MICHELE *face each other over a rectangle of black velvet on the stage floor.* HAL *stands close to the rectangle;* MICHELE, *at a distance.*)

HAL: The ways of the heart I tell ya are goddam mysterious 'cause here the old man's getting buried, Mom's outta control, I'm standing there in one of the old man's suits, any second it's gonna fucking pour, one of the old man's pals is saying what a great human being he was—easy for him to say, they played golf—and I'm cruising this chick. What can I say? I know this isn't appropriate behavior but . . . even with the hair back, even in all that cemetery drag . . . she's looking back is the thing, with these eyes, and they are hot . . . with sympathy? Maybe. Maybe. Rain. Just a coupla drops, but they sorta grease the preacher's gears—he's still got the slow rolling tones, but you can tell he's wrapping it up—he hits the "Amen," the storm breaks, the crowd breaks, me an' Mom go for the limo, and we're tooling outta the cemetery, and I look out the window—and the girl, she's still there, standing up by the grave, alone, in the rain. (*Beat, as he looks at* MICHELE.) She had my interest. Definitely.

(HAL *exits.* MICHELE *has stepped to the side of the grave as the sound of rain fades up. She pulls out a set of keys, holds them out for a moment, and then drops them into the grave.*)

2. Legacy

(*Sound of a city street.* HAL *is driving his cab.*)

HAL: Bastard! . . . That's the virtue of bombing 'round the isle of Manhattan in this canary—ya know where ya stand. In family matters, this isn't always the case. With family sometimes someone's gotta croak before ya get the bottom line, and in this case the bottom line is a big, red ink fuck you. Long as I remember, there was this money stashed for me. My trust fund. Love that word trust. The will gets read and guess who's left out in the cold. Then guess who wiggles in and wiggles off with 100 thousand bucks. The number from the cemetery. She's in. I'm out. (*Laughs*) The big laugh, though, is we're at the house after the funeral, everyone sucking down the schnapps, this major jerk, Dr. Emil Nash, old friend of the family, corners me, lays this fat hand on me, breathes booze in my face, and says, "A boy should know the truth about his father." So. Turns out the old man didn't check out at the hospital. Nash gets him delivered there "after the fact." And the fact is, he bought it while he was in bed with this 100-thousand dollar . . . individual. And there are a few details make a guy wonder just what went down. But no one's asking questions. Gotta think about Mom—far as she knows, he died kosher, laid out on those clean, white, hospital sheets. More important, though, ya gotta think of the practice. The surviving partners. God knows we don't wanna jeopardize the integrity of the firm. So the jerk gives me the rap, slaps me on the back, and I get the feeling I'm s'posed to feel proud the old man got away with something—even in his last earthly act. (*Laughs*)

(MICHELE *appears: she has switched on a lamp. She wears a night dress; her hair is wild, her face glistens with sweat. There is a bandage around her wrist. She reaches for the telephone by the lamp, stops.*)

HAL: But what I'm thinking, for some reason can't stop wondering, is about that girl—and just who got away with what . . .

(MICHELE *reaches again for the phone, punches buttons. After a moment:*)

MICHELE: Nathan. . . . Yes, but I have to talk . . . Nathan, please, I had this dream . . .

(*Sound of line going dead.* MICHELE *lets the hand with receiver drop, but does not hang up. Sound continues as stage goes to black.*)

3. Screamer

(HAL *sits in his cab, drinking coffee from a take-out container, looking out the window from time to time. He is waiting for someone.*)

HAL: I'm driving nightside, I'm driving dayside, and maybe I'm driving myself a little to the left of bananas 'cause last night—afternoon, whatever the fuck it was—I get this bizzaro number about that chick. She's in black, wearing sunglasses, and we're up against this dead-end place, concrete area of some sort, and I'm ripping off her clothes. She's got this great little body, white though, like blinding, gotta squint just to look, and I tell her, take off the sunglasses, but she won't. I try and rip 'em off, and we slip to the ground, she's under me, squirming, arms, legs, and to be honest, it's got me excited, but I'm still going for the glasses, really zeroed on those glasses, and I grab 'em, yank 'em off, she lets loose this howl, and I look and, Christ, there's nothing there, man, nothing but these two black holes, and I pull back and her face, there's no face at all, just bone, and this smile, this skull smile and I push her away, man, but she's got her arms around me, legs twisted around me and they are ice and she's pulling my face to that face and I can't fight it, and the holes move right over my head, swallow it, and I'm falling, spinning, being sucked down, screaming like hell and I know it's the end and then boom! I wake up with my ass on the floor. (*Beat*) Now this I can live without. Figure this babe stole enough, I'm not gonna let her get my sleep. (*Checks the window again.*) Well here it is. The golden moment.

4. Ouija Ride

(MICHELE *comes out the door of the hospital, wearing her nurse's uniform.* HAL *honks, leans out his window.*)

HAL: Hey! You *believe* this? A miracle on the sidewalks of New York! Almost didn't recognize you, you look so . . . hygenic. . . . Hello? You recognize me, right?

MICHELE: (*A croak*) Right.

HAL: 'Course you do. But, the way you looked at me . . . the way you're still looking at me . . . Aw, the surprise element, right? I'm *sorry*. Lemme tell ya, this is a great shock to me too. I'm real glad, though, 'cause, well, we got introduced when they read the will, but there you were in that crappy folding chair almost out in the hallway, and there was no opportunity for human contact. So now here's the opportunity, and I wanna extend the hand of friendship. Hal Gaines. (*Offers his hand.*) . . . What? Afraid I got bacteria?

MICHELE: This coincidence . . . rather lacks . . . credibility.

HAL: 'Scuse me?

MICHELE: I believe you understand me.

HAL: Before I get maybe offended, let me tell ya something. There's a principle here you don't understand. I'm driving a cab, and in this city you're not just driving on streets, you're driving on energy, and lotsa times when something's ripe, when I should run inta someone, I do, 'cause there's some fate element here, like that ouija board bit, I just put my hands on this wheel, and there's something pulling me, wherever, whyever, I don't know—but here you are and that is totally within the realm of everyday possibility—

MICHELE: Mr. Gaines, they told me yesterday, at Reception, you were asking about me.

HAL: (*Uncomprehending*) Me? (*Beat*) All right. I been wanting to run into you. I took a little affirmative action. Maybe you think I got hard feelings. Relax. The old man and me didn't see eye to eye, but what's that got to do with you? . . . Another few minutes with this hand here, they're gonna have to amputate.

(MICHELE *takes his hand*.)

HAL: Hallelujah! . . . This is a *wet* hand. Did I do that? Give you a case of clammy hands?

MICHELE: You were lying in wait for me. For all I know, you could be mentally unbalanced.

HAL: I been "lying in wait" hoping I could maybe give you a lift when you got off your shift. C'mon, hop in. I'll take you where you're going. Uptown, crosstown, the moon, you name it, it's on me.

MICHELE: Thank you. Very much. I walk.

HAL: Six a.m. You been on your feet all night and you're gonna walk?

MICHELE: Yes.

HAL: C'mon. I picked up tons of nurses, all they talk about is how much they wanna get off their feet. It's one of their big motivations in life. Right?

(MICHELE *tries to free her hand from* HAL's *grasp*.)

HAL: C'mon, it's the smallest thing I can do. For all you did for the old man.

MICHELE: I didn't do anything. Much. I did extremely little, actually.

HAL: Aw, what modesty! The way I understand it, you did everything humanly possible. (*Smiles*)

MICHELE: (*Jerks her hand free*.) Goodbye. I'm sorry about your loss.

HAL: (*Gets out of his cab, follows*.) Hey, wait! Is your time so valuable—

MICHELE: Please.

HAL: What's the situation! I offered you a ride.

MICHELE: Is that what you're offering?

HAL: What else? Jesus. Did I even hint I wanted anything else? What would I want? . . . Wow! If you'd stop to think of the *ego* involved in that. The paranoia. Lemme illustrate something—(*Taking out matchbooks, scraps of paper*.) Here. Liz. Great kid, great body. Macrobiotic . . . Jayme! N.Y.U. film student . . . Pat? Pam? Who is this? Doesn't jog the memory. But here's my point—every time I go to the laundromat, phone numbers fall out, it looks like autumn in Central Park. What do I need with you? All you are is . . . human interest. I make a gesture, purely outta courtesy, you act like I'm contaminated. What is it? Some bad press I got from the old man, right?

MICHELE: We di- . . . He didn't discuss you. I never even thought of you, until the funeral.

HAL: Ah, and then what did you think?

MICHELE: That . . .

HAL: Yeah?

MICHELE: That this would happen.

HAL: What's happened?

MICHELE: You're harrassing me.

HAL: I . . . whew! I'm offering you a ride, that to you is harrassment? I think it's just that maybe you're overwrought, you know? You're shaking, you look totally shot—

MICHELE: I'm fine.

HAL: You should see your eyes.

MICHELE: I happen to be perfectly fine!

HAL: You're fine, you just happen to look like a raccoon.

MICHELE: Maybe it's been a rather trying week!

HAL: Maybe it has. Maybe it has . . . (*Sighs*) I know it's been kind of a drain on me . . . But look, there's no reason for any negative energy between you and me, is there? I mean, can ya just see this for what it is: a guy who was a little curious to meet you, a guy who felt bad when his entire family gave you the evil eye when they heard what a slice of the estate you got? A guy who just wants to offer you a courtesy, to be a big man in his little way. For my sake, even maybe for yours, take the ride. A five minute ride. We'll have a civilized word, and that will be that. We'll part on a nice note, and if we ever see each other again, maybe we'll wave.

(*Beat*)

MICHELE: If . . . I were to accept this ride, I would want this very clear. I would be accepting it as a civil gesture. After this, I would expect you would not continue to—

HAL: Yeah, yeah—you take the ride, I buzz off.

MICHELE: Yes . . . rather . . . permanently. Tell me you understand.

HAL: Sure, sure, isn't that what I been saying?

(*They cross to the cab.* HAL *opens the front door for her, but* MICHELE *gets in the back.*)

HAL: So, where to?

MICHELE: Don't you know?

HAL: How would I know?

MICHELE: Columbus Circle.

HAL: Columbus Circle. That's good. Now at least I know it's in the western hemisphere.

MICHELE: I live right there. Very close by.

HAL: And you were gonna walk.

MICHELE: Why not?

HAL: Long way in your condition.

(MICHELE *opens her mouth to say something, does not.*)

(HAL *starts the cab. After a moment:*)

HAL: So . . . you're a nurse. Not to pry here . . .

MICHELE: Yes, I am a nurse.

HAL: Ah. Must be interesting, being a nurse . . . How 'bout all that blood? Doesn't it get to ya?

MICHELE: Blood is blood.

HAL: Spoken like a true nurse. But, I tell ya, blood has always had a real negative effect on me . . . You're not real old, are ya?

MICHELE: Not *real* old, no.

HAL: Twenty-three?

MICHELE: That's a fair approximation.

HAL: Michele Larson . . . That name sorta harks of the Great Midwest. Where you from? Sioux City?

MICHELE: Pennsylvania.

HAL: Pittsburgh?

MICHELE: Bradford.

HAL: Where's that?

MICHELE: Nowhere.

HAL: How'd ya make your escape?

MICHELE: Savings.

HAL: From nursing? Were you a nurse in Bradford?

MICHELE: Yes. Bradford Pavillion Hospital. I was assistant floor supervisor—if you want to check up on me.

HAL: Aw, c'mon, be loose, I'm not gonna . . . So it was like in this capacity of being like a nurse that you first met the old man, right?

MICHELE: Was that a raindrop?

HAL: Where?

MICHELE: On the windshield.

HAL: (*Looks closely*) No, it is something very small, now very dead.

MICHELE: The sky looks somewhat threatening.

HAL: Now aren't you glad you're riding with me?

MICHELE: I carry a foldaway raincoat.

HAL: . . . Right. So. You were saying how ya met the old man.

MICHELE: What do you do?

HAL: I play third base for the Mets. Whaddaya—

MICHELE: He—your father—said . . .

HAL: He did talk about me, hm?

MICHELE: He made one comment once.

HAL: Can you repeat it?

MICHELE: He said you dropped out of college to become a thief.

HAL: Christ! He said . . . You know what *he* was?

MICHELE: Of course. A very prominent, successful, well-respected—

HAL: A goddam criminal lawyer. He made a living helping murderers, rapists and thieves ease their guilty asses through some legal loophole. The biggest rush he got was standing in that courtroom selling twelve suckers the concept that black is, ya know, really just dark grey, and grey is, ya know, really white when ya just dust it off and *look* at it . . . So I'm not some pinstripe wimp, tie knotted around my neck, scribbling on a yellow pad, lying through my teeth in pig Latin. So maybe I've done a few hustles in my time, but this is life on the street, man, everyone hustles, it's out front. That's why I got this cab. 'Cause everyday the're possibilities, and I latch on when I like, see, in my own time . . . and one day, I'll be set up just fine . . . Ha, I'm crazy, spilling this to you . . . You were telling me, you met him at the hospital when he had that first heart attack six months ago, right? What was it that made you two cook?

MICHELE: I was doing my job. I wasn't "cooking."

HAL: Everybody in cardiac care was doing their job, I assume. He didn't leave *them* 100 grand. So come on, level with me. What was it attracted you to him? His suave manner?

MICHELE: He didn't have a sauve manner. He had tubes up his nose and wires practically everywhere else. He was frightened.

HAL: Yeah? Scared? You could see that?

MICHELE: Anyone could have. But his friends, and Marsha—your mother—

HAL: Yeah, I'm familiar with her.

MICHELE: She alternated crying with talk about buying clothes for winter in Miami. His friends talked law. And golf.

HAL: (*Simultaneously with* MICHELE) Golf.

MICHELE: He had nearly died. He needed someone to talk to, to help him come to terms with his mortality.

HAL: And you helped him in that direction. (*Beat*) So. He's lying there, tubes running out all available exits, scared to death, and this attracts you?

MICHELE: (*Looks out window. Alarmed:*) This is wrong.

HAL: It's okay. You can be frank. I understand human quirks. I figured out there's nothing more human *than* quirks. If fear turns you on—

MICHELE: You're . . . this . . .

HAL: It's a natural instinct. I mean, things that are wild can smell fear, they go right—

MICHELE: This is the wrong way. Where are we going?

HAL: Hm? Oops. This is what happens when you're coming off a sixteen-hour shift. Ya got this little voice in your head, your private dispatcher, ya just go where it says, ya forget no one else can hear it. I'm *sorry*. I just thought, since here we are cooking with this conversation—

MICHELE: You said—promised—

HAL: Yep! I'm taking ya home! We're just, uh, taking a more expansive route.

MICHELE: No! Take me home, now!

HAL: Hey, no big deal. You were gonna *walk*, ya can't be in a hurry, right?

MICHELE: Where is this? This gets bad.

HAL: Yeah? Well, guess this part of town does get a little intense for little girls in white rubber shoes.

MICHELE: Take me home!

HAL: Right. But I had this idea.

MICHELE: Forget it.

HAL: But you don't know what it is.

MICHELE: I don't want to! Stop! Now! Let me out!

HAL: Where? Jesus. See those rusted-out truck trailers? Ya know what goes *on* inside those things?

MICHELE: I have to get home. There's someone waiting for me!

HAL: Waiting for you? At the crack of dawn?

MICHELE: Yes! Right now!

HAL: Ah. Keeping the bed warm.

MICHELE: Yes!

HAL: Waiting for you in a warm bed this Sunday morning.

MICHELE: Yes! He is!

HAL: Last Sunday you were at a funeral. You didn't let the sheets get too cold.

MICHELE: What?

HAL: Who'd you find to take the old man's place?

MICHELE: We never . . . I have a boyfriend.

HAL: A boyfriend.

MICHELE: He's my fiancé!

HAL: In two seconds, he went from boyfriend to fiancé.

MICHELE: We're getting married in two weeks! Look! Look at the damn ring!

HAL: Whoa. Definitely not Woolworth's. How long ya had it?

MICHELE: Months!

HAL: You were wearing that and going at it with the old man? You got a spacious heart. Guess ya must have different niches to fill, huh. What niche was the old man filling, exactly?

MICHELE: None! I knew him strictly in a professional capacity!

HAL: What profession are we talking about here?

MICHELE: You . . . You have no right to—

HAL: I have a right to be curious, don't I? Curious about the old man's curious demise?

MICHELE: He had a coronary.

HAL: In your bed.

MICHELE: At the hospital!

HAL: Don't bother with the authorized version. I've been briefed by the eminent Dr. Emil Nash.

MICHELE: He . . . insinuated . . .

HAL: He didn't insinuate shit. He told me the old man croaked in your bed and that's where he found him. He figured I had a genetic right to know.

(*Beat*)

MICHELE: Where are you taking me?

HAL: Right here.

5. No-show Sunrise

(HAL *gets out of the cab. The sounds of water lapping and an occasional gull are heard.*)

HAL: The river. And beyond, the ocean. If ya walk to the end of the pier ya can just make out the Statue of Liberty. 'Course mostly what you're looking at is Hoboken. But I thought we could maybe stand here, have a heart-to-heart as we contemplate the sunrise. Now, how's that? . . . Hello?

MICHELE: (*Stays in cab*) It's not going to happen.

HAL: What?

MICHELE: The sunrise.

HAL: Isn't that being a little pessimistic? I know it's sorta grey out—

MICHELE: This is the West Side. The sun, for some billions of years, has shown a rather firm preference for rising in the east.

HAL: Goddam. Ya know, I think you're right. I'm *sorry*. It's been a weird time for me. Day, night, it gets twisted. All that happens here is the sunset, and we're just a little early for the show . . . Nice setting, though, don't ya think? Why don't you step out? (*Moves to open her door.*)

(MICHELE *slinks quickly across the seat, gets out the opposite door.*)

(*They stand with the cab between them.*)

MICHELE: You lied.

HAL: And you've been nothing but truthful down to the laces on your goodie-two-shoes. . . . Look, I just thought . . . it's not exactly a Hallmark card—ya got the smell, and Hoboken over there—but it's quiet. Peaceful. Inspires an individual to think: what's it all about. Life. Love. Loss . . .

MICHELE: It inspires me to think you are quite possibly deranged.

(HAL *starts around the cab, unzipping his jacket.* MICHELE *bolts away.*)

HAL: I just wanna give ya the jacket. Ya look cold.

MICHELE: Keep it. I'm fine.

HAL: You're fine. Christ. That's gonna be your epitaphy: "Michele Larson, 19 . . . 62 to 1985. I'm fine."

(*They move along the edge of the stage, which has become the "pier".*)

MICHELE: Will you please inform me just why you have abducted me?

HAL: Gee, is that how you perceive this? If that's the case, I'm really—

MICHELE: Please. Perhaps we'd both cope with this more effectively if you'd just concentrate, put whatever mental facilities you have to work, and give me a precise statement of your purpose in bringing me out here to freeze.

HAL: Sometimes when ya talk, I don't know, it sounds like a taped message from the phone company.

MICHELE: All right. Listen closely. What—the—fuck—do—you—want?

HAL: Good. Good. You're learning to communicate. Well, to respond to your query, what I want is to know a little more about how the old man "came to terms with his mortality."

MICHELE: Well. As you say—you've been briefed.

HAL: Yeah. I got what ya might call the bold stokes. But the're some details that're a little hazy.

MICHELE: He died of a coronary. He . . . did . . . happen to be with me.

HAL: That's where it happened to happen.

MICHELE: Are you saying . . . something?

HAL: I'm saying it would interest me to know how it happened. Precisely.

MICHELE: I would think decency would . . . constrain your curiosity about details.

HAL: I think you should tell me.

MICHELE: Why?

HAL: I'm the man's son. His flesh and blood.

MICHELE: It's not as if you loved him.

HAL: You did.

MICHELE: Yes.

HAL: Deeply.

MICHELE: You'll never know how much.

HAL: But I want to know how much. In fact, I want to know how, period.

MICHELE: You expect me to *explain* it to you? A son who never came to see him at the hospital?

HAL: Oh, I was there. I hadn't seen him for a couple years, but I came. I see 'm lying there, looking so . . . tired—I mean the man already looks like a memory—the first thing outta my mouth for some goddam reason is, "I'm sorry." Fuck. Sorry, he says, you're *sorry*. He looks at these flowers I'm holding—not even my idea, these flowers, Mom felt I shouldn't go in there empty-handed, this being a very big deal reunion, and he says, were ya hoping to put those on my grave? I'm s'posed to deal with that? So I say yeah, *yeah*, and I throw the goddam things on 'm. Walk out. I get to the cab, I figure, shit, so I go back, but I get to the room and there's this little ass bending over him, this I realize now, belongs to you, and he is engrossed, I'm gone from his mind. 'Course he remembers well enough to tell Mom I'm out to bury him. This was the man. A prince.

MICHELE: Obviously, you were alienated from him. May I point out that possibly this was *your* problem, not his? You must have noticed the number of people at the funeral. These were all people who cared—

Hal: Babe, there were two kinds of people there. Zombies and sharks. The zombies got a sensual thrill from having their blood sucked. All his life the old man attracted 'em. The sharks, the old man's pals, they were the ones that looked a little edgy. They made whole lives outta fucking the world, and looking down into that hole, I think they got this idea: the world fucks back.

Michele: Your father was never anything but generous with me.

Hal: Yeah. It makes a guy wonder.

Michele: What, precisely, does it make you wonder?

Hal: Just what is it you do that arouses such generosity.

Michele: Are you implying . . . that I am . . . in some sense . . . a whore?

Hal: Did I say that?

Michele: You are disgusting.

Hal: And what are you, nurse? You loved him and *I* just can't understand, it's my problem. Well, what gets in the way of my understanding is the thirty years I knew the man. This clouds my thinking, 'cause what those thirty years taught me is that the love he had in his heart couldn't fill a shot glass.

Michele: I can't help it if he didn't love *you*! Who possibly could?

Hal: Who fucking cares if he loved me! I don't, goddammit, I'm an adult for Chrissakes, think I give a goddam fuck whether my daddy loved me?

Michele: Then just what is your point?

Hal: My point is don't talk to me about love, the man was sentimental as a shark. Talk to me about how it really was, babe, and how it was that night, when he was found in your bed, arms folded, real peaceful, like he died in his sleep—but he didn't, did he? He had this bruise on his head, no one knows from what, it's *hours* before you call anyone—by the time our friendly doctor gets there with the ambulance, he's already the color of cement. So tell me, babe, about the picture I see, 'cause what I see is a man so used to twisting everyone around his finger he couldn't see how much twisting this little girl was doing, a little girl who creeps away on her crepe soles with 100 gees and is getting married in two weeks.

Michele: You're insane!

Hal: (*Advancing*) Am I? Am I?

(MICHELE *clutches her keys in her fist; they stick out between her fingers; she draws her fist back.*)

MICHELE: Don't!

HAL: Ho! Cool move! YWCA self-defense graduate, right? Ya drive 'm in like that, sorta let the IQ dribble out through the eyes . . . Whoa, easy, you're running outta pier there . . . Listen, I got extreme . . . accept my apology . . . accept my jacket . . . C'mon, it's windy out here . . . Now I'm offering a coat, you're offering to sink an inch of steel in my eye. Can we come to some understanding here? Go ahead, unlock my brain if ya want . . . but I think there's an understanding here, isn't there . . . some sort of understanding . . .

MICHELE: No. None. You're . . . (*She turns suddenly—she is at the end of the pier. She screams and nearly falls, teetering dizzily on the edge.*)

(HAL *throws his arms around her.*)

HAL: Whoa . . . Almost lost ya there . . . ooo, you're shaking . . .

MICHELE: (*Looking down into the water.*) I don't like the edge of things . . .

HAL: It's all right, I've got you.

MICHELE: It's not all right.

HAL: What's wrong with it?

MICHELE: Every . . . possible . . . thing.

HAL: (*Drapes his jacket around her.*) I thought you'd appreciate the warmth.

(*She tries to move back from the edge of the pier but* HAL, *still right behind her, does not let her.*)

MICHELE: Let me go. (*Beat*) I demand you take me home. This instant.

HAL: What is it ya gotta hurry home to?

MICHELE: My real life.

HAL: Is the bedwarmer real?

MICHELE: Yes.

HAL: Isn't this real?

(MICHELE *shakes her head, "no".*)

HAL: I gotta disagree with ya there. This feels real ta me, realer than anything that's happened this whole goddam week . . . This grey light makes everything sharp. Just the two of us, sticking way out on this river. (*Points over her shoulder.*) Statue of Liberty . . . Maybe this would seem more real if ya turned around. C'mon. Whaddaya think. Just look at me. (*Still holding her, he moves her back from the edge.*)

MICHELE: It's very obvious what you want.

HAL: What do I want?

MICHELE: I don't like to say the word for what you want . . .

HAL: And what do you want?

MICHELE: To go home.

HAL: Really? Really? (*Pulls her close for a kiss.*)

(MICHELE, *at the last moment, breaks away, slipping out of* HAL's *coat and racing a few steps before turning to see that* HAL *has not moved. She rushes offstage. A beat, then:*)

HAL: (*Calling*) I have a confession to make . . . I'm really ashamed of this . . . but the fact is . . . I stole your wallet. (*Holds it up*) I'm *sorry.* I dunno what possessed me. Haven't stolen a goddam wallet in years . . .

MICHELE's VOICE: Give it to me.

HAL: Oh, yeah, okay. (*Extends it.*)

MICHELE's VOICE: Throw it.

HAL: Bad arm.

MICHELE's VOICE: You have two.

HAL: (*Hefts wallet in his hand.*) Hea-vy. Lotta pictures in here. The Illustrated Michele Larson. Can I . . . just take a peek?

MICHELE: (*Appearing*) No.

HAL: Is it true when girls say no they mean yes?

MICHELE: No.

HAL: That's what I thought. (*Snaps open the wallet.*)

(MICHELE *comes cautiously forward, afraid to get too close.*)

HAL: Aw, c'mon. Just what is so private about your private life?

MICHELE: Don't you dare.

HAL: All I really want is a look at this fiancé. That would help me put the pieces together. Is this guy a moron, didn't *know* what was going on? Or is he a little sharper than that? A guy who saw 100 gees would make a helluva wedding present? Who was maybe even encouraging you . . .

MICHELE: You're sick! Totally sick! You give me my—

HAL: A nerve here? Is the *guy* the real mastermind?

MICHELE: He's not a mastermind, you idiot! He's a dentist!

HAL: Ha! An' he doesn't know a thing about it.

MICHELE: No!

HAL: Not even about the *money*? One hundred—

MICHELE: It's from a grateful patient! These things happen all the time!

HAL: The dentist doesn't know who this grateful patient was? Or where you were all those nights, making him grateful?

MICHELE: It's my life!

HAL: Sounds like you have a *couple* lives, baby. (*Lets the wallet fall open. An accordian strip of plastic-sheathed photos tumbles out.*)

MICHELE: (*Races forward*) No!

HAL: (*Sweeping photos out of her reach.*) Ah, Michele and her secrets, Michele and her niches . . .

(MICHELE *grabs at him.*)

HAL: I'm on to something, huh, getting warm . . .

(MICHELE *struggles for the wallet.* HAL *detaches the strip of photos and lets her take the wallet. He looks at a photo.*)

HAL: Jesus! That's him? This potbellied wimp? (*Looks at more photos.*) All of *him*! Must be the guy. Christ. Think I believe ya. He looks like a dentist. And a moron. (*Laughs*) She says "I do" to one guy while she's doing another guy to death. Old men, fat dentists—our little night nurse, on duty, in control, 24 hours a day. White on the outside but, baby, what color are you inside?

(MICHELE *grabs the strip of photos; there is a tug of war before* HAL *finally lets go.* MICHELE *bunches the photos together, and throws them off the pier.*)

MICHELE: Don't ever touch me! Or any part of my life! Never!

HAL: (*Angry*) What is it? I got something contagious?

MICHELE: (*Backs away.*) You heard me.

HAL: Yeah! Now hear me! You say the dentist isn't on to ya. Yet. I can't help wondering what would happen . . . if he knew.

(MICHELE *stops dead.*)

HAL: Does that throw a wrench in your clockwork?

MICHELE: You . . . (*Beat*) This doesn't involve him.

HAL: Well, once he hears a few brief facts, I think he'll be very involved.

MICHELE: What is it you want?

HAL: Just one thing. One little thing. (*Pulls her face roughly to his.*)

(MICHELE *screams.* HAL *puts a hand over her mouth.*)

HAL: Shh. Jesus, you'll wake New Jersey. Listen. All I want is for you to take me to the place the old man kept ya. That's all.

(MICHELE *shakes her head "no".*)

HAL: Think my being there will . . . defile shrine? Deep love being so far beyond my intellectual grasp? . . . I wanna see it. Is that, be honest, too much to ask? (*Cautiously takes his hand from her mouth.*)

MICHELE: I won't.

HAL: That would be real disappointing to me.

MICHELE: I won't.

HAL: It's that tough? You'd rather the dentist knew, for example, then ta go there.

MICHELE: I can't. I can't . . .

HAL: Why?

MICHELE: The keys. I don't have the keys.

HAL: Ah. Maybe they'll turn up. We'll go there and maybe they'll turn up.

MICHELE: No. They're gone. Forever.

HAL: Well, locks never really hung me up much anyway.

MICHELE: I'll tell you where it is . . . You can go.

HAL: Alone? Wouldn't be the same. Together. We'll go together. (*He releases* MICHELE.)

(*She walks to the end of the pier, looks out.*)

HAL: Thinking of swimming out ta the Statue?

(*A moment; she pulls her ring; says something inaudible.*)

HAL: Pardon?

MICHELE: I'll go with you.

HAL: Good girl.

MICHELE: Somewhere else.

HAL: What . . . Aw, kinky, but not what I had in mind. I wanna see the *place*, baby, not roll around with you at the Ramada Inn.

MICHELE: (*After a moment*) If . . . then I'm through with you. Forever.

HAL: Yeah. Sure.

MICHELE: Swear it.

HAL: I swear it. On the old man's grave.

(*She takes a deep breath; gets in the cab. He gets in, starts the engine.*)

HAL: Where we going?

MICHELE: 160 Riverside.

HAL: Nice address. What's the place like now? I mean, did ya remove any furnishings that seemed suitable for your new marital abode?

MICHELE: It's exactly as it was.

HAL: Big place? One bedroom? (*Beat*) Studio?

(*She doesn't respond, and he turns to face her.*)

MICHELE: A room. It's just a room. Just a room . . . (*When* HAL *turns away, she mouths the words to herself:*) Just a room . . . just a room . . .

6. The Room

(*Grey light fades up through the windows of the room. There is a bed with a chrome-rail headboard; the other furnishings—hi-tech chrome, leather, and plexiglass—include a table and chairs, armchair, vanity, liquor cabinet, bookcases. Plants, dying or dead, fill the bookcases and hang from the skylight.*)

(*A doorway leads off to the kitchen and bath; there is a closet, and French doors leading onto a walled terrace.*)

(The sound of banging and splintering at the door is heard.)

HAL'S VOICE: (*Muffled*) Don't worry, miss, people are always losing keys. That's why we got 24-hour service at Ace Locksmiths . . . unh!

Any fool can slip the lock on the door to the building, but these Medeco cylinders require a little more *so-phis-ti-ca-tion!*

(*Rending sound.* HAL *appears in the doorway, crowbar in one hand, lock cylinder in the other.*)

HAL: After you.

(MICHELE *enters, leans against the wall by the door.*)

HAL: Jesus . . . Planet of the Dead Plants. . . . Hey, you all right?

MICHELE: Just short of breath.

HAL: Gee I'm sorry. Would you like to lie down?

MICHELE: (*Quickly*) I'm fine.

HAL: Right.

MICHELE: It's close in here, that's all.

HAL: A little air in here wouldn't hurt. (*Crosses to French doors*) Ooo, quite a view from up here. (*Can't open the doors.*) How ya open this?

MICHELE: You don't. The key's missing.

HAL: Seems to be a problem of yours, keys. (*Stalks the room; referring to the plants:*) This jungle motif your idea?

MICHELE: Patients always leave plants . . . If I don't take them, they get thrown out.

HAL: (*Picks up a plant*) Very big-hearted of you. (*Shakes plant; leaves fall off*) I feel I should tell you, though: you don't exactly have a green thumb.

MICHELE: I haven't been back since . . .

HAL: You haven't been back. (*Points to bed*) What did ya do, strip that and make it as soon as they carried him outta here?

(MICHELE *looks away.*)

HAL: How very nurselike of you. (*At bed; runs a hand over the leopard skin coverlet.*) You like sleeping with animals? (*His shoe kicks something; he bends down to pick up a broken piece of glass, reflectively places it on nightstand. Sniffs at a candle on the nightstand.*) Mm . . . Cherry? (*Pulls at the candle, which is melted against the chrome bar of the headboard. Pulls it loose.*) This happen that night? I get the impression things burned a little outta control here . . . (*Opens nightstand drawer, finds bottles of pills.*) For the old man? Never liked· taking pills . . . Did ya have to twist his arm? (*Pulls pistol from the drawer.*) That's more his style. Ya should see the house. Guns, alarms, sonic beams. Not fair such a security-minded individual should turn out to be attacked by his own goddam heart . . . Here I am talking, and look at poor you. Still short of breath?

(*As* MICHELE *opens her mouth to respond:*)

You're fine. . . . Sit. (*Approaches her*) I insist.

(MICHELE *sits at the table in order to avoid him. A saucer filled with cigarette butts is in front of her; she pushes it away.*)

HAL: Want water?

(*She shakes her head.*)

HAL: Aspirin? (*Taking off his jacket*) Maybe you'd like to slip into something more, uh . . .

MICHELE: No.

HAL: (*He opens the closet. There are few articles—mostly lingerie.*) A well-rounded wardrobe . . . Christ, that one could stop a heart right there . . . (*Notices a man's robe with something protruding from the pocket: pulls out torn red panties.*) What happened here? Know ya don't wanna give me *details*. I'd settle for just a synopsis.

(MICHELE *pushes the saucer with cigarettes further away.*)

(HAL *crosses to the vanity, drapes panties over lamp. He picks up jewelry.*)

HAL: Good stuff. You're not *leaving* this here?

MICHELE: Take it.

HAL: (*Considers it. Holds up earrings.*) Not my style. (*Finds photo stuck in the vanity mirror.*) This is an oldie. *I* never saw him that young . . . guess all the later ones had my mom cluttering up the scenery. (*Turns photo over*) "To Mickey." . . . They call you Mickey.

MICHELE: They don't. He did.

HAL: Sweet. "To Mickey, my angel in white. Robert." Hey, that's poetry. (*Looks to* MICHELE) Didn't know he had it in 'm. I'm impressed. Maybe some people just have ways. Hell, some people can make bears dance. (*Jams picture back into mirror frame.*) Ya got the old man here, pictures of the dentist—now floating in the Hudson . . . Haven't seen any pictures of the family. How 'bout Mom. Dad . . .

MICHELE: They're gone.

HAL: How?

MICHELE: Car.

HAL: Sorry.

MICHELE: Don't be. Nathan is my family.

HAL: Dynamic guy. . . . So what exactly was the old man? Was he family, too?

(MICHELE *shakes her head.*)

HAL: Then what was he?

MICHELE: A . . . very . . . forceful, and special man.

HAL: Whom it was your good fortune to have known. (*Looks at the cigarettes in the ashtray* MICHELE *has pushed away.*) Luckies your brand?

MICHELE: Don't smoke.

HAL: Who smokes them?

MICHELE: One of the men who came for him, I suppose.

HAL: . . . So what's it feel like, this place, without him? My mom is rattling around fifteen rooms in Westchester, reaching for sedatives like they were bar nuts. She's got what you call a difficult transition ahead: from being a wife to being . . . nothin. 'Cause her life was for him. Everything for him. (*Laughs, plucks his windbreaker.*) Fuck. This *jacket* was for him. He didn't like the lining. (*Beat*) Ya look like ya been up since the Dark Ages.

MICHELE: You too.

HAL: Maybe we need rest. (*Reaches for her hand.*)

(*She rises;* HAL *crowds her.*)

HAL: What's been keeping ya up, babe? Hm? What is it, makes you toss and turn . . . (*Backs her into the bed.*)

(*She collapses in a sitting position on the bed, tries to leap up;* HAL *holds her by the shoulders. After a beat:*)

HAL: You seem tense . . . Maybe you'd like a drink.

MICHELE: I don't drink.

HAL: Don't drink, don't smoke . . . Do you . . . know how to relax? (*Massages her shoulders.*)

(*The sound of rain on the skylight is heard.*)

HAL: There's the rain . . . Must be nice having that skylight. Look up and see the stars. Ya musta spent a lotta time, just counting those stars.

MICHELE: You don't see stars. It's opaque. You see black.

HAL: You can look at me . . . Look at me . . . It's all right here . . . there's something about this place . . . I'm even thinking . . . I got myself in this situation again where I'm living outta just a bag, got toothbrushes all over town. I been staying mostly with this chick in the East Village, but she gets to me. Killer figure, but think she's got brown rice for brains . . . If the old man took this place, he got a deal on it. And being family, I bet I could take over the lease. Whaddaya think? It'd be great, to come into something 'cause of the old man after all. 'Course . . . the furniture would have to go . . . except for you.

MICHELE: You said . . . once.

HAL: Yeah but . . . you're already installed here . . . all your nighties, bracelets and chains. We'll talk, we got lots to talk about. But for now . . . Relax . . . relax . . . and just say, I want to be here. Because you do, don't ya. You want to be here.

(*She shakes her head.*)

HAL: Then why are you here?

MICHELE: For Nathan.

HAL: (*Laughs*) Look at me. You want this. You know. So say it. Say yes. Say it. Yes . . . (*Whispers in her ear.*) Yes . . . yes . . . (*Beat*) You stopped shaking.

MICHELE: I'm still cold.

HAL: I'll warm you. (*Starts to push her back on the bed.*)

MICHELE: Could . . . I have something to drink?

HAL: *Now* you want something to drink. (*Laughs*) Sure. Whaddaya want?

MICHELE: Tea.

HAL: Tea?

MICHELE: A cup of hot tea.

HAL: You really need this?

MICHELE: I would very much appreciate a cup of hot tea.

HAL: Right. Great. Tea. (*Exits to kitchen. Mutters from off:*) Where the fuck do I find . . .

(*A clattering sound is heard from the kitchen. Meanwhile,* MICHELE *opens the nightstand drawer, takes out the gun, and regards it.*)

HAL'S VOICE: All right, it's under control.

(*The sound of water running is heard.* MICHELE *sits down on the bed.*)

HAL'S VOICE: Did you have in mind the . . . (*Reads with difficulty:*) Camel-meel or the English Breakfast?

(*He appears in the kitchen doorway. She moves the gun behind her back. He crosses to her and puts the tea boxes on the nightstand. He sits beside her, then touches her face.*)

HAL: You are cold. Here . . . (*he puts his arm around her. He takes her hand, then puts it on his thigh.*)

(MICHELE *flinches, pulling her hand back.*)

HAL: It's nothing. Quarters in my pocket. I'm a communicator. Very dependent on quarters . . . (*Hand near her breast*) Your heart feels like the cavalry charging . . . What's this look? Whaddaya see?

MICHELE: Hate.

HAL: What hate?

MICHELE: Your hate.

HAL: I don't hate you. I understand you.

MICHELE: (*Starts to bring the gun from behind her back.*) I don't think so.

HAL: I think so. Think I can even prove it. (*Leans in to kiss her.*)

MICHELE: I don't want you.

(HAL *kisses her, pushing her down onto the bed.* MICHELE *lifts the gun. We hear the sound of a tea kettle whistling.*)

(*The kiss becomes tender. The gun falls to* MICHELE'S *side; she slips it under* HAL'S *jacket, which lays next to her.*)

(*They separate. A moment, as they look at each other.*)

HAL: Wh . . . which tea?

MICHELE: No preference.

(HAL *gets up, fumbles with the tea boxes, exits.*)

(MICHELE *sits up and, after a moment, stands. She looks off toward kitchen. She grabs her purse and runs out the door.*)

(HAL *enters, balancing a cup of tea.*)

HAL: Delicate operation here . . . (*Looks around, finds her gone.*) Christ . . . that . . . (*Sets down tea. He grabs his jacket from the bed, to chase after* MICHELE. *Sees gun.*) Oh shit . . . (*Picks up gun. Looks off toward door.*) What's the story here? What the fuck is the story?

(Act break if desired)

7. Trust Exercise

(HAL *drags himself, exhausted, into a phone booth. We hear the sound of rain.*)

HAL: So I chase that lethal bitch, all the way to Columbus Circle, like I'm gonna be able to find her for Chrissake, but I don't even catch sight of her. (*Picks up receiver, punches 411.*) St. Vincent's Cardiac Care Unit please . . . (*Takes out a pen and matchbook, then jots down number.*) Thanks, doll. (*Deposits quarter, pushes buttons.*) This better work . . . (*With effeminate inflection:*) Hello, may I speak to Nurse Larson? Oh no! Can you tell me where she might be reached? Policy, smolicy, darling, this is an emergency! I'm altering the bridal gown—you are aware she's getting married, to that marvelous man with the drill—mmm. Well, I've misplaced the measurements. I know, call me hopeless, but they're *gone!* And with a girl like that, such a wisp as it were, one needs to be absolutely *precise.* So . . . Oh pleeease, I'm on my virtual knees . . . Oh, bless you! (*Takes down number. Suddenly macho:*) Sweetheart, you're probably a great kid, but suspicion, it's a disease. It comes between people. Ya gotta learn to trust. Baby, the lesson for the day is: trust. (*Blows kiss into the receiver, then hangs up.*)

(*Lights up on* MICHELE, *sitting by the phone, in her bathrobe. A bottle of scotch and a glass are on the table, by the phone. She contemplates a razor blade, which she holds up, then sets on her knee.*)

(*The phone rings.* MICHELE *grabs the receiver.*)

MICHELE: Hello? . . . Hello? (*Long pause*) Nathan?

HAL: I take it the doctor isn't in. Too bad. I got this real nasty case of decay . . . (*Beat*) Hello? (*Beat*) Mickey?

MICHELE: (*After a moment*) You won't leave me alone.

HAL: Listen, no one should be alone.

MICHELE: (*After another moment*) All right.

HAL: All right what?

MICHELE: Tonight.

HAL: What about now?

MICHELE: No.

HAL: Why.

MICHELE: I have things to take care of.

HAL: What kind of things.

MICHELE: Personal.

HAL: All right. Tonight. At the place. Kiss kiss.

(MICHELE *hangs up.*)

HAL: Yeah, little girl. Tonight.

(*Lights fade on* HAL)

(MICHELE *takes off her ring, looks at it, then drops it in her glass of scotch. She picks up the razor blade, moves it toward her wrist, and slips it under the ace bandage there. She sits silently; then, softly:*)

MICHELE: Mickey . . . Mickey . . .

8. The Edge

(HAL, *with his shirt off, stands on the terrace outside the room.*)

HAL: The old man always liked a high floor. It gave him the opportunity to look down on a lot of people at once. (*Lingers over view; then:*) The're no answers out here, Hal boy. (*Turns, crosses into room.*)

(*Rubbing his arms, chilled, he goes to the closet. He pulls out a grey robe; its hanger is entwined with that of a black negligee.*)

HAL: Christ, can't keep 'em apart. (*He regards the robe, smells it, hesitates, then puts it on, grimacing. He notes a "G" on the pocket.*) Property of Mr. Monogram. (*He pulls a folded paper out of the pocket. Reads:*) "Sung Chu Mei—Free Fast Delivery!" (*He crosses to the bed. He picks up the gun, contemplates it, then slips it into his waistband. He pulls the covers off the bed. The sheets are red.*) Satin yet. (*He flips the covers back and finds a tie, burned at one end and knotted a few inches above the burn. He regards it, then leaves it on the bed.*)

(*He crosses to the vanity; looks through drawers, in wastebasket. Takes out* The Wall Street Journal, *reaches back in, and:*)

HAL: Ouch!

(*He sucks at his finger. He then pulls out a broken lamp. He puts it on the nightstand and matches it with the piece of broken glass he found that morning by the bed. He looks from the lamp to the tie.*)

HAL: Well, put it together, Sherlock . . . Looks like he tried to hang himself from a table lamp.

(*We hear the sound of the buzzer.* HAL *starts, then locates the intercom.*)

HAL: Yeah.

MICHELE'S VOICE: It's me.

HAL: You.

MICHELE'S VOICE: Mickey.

HAL: What is it, like six?

MICHELE'S VOICE: I imagine.

HAL: Just couldn't wait, huh?

MICHELE'S VOICE: May I come up?

(HAL *presses the door button. He stands still for a moment, then crosses to the vanity. He adjusts the robe, then combs his hair.*)

HAL: Whaddaya doing? This isn't your goddam first date. Could be your last. (*He crosses to the table and tries to sit casually. He then moves to bed, reclines.*)

(*The sound of a knock is heard.* HAL *moves quickly to the armchair and arranges himself.*)

HAL: It's not locked.

(MICHELE *opens the door. She is wearing a sweatsuit and track shoes.*)

MICHELE: Hello.

HAL: Hello.

MICHELE: May I come in?

HAL: Do.

(*She steps in and closes the door.*)

HAL: Can ya stay, or will ya have to run?

MICHELE: Pardon my attire. I thought I would change here.

HAL: Change to what?

MICHELE: To something more appealing.

HAL: You wanna appeal to me?

MICHELE: It stopped raining but my shoes are soaked. May I take them off?

HAL: Yeah. And we might as well stop playing Captain May I. Come the fuck in.

MICHELE: Thank you. (*She takes off her shoes and socks.*)

(*He moves to the door, slides a bookcase in front of it, then sits on it.*)

HAL: So. The night nurse returns.

MICHELE: I shouldn't have left.

HAL: Yeah, I noticed after ya went, there seemed to be a few unresolved details. (*He takes out the gun and places it in his lap.*)

MICHELE: I . . . you made me nervous. (*She crosses to the vanity.*)

HAL: Now you're not nervous.

MICHELE: (*She turns on the lamp, which is still covered by the panties* HAL *put there; it casts a reddish glow.*) No.

HAL: (*Joins her at the vanity.*) That's good.

(HAL *watches raptly as* MICHELE *prepares to do her makeup.*)

MICHELE: (*Meeting* HAL's *eyes in the mirror.*) Maybe you could get me a drink.

HAL: Thought you didn't drink.

MICHELE: Not as a rule. Only as an exception.

HAL: Hey. Right. Nothing like a cocktail to take the edge off an awkward social situation. (*He places the gun on the vanity then moves to the liquor cabinet, watching her. He freezes as she slides the gun across the vanity. He resumes crossing the room as he sees she is just getting the gun out of her way.*)

HAL: What's your poison? Tea, straight up?

MICHELE: Scotch.

(HAL *pours the drinks.* MICHELE *begins applying makeup. She meets* HAL's *glance in the mirror and takes the drink from him. She kicks it back in a few gulps. With a controlled gasp:*)

MICHELE: Thank you.

HAL: Would you like another for a chaser?

(Michele *holds out her glass.*)

Hal: Maybe you should wait for the first one to hit.

Michele: Maybe I don't want to wait.

(*He pours, then perches on the vanity, playing with the gun. She stops putting on her makeup to glare at him.*)

Hal: Gosh, I'm sorry. I got this high metabolism, always gotta be doing something. I know it's sortuva drag at a time like this when it's just a guy and a girl alone and ya wanna be laid back and casual.

(Michele *puts her hand over his to stop the twirling of the gun. She has finished her makeup; it is much more than we have seen her wear before—perhaps a little too much—but the effect is striking.*)

Hal: Ooo, look at this face. Baby, this face could launch a thousand heart attacks.

(*She turns back to the mirror. She unzips her sweatshirt part way to apply perfume to her neck and breasts.* Hal *leans in, sniffs.*)

Michele: Obsession.

Hal: It's very you.

(*She puts on jewelry.*)

Hal: Ya know, I'm beginning to feel seriously underdressed. (*He picks up the burnt tie, bends over her shoulder at the mirror, and knots it around his neck.*)

(Michele, *reaching to take off her headband, freezes.*)

Hal: Whaddaya think? Dashing?

(*She tears off the headband, shakes her hair loose, brushes it.*)

Hal: You're real businesslike . . . but just what kind of transaction do you have in mind?

(*She rises from the vanity and turns off the lamp. He puts his hand on the zipper of her sweatshirt and unzips it slowly as he talks.*)

Hal: Might as well be upfront about it. 'Cause before you leave this time, we're gonna get to the bottom line . . . (*He has unzipped her sweatshirt; he let his hand fall.*)

Michele: Give me a moment.

Hal: A moment for what?

Michele: (*Skirts him*) To prepare. (*She takes items from the closet and moves toward the bath.*)

Hal: (*Follows her*) Babe, you are the most prepared chick I ever met.

Michele: (*Turns to face him*) A moment. (*Exits to bath*)

(Hal *looks after her, then sits at the vanity. He picks up the picture of his father then looks at himself in the mirror. He throws the picture down and gets up. He pours himself another drink, raises it, stops. He pours it into a dead plant.*)

(Michele *appears, wearing a black negligee and high heels.*)

Michele: Is there something you'd rather I wore?

Hal: No . . . ya look just fine in full combat gear.

Michele: Please. Look.

(Hal *goes to the closet and pulls out a risqué red nightie. He holds it up, looking from it to* Michele.)

Hal: Naw, I s'pose this is more something two people gotta sorta work toward in their relationship. (*He returns it to the closet, then moves toward* Michele.)

(*The broken lamp is between them.* Michele's *eyes fix on it.*)

Hal: Yeah, dug out this lamp . . . Unfortunately, it doesn't shed much light . . . Hey, don't worry about it. You're gonna shed the light . . . Why don't ya start by telling me what your scheme is, hm? Ya figure ya can get me to stop asking questions, get me outta your life with one hot little command performance? Is that the concept?

(Michele *crosses to the French doors; a reddish light comes through them. She stands in the threshold.*)

Michele: You found the key.

Hal: Where you hid it.

(*Pulls key from the dirt of a dead plant by the doors and lays the key in* Michele's *hand.*)

Michele: I didn't hide it.

Hal: You mean he hid it?

Michele: I always wanted to see the river . . . the lights . . . but he wanted me in the room. (*She throws the key back in plant and wipes her hands. She steps onto the terrace.*)

Michele: Rather spectacular. The sunset.

Hal: (*Joins her*) Yeah, nothing moves me like a picturesque sunset. (*Beat*) You didn't come to watch the sunset.

MICHELE: No.

HAL: Why did you come?

MICHELE: To be here.

HAL: Why?

MICHELE: This is where I belong.

HAL: That's no answer.

MICHELE: I don't have answers.

HAL: Yes ya do, baby . . . All the answers . . . if a guy could just plumb your depths . . . (*He kisses her—a long kiss*) Nice . . . I mean that sincerely. You do nice work . . .

(MICHELE *caresses him; he notices the bandage around her wrist.*)

HAL: How'd ya get that?

MICHELE: Sometimes . . . I get hurt.

HAL: Sometimes?

MICHELE: When I'm bad.

HAL: Little you?

(*She leans into him, bites his neck.*)

HAL: Ah!

(*He grabs her wrist and pulls her into the room, pushes her toward the bed. She lands on the bed in a provocative pose, half sitting, half lying. He moves to her, then stops short.*)

HAL: Oh those wide eyes . . . and that hustler's heart beating so fast . . . You're home now, aren't you, right at home . . .

MICHELE: Yes.

HAL: This is all there was to it, right, your . . . "deep love." Just this. Two hustlers, hot for the game.

(*She reaches for him.*)

HAL: No, babe. Things seem to happen when you lie down on that bed.

MICHELE: We want things to happen.

HAL: I wanna make sure I know what's happening.

MICHELE: I'm sure you'll figure it out.

HAL: (*He laughs, then takes her face in his hands.*) Ya think ya got it all. Ring on your finger, 100 gees in the bank . . . Too bad for you, there's me—a guy with nothing, and I don't care what it takes, I'm gonna know what happened between you and him, and when I've got the dirty facts, I'll make the deals, and your ass'll be mine.

MICHELE: I *am* yours.

HAL: Then tell me . . . love . . . how'd ya do it that night?

MICHELE: The way it's customarily done . . . more or less . . .

HAL: Except for the end, baby. It can only end that way once.

MICHELE: Shhh . . . Any way you want it . . . Any way . . .

HAL: What he didn't know killed him. I'm not making the same mistake. (*He rips the tie from his neck.*) What's this?

(MICHELE *moves to kiss him, closing her eyes.* HAL *yanks her hair back.*)

HAL: No more games. Now we get serious.

MICHELE: Yes . . . yes, lover . . .

HAL: What is this?

MICHELE: Tie.

HAL: How'd it get burned?

MICHELE: Fire.

HAL: Explain. (*He throws the tie around her neck, then pulls her to him.*) Explain.

(*She puts a finger to her lips, then to his. She tries to kiss him. He twists the tie, pulls her away from him.*)

HAL: You know who you're dealing with? Hm?

MICHELE: Yes.

HAL: I don't think you do.

MICHELE: Yes . . .

HAL: (*He releases the tie, straddling her.*) Do you?

MICHELE: Yes . . . I do . . . I do . . .

HAL: Good, baby, good.

MICHELE: I know . . .

HAL: But who am *I* dealing with? Hm?

MICHELE: You know . . . you know, lover . . .

HAL: Yeah? But with this . . . (*He wipes roughly at her lipstick.*) All that perfume . . . it's hard to tell . . .

MICHELE: Not for you . . . (*She throws her arms around him.*)

(*He pushes her back down, hard. He takes his drink from the nightstand and splashes it on her.*)

HAL: Now let's see who's here . . .

(*She twists under him as he rubs off her makeup.*)

HAL: The romance rubs off, baby . . .

(*She bites his hand.*)

HAL: Ah! (*He slaps her; and grasps her by the hair.*) Yeah . . . now this is a face I can believe, I can relate to this . . . these eyes . . . what's making those little black circles . . . a little black soul . . . (*He seizes her jaw.*) If I have to rip away this face to get behind it, I will, understand? Christ, what was I seeing this morning . . . kissed this face . . . thought maybe I even *felt* something . . . but now I see what you are . . . and you are nothing . . . nothing but a whore . . . even smell like a whore, booze for perfume . . . (*He picks up a shard of glass from the broken lamp and sticks it under her throat.*) What is this?

MICHELE: Glass.

HAL: The lamp broke. How?

MICHELE: It fell.

HAL: Accidents happen, hon, and the way my hand is shaking, we could have one right here . . .

MICHELE: Just tell me what you want . . .

HAL: You know what I want . . .

MICHELE: Yes . . . I can feel it, I feel you . . .

HAL: What I want bitch is—what happened that night?

MICHELE: Yes . . . all right . . .

HAL: (*He traces the glass along her neck and cheek.*) The next word out of you mouth, bitch, better be the right one. What happened that night?

MICHELE: This, lover . . . this is what happened . . . Here we are, just like the first time I came here to . . . (*Laughs*) Talk . . . He reached for me . . . I said no . . . He kissed me . . . I thought how awful this was, how awful *I* was, but . . . then there was nothing . . . but him . . . and now you . . . with his eyes . . .

HAL: I don't have his eyes.

MICHELE: Oh yes.

HAL: I have nothing to do with him.

MICHELE: Mm.

HAL: I don't.

MICHELE: Same eyes . . . same ways . . .

HAL: (*He tries to push her away.*) All—all I want from you—

MICHELE: Is that night . . . yes? I'll give you that night . . . just . . . hold me . . . please . . . will you do that? Just . . .

(*She embraces him. Behind his back, she slips the razor blade out of her wrist bandage.*)

(*HAL disentangles himself from her, then sees her trying to conceal something in her fist.*)

(*He looks in her eyes; makes a grab for her wrist.*)

HAL: Open. . . . Open! (*He tries to tear her fingers open.*)

(*The struggle is wordless; then:*)

MICHELE: No. . . . No . . . (*Blood begins to stream down her arm.*)

HAL: Fucking Christ . . . (*He pries her fingers open, then shakes out the bloody blade; it falls to the floor. He goes after it.*)

MICHELE *goes for the gun.* HAL *flings the razor onto the terrace and straightens to find* MICHELE *leveling the gun at him. He makes a move toward her.*)

MICHELE: Stay!

HAL: Drop it, baby.

MICHELE: I hate baby.

HAL: Mickey.

MICHELE: I hate Mickey.

HAL: Michele.

MICHELE: I hate Michele.

HAL: What should I call you?

MICHELE: Nothing.

HAL: I have to call you somethi—

MICHELE: Shhh . . . I don't want to hear you, your words, no . . .

HAL: Michele . . . it's a good name—just maybe I don't say it right . . . I'll just keep saying it till maybe I—

MICHELE: Shhh . . . his words got me here, to this room, got me to do things . . . he called love . . . And when I told him I wouldn't see him, I was getting married and I would never come back, he used his words, his words to tell Nathan, tell Nathan what we did here . . .

HAL: Michele, listen—

MICHELE: No! You wanted that night . . . That night I came here, asked him why he told Nathan, and he said, "I did it for you. I know you, what you really are, what you are . . . is mine." He reached for me, I hit him, fought him, but he got me on the bed, tied me to it, fucked me, cursing me, his bitch, his whore, choking me, but then . . . stopped . . . tried to untie me . . . his hands shook . . . he went for the phone . . . fell. I slid the tie to the candle, burned through it . . . stood . . . watched him . . . gasping, convulsing, eyes . . . on me . . . He knew . . . I knew . . . I could save him . . . But I watched . . . waited . . . for him to die . . . I thought, that night, it was over, thought . . . with the money, maybe, start somewhere else . . . but the money wasn't mine . . . it was a curse, a curse to bring you after me . . . if you can see for him . . . look . . . look, you bastard, look at her . . . (*She puts the gun to her head.*)

HAL: No! (*He leaps forward.*)

(*They wrestle for the gun; it goes off. They are both very still. They look to see if either of them is injured: they are not.*)

(MICHELE *backs away from* HAL; *winded, with the gun, he stays on the bed, breathing hard.*)

HAL: Jesus . . .

(MICHELE *backs toward the terrace, and goes out onto it.*)

HAL: Michele . . .

(MICHELE *steps up on the terrace ledge.*)

HAL: No! (*He leaps up, but does not rush her; advancing cautiously:*) Michele!

(MICHELE *looks down at the street. We hear the sound of traffic below.*)

HAL: Michele! Look, look at me! Please, just . . . Look . . . Michele . . . don't let him pull you . . . because that's what it is, Michele . . . *Him.* The old man. He's got us up here like a puppet show . . . Michele . . .

MICHELE: (*Softly*) . . . Forgive . . .

HAL: No. No. You just didn't save him. But, Michele, you can save *me* . . . Please . . . will you . . . will you just take this hand . . . Michele . . . you think there's something bad in you, something black and cold but, Michele, no, it's not, it's just this empty place, this aching place, and some bastard comes along, so full of blackness, he's overflowing with it, it's all he gives you . . . it fills you . . . you think it is you, but, Michele, it's not . . . Michele . . . if you just take this hand . . . take it, just for a second, I promise, I'll never come near you again, never, I promise . . .

(*He inches toward her. She moves away, swaying dizzily.* HAL *drops to his knees.*)

HAL: *Nooo!* (*He sees the razor and picks it up.*) Please . . . please . . . take the hand . . . (*He slashes his palm.*) Please take this . . . this . . . damn hand . . .

(*She is looking away. He slashes his hand more deeply and deliberately; a sound of pain escapes him.* MICHELE *turns.*)

HAL: This damn . . . damn . . . hand . . . (*He holds it toward her.*) For a second, a second, and it'll never touch you again. (*A sob*) Mi . . . chele . . .

(*From below there is the flashing red light of a squad car.* MICHELE's *injured hand moves slowly, as of its own will, toward* HAL's. *Their fingers touch, curve into each other's and slip into a strong, interlocking grasp.*)

HAL: Thank you . . . thank . . . you . . .

(HAL *stays low as he brings her off the ledge; as she steps onto the terrace, he is on his knees.*)

(*The sound of the street fades; lights fade till* HAL *and* MICHELE, *hands clasped, are lit solely by the blue moonlight above and the flashing red light below.*)

CURTAIN

Poisonous mushrooms, red herrings, marital infidelities, and a mysterious Merchant of Death are elements in this English style **thriller** with a fascinating, intricate plot. Four males, two females; single interior set.

Dead Souls

A COMIC EPIC IN TWO PARTS
By
LAURENCE SENELICK
Based on the novel by
NIKOLAY GOGOL

A **theatrical extravaganza** drawn from Nikolay Gogol's comic epic of greed and gluttony in Tsarist Russia. The **picaresque adventures** of its conman hero lend themselves to a broad pageant of grotesque characters and events. Over one hundred characters can be played with any number of actors from fifteen on up. It can be staged with a bare set and a few props, or as elaborately as you choose.

SHORT PIECES

FROM

THE

NEW

DRAMATISTS

The New Dramatists is a major American arts organization dedicated to developing and promoting the work of **new playwrights**. Its present and past membership includes an impressive array of playwrighting talent. For two recent ND fundraising events, member playwrights contributed mini-plays of no longer than four minutes. We have collected these delightful dramatic dollops by writers such as **Steve Carter, Jack Heifner, Eric Overmyer, Mac Wellman, and August Wilson.** Many of these short plays make excellent audition material.

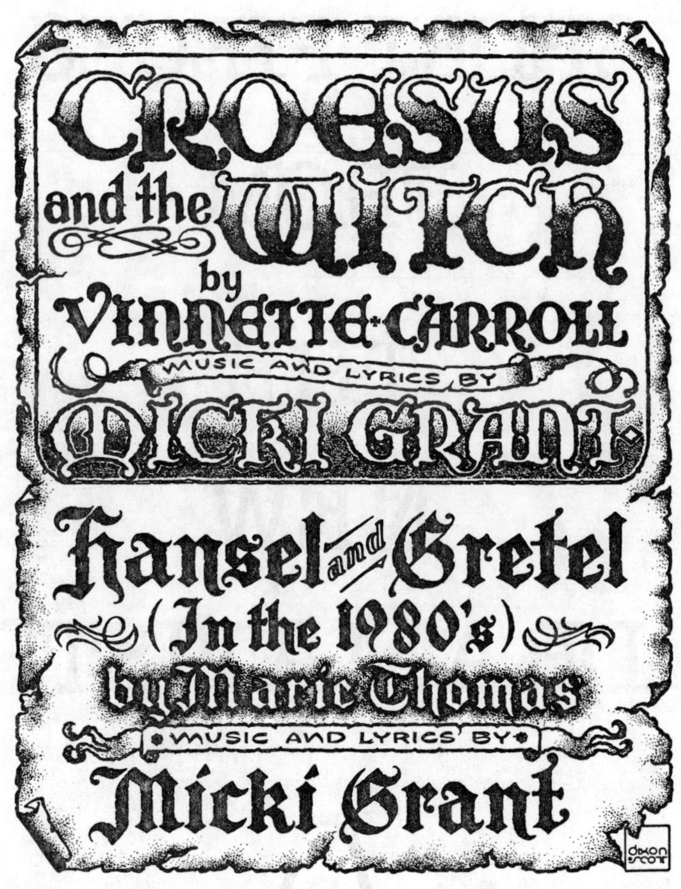

There is little question that **Micki Grant** is one of the most talented people writing music in the American theater today. With **Vinnette Carroll**, at the **Urban Arts Theater**, she has created wonderful shows like YOUR ARMS TOO SHORT TO BOX WITH GOD and DON'T BOTHER ME I CAN'T COPE. This large format book contains both the book and music to two modern reworkings of fairy tales, one done in collaboration with Vinnette Carroll and the other with Marie Thomas. Both plays can use flexible sized casts and young actors.

In this **one-man show** set in a Monte Carlo villa at the end of the last century, the grand master of the kitchen, Escoffier, ponders a glorious return from retirement. In doing so, he relates anecdotes about the famous and shares his mouth-watering recipes with the audience. One male; single interior set.

Set in **rural Alabama** in 1968, the play is a bittersweet tale of a middle-aged waitress whose ability to love and be loved is re-kindled by **her** chance encounter with a young drifter. This play was developed at the **Eugene O'Neill Theater Center's** National Playwrights Conference in 1982. Two males, one female; single interior and exterior set.